Understanding
The Crucible

The Greenwood Press "Literature in Context" Series

Understanding *To Kill a Mockingbird*: A Student Casebook to Issues, Sources, and Historical Documents
Claudia Durst Johnson

Understanding *The Scarlet Letter*: A Student Casebook to Issues, Sources, and Historical Documents
Claudia Durst Johnson

Understanding *Adventures of Huckleberry Finn*: A Student Casebook to Issues, Sources, and Historical Documents
Claudia Durst Johnson

Understanding *Macbeth*: A Student Casebook to Issues, Sources, and Historical Documents
Faith Nostbakken

Understanding *Of Mice and Men*, *The Red Pony*, and *The Pearl*: A Student Casebook to Issues, Sources, and Historical Documents
Claudia Durst Johnson

Understanding Anne Frank's *The Diary of a Young Girl*: A Student Casebook to Issues, Sources, and Historical Documents
Hedda Rosner Kopf

Understanding *Pride and Prejudice*: A Student Casebook to Issues, Sources, and Historical Documents
Debra Teachman

Understanding *The Red Badge of Courage*: A Student Casebook to Issues, Sources, and Historical Documents
Claudia Durst Johnson

Understanding Richard Wright's *Black Boy*: A Student Casebook to Issues, Sources, and Historical Documents
Robert Felgar

Understanding *I Know Why the Caged Bird Sings*: A Student Casebook to Issues, Sources, and Historical Documents
Joanne Megna-Wallace

UNDERSTANDING
The Crucible

A STUDENT CASEBOOK TO ISSUES, SOURCES, AND HISTORICAL DOCUMENTS

Claudia Durst Johnson and Vernon E. Johnson

The Greenwood Press
"Literature in Context" Series

GREENWOOD PRESS
Westport, Connecticut • London

Library of Congress Cataloging-in-Publication Data

Johnson, Claudia D.
    Understanding The Crucible : a student casebook to issues,
sources, and historical documents / Claudia Durst Johnson and Vernon
E. Johnson.
        p.   cm.—(The Greenwood Press "Literature in context"
series, ISSN 1074–598X)
    Includes bibliographical references and index.
    ISBN 0–313–30121–2 (alk. paper)
    1. Miller, Arthur, 1915–   Crucible.   2. Miller, Arthur, 1915–
Crucible—Sources.   3. Historical drama, American—History and
criticism.   4. Hysteria (Social psychology) in literature.
5. Witchcraft—Massachusetts—Salem—History.   6. Subversive
activities—United States.   7. Salem (Mass.)—In literature.
8. Witchcraft in literature.   9. Communism—United States.
I. Johnson, Vernon E. (Vernon Elso), 1921–   .   II. Title.
III. Series.
PS3525.I5156C7345   1998
812'.52—DC21   98–10703

British Library Cataloguing in Publication Data is available.

Library of Congress Catalog Card Number: 98–10703
ISBN: 0–313–30121–2
ISSN: 1074–598X

First published in 1998

Greenwood Press, 88 Post Road West, Westport, CT 06881
An imprint of Greenwood Publishing Group, Inc.

Printed in the United States of America

The paper used in this book complies with the
Permanent Paper Standard issued by the National
Information Standards Organization (Z39.48–1984).

10 9 8 7 6 5 4 3 2 1

Contents

Preface

On the evening of January 22, 1953, after the curtain came down on the opening Broadway performance of Arthur Miller's *The Crucible*, the author walked into the lobby of the Martin Beck Theatre in New York City to mingle with friends and other playgoers who had come to see this, the fourth Broadway production of a Pulitzer Prize–winning playwright. The mood he encountered there scarcely gave him cause to celebrate, however, for, as Miller explains in *Timebends*, his autobiography, "In the lobby at the end, people with whom I had some fairly close professional acquaintanceships passed me by as though I were invisible" (New York: Penguin, 1995, 347). To make matters worse, *Variety*, the show-business newspaper regarded as the bible of the theatre district, listed *The Crucible* among the year's prominent flops, and several highly respected reviewers, to whom many playgoers looked for guidance, panned the play. One of the most respected theatre critics in New York, George Jean Nathan, excoriated the play in the April edition of *Theatre Arts*, criticizing it for being a play with little emotional warmth, its impersonal characters having as their only function to propagandize about the U.S. Senate hearings then in progress. As a sermon, he said, it was acceptable, but not as drama. Walter Kerr, another key critic, writing for the *New York Herald Tribune*, also panned the play and the production, claiming that the characters were no more than puppets serving Miller's politics. In *The New Republic*, Eric Bentley, the most famous theatre critic and historian of the modern theatre, denigrated the play as a melodrama that unsuccessfully tried to draw a parallel between witchcraft and the Senate hearings. Even though *The Crucible* was recognized as one of the best plays of 1952–1953 in *The Burns Mantle Best Plays and the Yearbook of the Drama in America*, the reviewer, Louis Kronenberger, called the characters merely mouthpieces for Miller's politics and asserted that Miller had failed to address the causes of the 1692 hysteria, had distorted and muddled history, and had founded the whole drama on a false parallel between 1692 and 1952.

In light of the climate that then prevailed, one suspects that many reviewers and playgoers believed that viewing and approving of the play might taint them as sympathetic to communism. People in those highly charged times had lost their jobs for less.

But time and circumstances have reversed the fortunes of *The Crucible*, for in the last quarter of the century it has become one of the most frequently read and most often produced plays of the modern theatre. It has a record of being one of the best-selling paperback books of fiction in America, Bantam Books and Penguin Books having sold over six million copies of the play. It is one of the works most frequently taught in schools in the United States. No play in this century has been more often chosen for production, especially by regional and educational theatres. Since its first appearances in 1952, it has had four runs on the professional stage in New York City and numerous performances on the professional stage in Britain. No American play in this century is so often chosen for production throughout the world. There is scarcely a country in the world with theatre that has not staged a production of *The Crucible*, one of the most famous being a production in Red China, where, ironically, it was taken to be a criticism of communism rather than a criticism of Communist hunters, as it had been perceived in the United States in 1952. Arthur Miller says, "I don't think there has been a week in the past forty-odd years when it hasn't been on a stage somewhere in the world" ("Why I Wrote the Crucible," *New Yorker*, October 21, 1996, 165). It has twice been made into a film and once into an opera.

Few works of fiction have been so decidedly engendered from historical events—in this case, the Salem witch-hunts of 1692 and, by implication, the "Red Scare" of the 1950s. The primary purpose of this volume is to explore the historical contexts of *The Crucible* and the issues it raises. Chapter One prepares for the contextual study that follows by presenting a literary analysis of the play's dramatic structure. Chapter Two is a study of the attitudes and circumstances leading up to the terrible persecutions for witchcraft in Salem, Massachusetts, in 1692. Chapter Three focuses on the actual trials themselves, with special attention being given to the historical characters on whom Miller based his play. In Chapter Four, attention turns to the implied subject of *The Crucible*, the government investigations in the 1950s, when the play appeared, that took the form of modern witch-hunts for subversives. Chapter Five looks at one of a number of current issues to which *The Crucible* speaks: the preposterous and hysterical cases in which whole groups of people have been accused of child molestation solely on the testimony of preschool-aged children.

The documents that tell these stories are as varied as they are riveting. Among them are excerpts from sermons, poems, histories, letters, colonial laws, court transcripts, appeals for mercy to the courts, petitions, eyewitness accounts, transcripts of local hearings, a government pamphlet, an executive order, a presidential veto, and an interview with two people who were actively engaged in most of the key political issues of the 1950s.

NOTE

Quotations from *The Crucible* refer to act and page numbers in the Penguin Books paperback edition (New York, 1995).

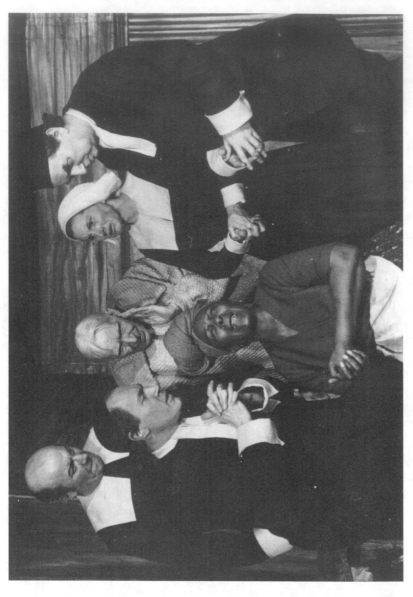

Fred Fehl's 1953 photo of a scene from Arthur Miller's first production of *The Crucible*. The Putnams and Reverends Hale and Parris press Tituba for a confession as Giles Corey looks on. Printed with permission from Margaret Fehl and the Billy Rose Theatre Collection, The New York Public Library for the Performing Arts, Astor, Lenox and Tilden Foundations.

1 ———————————————————

Literary Analysis

In a close examination of Arthur Miller's play *The Crucible* as a literary work, the title itself is the first vivid indicator of the thematic ideas on which the play is based. Several meanings of the word resonate throughout the play. A crucible is literally a metal or earthen vessel in which materials—metal or stone—are brought to extremely high temperatures for the purpose of changing their properties to produce something else. Thus the title suggests the setting of the play because this definition conjures up images, pertinent to Miller's play, of a witch's cauldron, wherein, according to tradition, the witch cooked up her eye of newt and heart of toad and other unappetizing ingredients in order to cast spells. Such a cauldron is mentioned in Act I when, in the initiating moment that begins the witch-hunt, Abigail Williams is challenged by the Reverend Parris because he saw a kettle in the forest containing what looked like a witch's brew, including a frog.

THE THEME

The word *crucible* suggests not only the setting of witch hysteria, but the fundamental theme of the play as well, for a crucible also refers to a severe test or trial. On one level, it refers to those tests to which the magistrates subjected accused witches. In Miller's play, for example, those accused of witchcraft were asked to repeat the Ten Commandments. The inability of the accused to recite them all correctly was often regarded as proof that they were witches. Note, for example, that John Proctor is asked to recite the Ten Commandments and leaves out "Thou shalt not commit adultery."

Another meaning of the crucible pertinent to the play is that the community itself is a crucible in which the citizens have been heated to red-hot panic and hysteria. In this crucible, the "metal" of ordinary citizens is tried and tested. How will they withstand this heated and unhealthy atmosphere? Will they confess like cowards and give the judges names of their friends and neighbors to save their own skins? Will they encourage this witch-hunt by cooperating in whatever way they can? Or will they become finer people in this fiery crucible?

How is character revealed in the face of the intense heat of the crucible? As a social playwright, Miller is not interested just in the character of the individual; he is concerned with the character of the society as a whole and particularly of its ruling class.

The crucible of 1692 has been brought to the white heat of destructiveness for a reason that thunders with irony in this church-dominated community. A group that pretends to have been founded on a religion of compassion has lost all love, both individually and collectively, in an orgy of greed, ambition, and lust. Without that foundation, everything is turned upside down and inside out. In the chaos that ensues, irrationality and fear begin to reign.

In a world turned chaotic and perverse, justice and faith are sacrificed. The characters' inability to appeal to simple justice and reason creates the real terror of 1692. As wise people began to observe after it was all over, the Devil actually had been in Massachusetts—not in the accused but in the accusers.

Because the Devil, or at least a form of evil, had taken over the loveless leaders of Massachusetts Bay, this religious community had become a witches' cauldron in which every member was put to the test. Miller's play explores how that crucible came into being and how society and its members endured the experience. The playwright develops his theme through a tightly constructed, traditional, realistic plot and through complex, multidimensional characters who, though subject to human weakness, have the capacity to evoke our sympathy and to achieve greatness.

THE PLOT

Exposition

The plot of *The Crucible* follows the realistic dramatic tradition. It begins with an exposition, followed by an initiating circumstance that brings on rising action, moves toward a climax, and ends with a denouement. The exposition begins with the first line: Betty, the Reverend Samuel Parris's daughter, is ill, seemingly on the point of death. Rumors of witchcraft are flying, and Betty has attempted to fly. All the major characters and the main threads of the plot are introduced. Most of the principal characters enter, including John Proctor, Giles Corey, Rebecca Nurse, Mercy Warren, the Putnams, and the Reverend John Hale.

In the first five pages of the exposition are roughly five units of action (sometimes called French scenes), in which different configurations of characters appear on stage. In just these brief five pages the playwright establishes the essential facts:

- Betty, the daughter of the Reverend Parris, has a strange sickness.
- Parris has caught several girls, including his daughter, his niece, and his servant Tituba in a forbidden activity, dancing in the forest.
- Abigail, his niece, who lives with his family and is a leader of the girls, has a questionable reputation for wildness and has been without a job since she was fired by John Proctor's wife Elizabeth.
- Abby and the other girls are afraid of being whipped should the truth of their activities in the forest be discovered.
- Their activities include taking off their clothes in the forest, and Abigail has drunk a charm (we later learn that it is chicken blood) to harm Elizabeth Proctor, John Proctor's wife.
- Parris has consulted a doctor and sent for a scholarly minister, the Reverend Hale, to determine if anything unnatural is afoot.
- Parris is worried about his own situation in the community, a community seriously divided between those who support him,

like the Putnams, and those who despise him, like the Nurses, the Proctors, and the Coreys.

- Parris is greedy as well as quarrelsome and ambitious.
- The whole village already fears that witchcraft is abroad.
- The powerful Putnams are pressing Parris to support an investigation largely because seven of Ann Putnam's infants have died at birth and their one daughter is sick.

The second major grouping around the child's bed includes John Proctor and Abigail Williams. Proctor, it is revealed, has had an affair with Abigail, Parris's niece, the leader of the pack. It is clear that while he still lusts after her, he is determined never to resume the affair, while Abby, a fiercely willful girl, sees him as her idol and liberator—one who has shown her the light, unleashed her passion, and unveiled the community's hypocrisy. It is clear in this scene that she is determined that she will have him and that his cold wife will be either eliminated or put aside.

The third major grouping embraces many of the major players in the drama and emphasizes the division in the community between pro- and anti-Parris members. By the end of this scene, the playwright has established a series of complex motives and community relationships that will feed the hysteria:

- Parris's hellfire sermons and love of money are so resented by many in the community that they refuse to attend church.
- There is a feud between Thomas Putnam and many others in the community (including John Proctor) over land.
- Rebecca Nurse's charities and down-to-earth style are resented by Ann Putnam, who is trying to come to terms with her babies' deaths and explain them supernaturally.
- Martha Corey's love of books is betrayed by her husband, Giles, in somewhat bumbling fashion.

Besides establishing a basic situation, the exposition provides a sketch of each character and establishes a fearful atmosphere that quickly intensifies. Thus we see Act I, Scene 1, begin with an atmosphere of tension and fear, fed by ambition, pride, greed, an obsession with status and land, the aftermath of adultery, and plain human evil, all of which set the stage for hysteria. Rampant evil has already been there for some time when the curtain opens. The Promised Land of the New World is a long way from Paradise.

Initiating Incident

The exposition has shown us that trouble has actually begun long before the curtain opens: the leading people in this community have lost (or at least desperately strayed from) the sense of community, the love of God, and the love of one's neighbor and the common good that their own beliefs had taught them to honor and that had led them to cross the ocean and to struggle to establish this new home in the wilderness in the first place. This is clear in a brief look at the motives of each. All, in one way or another, live in a fallen world. At this crucial moment, something happens to set the machinery for a witch-hunt into motion. The wealthy Putnams persuade the Reverend Parris that rather than being afraid that witchcraft in his household will besmirch his reputation, he should view it as an opportunity to further his status. At about the time that he is so persuaded, he turns to accuse Abigail of unholy activity in the forest and to threaten her. Prompted by the crazy Ann Putnam, Abby begins to make charges of witchcraft in order to divert attention from her own misbehavior. It is this charge of witchcraft that sets the tragedy in motion and begins an intense action that rises to the climax.

Up to this point, the trouble could have ended with only minor punishments meted out to the guilty girls; but after this, retreat is not possible. We have seen the iron will of Abby, who will not, who cannot let charges of witchcraft die, and the weakness of the other participants in the moonlight voodoo. With the introduction of Reverend Hale's decision, at Putnam's and Parris's request, to pursue witchcraft in the community, the charge takes on a life of its own.

Rising Action

The action rises from the end of Act I, Scene 1, when Tituba and the girls, out of pressing fear, join in the charges of witchcraft that have been prepared for after the Reverend Hale arrives officially to endorse supernaturalism and Ann Putnam admits that she has met with Tituba to contact the dead in order to find out who "murdered" her seven dead infants. The rising action proceeds through Scene 2 of Act I, the scene between John Proctor and his wife Elizabeth in the common room of their home. Miller here introduces subtle bits of business and action that show the still-lingering tension between the two, stemming originally from Proctor's past affair with Abigail Williams, but involving perhaps much more, things that might indicate a certain "coldness" in Elizabeth, a certain carelessness in John. At the same time, it is clear that each is attempting to mend fences; they are trying desperately to regain the solidity and trust that they once had. Complicating their own attempts to mend their marriage are rumors of many arrests and, finally, Elizabeth's own arrest after being accused by her husband's lover, Abigail Williams.

Scene 1 in Act II builds the action through a psychological unveiling of Abigail Williams in a forest encounter between the two former lovers. Abigail, who in the beginning had denied the widespread presence of witchcraft, has now in her madness come to believe her own lies. John Proctor begins to see that she and the community itself have fed each other's insanity.

The Climax

The climax or final turning point in a play is that moment of high feeling and revelation that makes the rest of the action inevitable. In this play it comes toward the end of Scene 2 of Act II. This occurs after Deputy-Governor Danforth has refused to consider the petition signed by her neighbors; after weak-minded Mary Warren's attempt to tell the truth has wilted under the pressure of hostility and disbelief from the court (when she cannot "faint" on cue), and after one more stirring performance by Abigail and the other girls, when they all turn "cold" and demonstrate the appearance of spirits once more; and after the Reverend Hale's belated and desperate attempt to turn the tide has failed.

Finally, Proctor, in a last effort to turn aside the disaster, confesses to lechery with Abigail and reveals that her accusation of his wife is vengeance for having been dismissed because of it. By this time, a hostile court is not willing to accept his word; they feel instead that he is lying. Thus they call Elizabeth into the court to answer the simple question: Did John Proctor have an affair with

Abigail and was that the reason you dismissed her? Elizabeth enters, forbidden by Danforth even to look at Proctor so as to receive no cue from her husband.

This and the following action provide the final turning point. Ironically, Proctor has already testified that his wife will never tell a lie (he has bet his life on this fact); but when Elizabeth Proctor is forced clearly to answer Danforth's repeated question, eventually she does lie in an effort to protect her husband. No, he did not commit lechery, she says, and with her only lie, she sends her husband to his death. This is the high point of the play, with the dramatic action rising to a crescendo, after which John Proctor's doom is certain.

This is also the final defeat for the Reverend Hale's belated crusade. Saying that this was a natural lie for a woman under such circumstances, he cries out against the court and charges that "private vengeance is working through this testimony" (Act III, p. 105).

As a coup de grace for truth, Abby begins to work on Mary, who had promised Proctor to reveal the truth and Abby's deceptiveness. In one of Abby's fits of screaming and shivering agony, she says that it is Mary's spectre who tortures her, and Mary at last completely changes her testimony, joining the triumphant Abby and charging that Proctor is the "Devil's man." At last, with death certain, Proctor violently condemns the entire court in a shout of fury, as Hale too denounces them all and walks out.

Denouement

Act IV provides the falling action or denouement and the final catastrophe. The entire act has the tone of a requiem. Proctor retracts a confession he has contemplated (which would have saved him) and marches to the gallows.

CHARACTERIZATION

Each of the characters passes through the crucible—the heat of personal testing created by the witchcraft hysteria. All are changed in some way. Some experience a moral collapse, giving way to fear and self-interest. Others, like John Proctor, emerge heroic.

John Proctor

John Proctor, the leading man of Miller's play, is the character on whose test within the crucible the playwright focuses most intently. Proctor is thirty years old. He is strong, perhaps handsome, perhaps congenial, certainly commanding. His first act upon coming on stage is to berate Mary Warren (now working at his house) for being away without his permission. He is accustomed to being obeyed, and he establishes a distinct but justified sense of authority and command.

He is also a practical, no-nonsense person. He gently mocks the rumors about Betty Parris's illness. He questions the wisdom of sending for Hale to look for devils, and he justifiably challenges Putnam's wild charge that children are dying in the village. He also has an ironic sense of humor regarding the absurdity of the witch charges and the secret cavorting of the young girls at night in the forest. To him, this is more a cause for amusement than for hysteria.

But in his scene with Abigail, we are introduced to a different side of Proctor. We see that while Abby, who is described as a "child," was working in the Proctor household, he had an affair with her. One tends to call it a "love affair," but it seems to have been more lust than love on Proctor's part. The stunningly beautiful Abby presents herself as the wronged maiden. Considering the strength of the two people—the young girl/child and the thirty-year-old man—Miller leads the reader to wonder who seduced whom. Nevertheless, the fact, damning to Proctor, is that he, the much older adult, seems to have been the first man she ever slept with.

Although Proctor has decisively ended the affair, he still lusts after her, a fact that does not escape Abby's notice: She tells him that by watching his face when he fired her, she could tell that he loved her then and loves her yet. Everything that we see tells us that this is true. When she triumphantly challenges him, he admits that perhaps he has wanted her.

This brief scene reveals Proctor, at least as he has been in the past, as dishonorable and self-centered. He is a grown, married man who has given in to his lust for a child whom he knew from the first should have been completely off limits. He wants the affair, wants her, yet does not want the situation, though he ultimately has given in to it. If one judged his conduct outside of a play, he would emerge as brutal and predatory, giving no thought about what he is doing to himself, his wife, or Abby. In this first scene, he still seems unconcerned about others and concerned only about himself.

He is determined to break off the affair now—a necessity, for he intensely desires to reestablish his marriage and to regain some sense of self-respect. The fact that he has done this by scorning the person he has seduced is part of the complexity of Miller's script. Proctor is forced now to face the inevitable consequences of his act and the forces that he has set in motion, for his spurning of Abby, who sees herself as wronged, has much to do with her determination to escalate the hysteria and everything to do with her accusation of his wife.

In a modern court, the onus would be ineluctably on John Proctor: the mature, middle-aged, and careless man who casually seduced his baby-sitter. Did John Proctor really ever plan to leave his wife and marry Abigail Williams? Did he ever really promise Abby that? The indications are that he did not. That, however, remains part of the "unwritten script" that a skilled actor would have to generate to add depth to this character in performance. But if he did not, then how did he lead Abby to dream so positively that he would? Did he deliberately say things to the young girl to make her think that he would do this, while secretly knowing that he would not? In either case, he is surely not "heroic" at this stage, but only determined to pull himself together at the child's expense.

At the conclusion of this early scene between Abby and Proctor (14), Proctor notes, with grim determination, that he will cut off his hand before he will ever touch Abby again. This is at once an admission of his guilt and a preview of his fate. It looks forward to the final scene, in which Proctor tears up the phony confession that would have "saved" him and instead deliberately chooses death. The things that he dies for later are clearly apparent here, in miniature: his name and his sense of virtue, his goodness. The terrible pressure of the witch-hunt, with its tortures and executions, is what, as in all moments of extreme pressure, reveals what these characters are truly made of.

This scene also achieves one other thing, in addition to furthering development of plot and character: if a watching audience needed anything to slant their sympathies toward Proctor, despite the weakness and casual destructiveness of his nature, as shown in his past affairs with Abby, it is this: the "enemies," the "antagonists," are Parris and the Putnams. They are about to start hunting "witches," and he is opposed to it. As a dramatic device, it should perhaps be noted that in a stage play, as in real life, one is judged not just by the stature of his friends or by what he does in the abstract, but also by who his enemies are.

Abigail Williams

Abigail Williams, the leader of the adolescent accusers and former lover of John Proctor, is early on caught in a crucible of her own. She is likely to be disciplined for her indiscretions in the forest and needs to find a way out. She has also just had an affair with John Proctor and desperately wants to hold on to him and get his wife out of the way. She faces these, her own crises, by helping to create and escalate a witch-hunt. In so doing, she shows herself to be a complex character, cunningly intelligent, insightful in many ways, manipulative, and possessing a toughness borne of excruciating frontier trials as a child, having seen her family killed in King Philip's War.

In the first, expository scene, it is revealed that she is regarded now as a "bad girl," a reputation she has only acquired since going into service with the Proctors. She was fired by Elizabeth Proctor and has since been unable to secure another position. She says too, perhaps with some justice (we never really know), that Elizabeth Proctor has been blackening her name.

In the same act, when she and Proctor are alone, we learn that Proctor has been her first and perhaps her only lover. She is intent on holding on to him and is devastated at his determination to end the affair. Her feelings for Proctor and his spurning of her lead her to identify Elizabeth Proctor as a witch.

Her second motivation is also apparent in the first act. Parris knows, partly through his traumatized daughter, that Abby has been playing at forbidden games in the woods with Tituba. To escape discovery and punishment, Abby fearfully diverts attention from discovery of her own misdeeds by pointing her finger at others. In a speech that warns the girls to remain silent, she reveals her hard, bloody experience on the raw frontier and demonstrates conclusively that she is the leader. Forced into a corner, she will do whatever is necessary to protect herself. She determines to mark the lines of their admissions and to limit the damage. "Now look you," she says, "We *danced*. And Tituba conjured Ruth Putnam's dead sisters. And that is all" (Act I, p. 19). She goes on to issue a dire threat, revealing that, having seen Indians smash in her parents' heads on the pillows next to her own, she is tough enough to do the girls serious harm should they talk. She is, or will be, a formidable opponent.

Abby is further revealed in a meeting with Proctor in the woods. Here Proctor makes another declaration that under no circumstances will he ever go back to her and that he will, instead, expose her and himself if necessary, in order to save his wife. But Abby is equally fierce in her determination, after being scorned, that she will see them all in hell before she will ever relent and confess that the witchcraft is a fraud. Indeed, she has come to believe her own lies. While Proctor has called this meeting with Abby for the purpose of breaking off their relationship once and for all and warning her that he will not permit her to destroy his wife, the entire scene conjures up echoes of previous meetings in the same place for entirely different reasons.

Though Abby is a skilled dissembler, the lines betraying her loneliness and inner despair have the ring of truth about them. There is a distinct madness about her. The hatred and frustration, along with the stress of the performances for the officials, have produced an inner misery that is not faked. She does not like it in the woods now, and certainly not alone. She sits close to Proctor in the lantern light. When he asks if she is troubled, she thinks that he is mocking her. When he notes that there are rumors about her wild behavior in the tavern with the deputy governor, she responds that the times are exaggerated and there is no pleasure at all for her in any of it. Hosts of boys mockingly follow her wherever she goes; she gets only lewd looks from them, a fact that tortures her now.

Proctor suddenly sees that she is insane when she says that her leg has been bruised by his wife Elizabeth and by George Jacobs, both of whom are in jail. Her insanity is also apparent in an outburst about hypocrisy. She declares that John is the only "good" person in town because he has taught her what goodness is and what frauds other people are.

There is madness in this speech, the half-truth of the wronged and disturbed girl who can see only the evil in the world and in the people around her. At the scene's close, when Proctor threatens to ruin her if she does not free his wife, Miller's stage directions reveal a truth about Abby: that she is still a child.

Elizabeth Proctor

Elizabeth Proctor, like Abigail Williams, is already being tried in her own crucible long before the witch-hunt begins—a crucible created by her husband, who has taken a young lover. The heavy consequences of his actions fall on Elizabeth and the only thing she has, her family, long before they descend upon the whole community when John's actions victimize her for a second time.

Although Elizabeth does not make an appearance on stage in Scene 1, her presence is felt there, for the clash between the two ex-lovers centers on her. We hear Abby excoriate her, among other things, using the telling word "cold," with the implication that she is describing Elizabeth sexually, and we are moved to ask, "Where would Abby have gotten this idea?" The natural conclusion is that she would have heard John Proctor's lips in a lover's confidence when he justified to Abby his betrayal of his wife. Now, however, Proctor has little to say about Elizabeth in response to Abby, and the audience must wait for his wife to reveal herself to be very different from the portrait of her painted by Abby.

Elizabeth does not actually enter the stage until Act I, Scene 2. The curtain rises on an empty stage in the Proctor house, a pleasant, domestic scene, with Elizabeth heard offstage softly singing to the children. As the action proceeds, we see her reaction to John as he comes home weary from the field, having been tramping about all day with spring planting while she has been preparing his dinner. She serves him two dishes, one of which is rabbit stew, and scrambles to bring him the glass of cider she had forgotten. She tells him about catching and skinning the rabbit for his stew after it ran into their kitchen. He talks of spring in Massachusetts, suggesting that on the following Sunday they should walk around the farm together to enjoy the flowers.

It is seemingly a normal conversation on a chilly May evening just before the shadows fall. But something is obviously wrong. The air is fraught with tension. There is the strained solicitation between two people who are trying hard to heal a relationship lacerated by betrayal and stinging quarrels. They still cannot quite trust each other, for the hurt has been too deep. It is the tone of two people walking on eggshells.

Elizabeth's first line, "What keeps you so late? It's almost dark" (Act II, p. 47), is fraught with hidden implications. Although it is perhaps delivered in a tone of solicitation, as if she is trying too hard to please, John probably freezes momentarily. Is she checking up on him? No sooner are the words out of her mouth than she likely regrets them because they might have struck John as distrust. John might think that she suspects that he has been out late with Abby. Perhaps immediately after her question, she is dragged down with self-doubt, wondering herself if her words came from true solicitation or distrust. He replies, "I were planting far out to the forest's edge." And she: "Oh, you're done then" (Act II, p. 47). Then Proctor asks about her health, and she replies that she is well.

Miller demonstrates great skill in the lines about the rabbit. In telling of its capture, Elizabeth shows a distinct sense of compassion for the poor thing that had wandered into the kitchen on its own, only to be killed for food. We see that she is a frontier woman and can perform her duties of capturing, killing, skinning, and cooking wild game. There is also in her line something of that melancholy vision of life that recognizes the death of innocent creatures as a constant fact of life: "It hurt my heart to strip her, poor rabbit" (Act II, p. 48). We see too that Proctor makes a point of telling her that the dish is "well seasoned," a thing, we suspect, that he does not normally do. She replies, "I took care," then asks him, "She's tender?" (Act II, p. 48).

The dialogue about the rabbit is especially tense because of the loaded meaning that husband and wife must both feel but try to ignore. This is introduced with the specific reference to the rabbit not as "it," but as "she," not just once but several times. Elizabeth's sympathy for the rabbit brings to the Proctor table her own victimization by John during his affair with Abby and foreshadows Abby's attempt to victimize her further by accusing her of the capital crime of witchcraft. The lines about the rabbit escalate the tension in an already tense household because they resonate with another double meaning: the rabbit is also Abby, the wild thing that found herself in the Proctor household and was served up (though not by Elizabeth) for the enjoyment of John Proctor.

The suspicion and recriminations come to the surface as the scene between the two closes, for she insists that he let the court know that Abigail had in the first scene denied any involvement with witchcraft. In the process, he reveals that Abigail had told him this while they were alone. When Elizabeth responds that he had concealed from her the fact that they were alone, he bursts out angrily, "Woman, I'll not have your suspicion any more. . . . I have gone tiptoe in this house all seven-month since she is gone; I have not moved from there to there without I think to please you, and still a . . . an everlasting funeral marches round your heart. I cannot speak but I am doubted; every moment judged for lies as though I come into a court when I come into this house" (Act II, p. 52).

There is a double edge to the whole scene in that this seems to have been regarded as an ideal marriage before the trouble set in. Does Elizabeth shoulder some responsibility for her husband's affair in having had her coldness drive him to Abby? We never know certainly, although in the final scene, when Proctor is facing imminent death, she says that she was, and he, in turn, as firmly denies it.

In the play's climactic scene, Elizabeth illustrates the impossibility of surviving this crucible. In the chaos, neither she nor anyone else can make the move that will save them, no matter how hard they might try. There is no way to outguess or outmaneuver the witch-hunters. They have always asked for the truth but required lies. When Elizabeth is put to the test with the question about John's lechery, she can only guess that a lie will save him, as lies have saved so many others.

The Reverend Samuel Parris

The Reverend Parris, without whom, we suspect, there would have been no witch hysteria and no crucible in which the town would be tried, is revealed as arrogant, stubborn, proud, and incompetent. His main concern is with status and his "authority" as a minister: power, control, reputation. Greed is also very much involved, for he is still angry because no one has brought "firewood" to his house, as his contract calls for.

Fear seems to motivate him from beginning to end. At first, he seems to fear that he will lose status if it is discovered that witchcraft began in his house, but he soon comes to fear that he will be damaged if he does not take an active role in the witch-hunt. Once thoroughly implicated in the proceedings, he is terrified of any challenge to the validity of the accusations and tries to insert protests into the conversation between Proctor and Danforth. By the last scenes, he is drained and hysterical with fear that his involvement will hurt his reputation on earth and his hope to avoid burning in hell in the hereafter. Now he frantically does what he can to get confessions from the accused and thus halt further executions.

Thomas and Ann Putnam

The Putnam family, as instigators and the chief accusers in the witchcraft trials, are also instrumental in heating up the community crucible. Ann Putnam, described as "twisted" and "death-ridden," is a woman seemingly rendered mentally disturbed by the death of seven of her children. In seeking answers to the deaths of so many children, she has secretly hired the West Indian slave Tituba to conjure up the dead in order to find out who (as she says) "murdered" her seven children who have died as unbaptized infants. Wanting desperately to know why God has punished her in this way, she frantically grasps the idea of witchcraft, which both provides her with a reason for her suffering and absolves her from any self-blame that her children's deaths may have been the result of her own neglect or her own sins, as Puritanism would have taught her.

Thomas Putnam, a rich landowner, is hard-headed, greedy, and malicious. It is the Putnams who are responsible for Parris's change from fearful denial of witchcraft to an eager participation in the idea. In the congregation's battle, Putnam is on Parris's side, and Parris, realizing Putnam's wealth, is eager to please him.

Immediately following the scene between Abby and Proctor at Parris's house, the Putnams make an appearance. He is harsh, vindictive, and land greedy. As the adults question Abby about the frolic in the forest, Abby accuses the Putnams' daughter Ruth. This gives Thomas Putnam an additional motive to push the minor problem into a serious charge of witchcraft and to push the threatened girls and Tituba into a position from which there is no backing out, from which, it seems, the girls' only means of escape is to become official victims—to name others, adults, who supposedly "bewitched" and tortured them.

Putnam's greed is in evidence when Giles Corey and Francis Nurse appear before Danforth with evidence. Corey charges that Putnam is accusing those with desirable land, in one case a man named George Jacobs, because anyone accused must forfeit his property to the state, and it is apparent to everyone that Putnam is the only one rich enough to buy such land. As Corey tells Danforth: "And there is none but Putnam with the coin to buy so great a piece. This man is killing his neighbors for their land!" (Act III, p. 59). He further tells Danforth that Putnam has been overheard saying, after his daughter named George Jacobs, that his daughter had given him "a fair gift of land." So, while his wife's motives are psychologically twisted and irrational, Thomas Putnam's motives are coldly rational and greedy.

Giles Corey

Giles Corey is a hard-headed, untrained, and tough eighty-three-year-old farmer. He emerges as a simple man, often bumbling, somewhat naïve despite his age, and trapped by the general rush of the tragedy. He is tested cruelly in the crucible of hysteria. First, he labors under a weight of guilt at naïvely having provided the court with evidence to accuse his wife, and second, he has to determine what his actions will be after he is arrested. In the first expository scene, he is trapped by his innate respect for the Reverend Hale, a highly educated scholar who has mastered the world of books and of formal knowledge, into revealing a harmless fact—that his wife reads books. He asks Hale, purely out of curiosity, what this signifies. Much later, he reacts with horror to the realization that this simple question has given the authorities grounds to arrest her for witchcraft. To this he reacts with violence and anger, fiercely determined to defy the court to free his wife. In the process, he accuses Thomas Putnam of charging Martha Corey, his wife, only to be able to take the Corey land, which Putnam has coveted for years. When that fails and he is challenged to name the man who has overheard Putnam crowing about the opportunity to acquire George Jacobs's land, he refuses, even though it places him in contempt of court.

The laws of the times permitted the state to take the land of anybody who was convicted; and the example of the others told Corey that to be accused was to be convicted. A loophole in the law provided that if one did not plead "guilty" or "not guilty," his land could not be taken. However, the law did allow the state to torture an accused person to make him or her enter a plea. The torture in this case was being pressed under an increasingly heavy weight of boulders. After refusing to enter a plea in order to save his land for his family, Giles Corey was slowly pressed to death over a period of days. His last words, when asked if he had any request, were "More weight." The brief story of Corey may be called a kind of subplot, a parallel plot to Proctor's, echoing and prefiguring his own death.

The Reverend John Hale

The Reverend John Hale, like Giles Corey, provides a subplot to the story of the Proctors and Abigail Williams. More than any of the others, this young man is tried intellectually in the crucible of hysteria. Harvard trained and with a confidence that gives him that unassailable air of authority, by his presence, he initiates and puts the stamp of authority upon the problem he finds in Parris's house. He, in effect, ignites the situation, like a spark in a tinder box.

Hale, a bright, scholarly young man of thirty-five, enters with his ancient books, his "authorities," ready to combat the forces of the Devil. In the beginning, he is arrogant, almost jovial in his self-assurance, having no doubt that with his knowledge and his experience, he can solve the riddles and rout the Devil. He honors ancient scholarship so highly that he cannot see reality and makes no effort to perceive possible falsity in the character of Thomas Putnam. It never occurs to him, as it does not occur to Parris, that Betty Parris and the other children might be putting on an act, or at best might be suffering from self-induced hysteria.

Betty Parris has "tried to fly." Hale accepts this without question. Hale, in examining Betty Parris (who is still in bed through all this), further notes his total acceptance of the charges by telling Putnam to "stand close in case she flies" (Act I, p. 38). She cannot bear to hear the Lord's name. He accepts this without question, and to validate it, he turns to his books. Seven children have died in childbirth. He accepts Ann Putnam's explanation of witchcraft, on the face of it, supernatural and devilish, and immediately, instead of examining the facts, leafs through his books, declaring that he will search out the Devil and crush him.

He notes with pride, too, that in his books he finds all knowledge of the invisible world. He loves being the visiting expert and the center of this enthralled group. In these books, he notes, the Devil is stripped of all disguises. The practical common sense of Rebecca Nurse and of John Proctor stands in stark contrast to Hale's gullibility.

In Scene 2, in Proctor's house, Hale is still the pedant, still the obtuse, plodding man of books who gleans all his knowledge from authority and virtually none from the world of real people. There are hints, even at this early stage, that he is beginning to experience some inner doubts about what he has helped put in motion. He has been visiting people around Salem to learn more about the situation. He has also been visiting Rebecca Nurse, a woman who, as he revealed in Scene 1 when he first met her, had earned a wide reputation for kindness and charitable works. She has not yet been "charged," but she has been "mentioned," and this disturbs him. Still, he puts on a show of adamantly insisting that he himself has examined Tituba, Sarah Good, and others and that they have "confessed." He now demands that Proctor prove his own piety by quoting all of the Ten Commandments.

A few lines later, Francis Nurse enters to reveal that Rebecca has indeed been charged—with murder. This time Hale is truly appalled. Nevertheless, even with this, he still clings with desperation to the hope that the "court" represents God and that the innocent will not suffer.

As the hysteria continues to build, however, and especially when his own wife is charged, Hale has a change of heart. By the end of the courtroom scene, Hale has completely reversed himself. Indeed, Hale undergoes the most profound change in the play. He has a formal and earth-shattering enlightenment that the court is not from God. At the end of the scene, he shouts out bitterly that the girls are not bewitched, that they are frauds and are condemning innocent people, and he storms out, denouncing the proceedings.

In the very last scene, it is revealed that Hale has been trying to save as many lives as he can; he is a man of great "sorrow," and he shows signs of exhaustion when he enters. Danforth, of course, will not change his verdict and will not pardon anyone, for twelve people have already been hanged. To pardon the rest would undermine and invalidate all the horror that Danforth has perpetrated. It is Hale too who has the lines depicting the countrywide desolation resulting from the court's reign of terror: the children wandering the streets without parents or homes, the abandoned animals in the road, the crops rotting in the fields, and the universal fear of being the next one named by the girls.

Hale has all the characteristics of a tragic hero: He is a man of substance. While not a king, he is distinctly a leader in the community and a man with almost kingly powers, at least in the beginning. He is proud and capable; he is a scholar, with a substantial reputation, a graduate of Harvard College, the man they all look up to for light and guidance. He finally undergoes a genuine enlightenment, a genuine change. But it is knowledge too late gained. In the end, he sees that all his efforts to rectify or even to ameliorate the great wrong have come to naught. His only reward is that he has seen the truth.

Rebecca Nurse

Unlike the Reverend Hale, Rebecca Nurse endures the test of the crucible with the strength she has maintained in living her day-to-day life all along. She begins with a clearheaded view of the children's disorders and of Ann Putnam's sufferings; she sticks to the truth throughout; and she refuses to confess or name names to save her own life.

When she is first introduced, she is seventy-two years old. Her reputation as a good and charitable woman has reached even as far away as the town of Beverly and the ears of the Reverend Hale. She serves as a foil for all those people who initiate the machinery of witch-hunting, either from good motives or ill, and for those who keep it moving by cooperating. She is probably the one truly virtuous and unstained person in the entire play. As Hale says in Act II, it is preposterous that a person such as Rebecca Nurse should be charged (61); and a short time later, after she has indeed been charged, he asserts, "Believe me, sir, if Rebecca Nurse be tainted, then nothing's left to stop the whole green world from burning" (Act II, p. 67). Her fate and the excellence of her character lead the audience to feel the extent of the destructive malice at work here.

THE TRAGIC HERO

Arthur Miller's characterization of one who is tried in the fiery crucible results in a specific dramatic form, our highest one: the tragedy. With the tragedy, the playwright also gives us the highest type of dramatic character: the tragic hero. Traditionally, the tragic hero is one who fights against overwhelming odds even though he may sense that he is going to lose. The forces he struggles against may be tremendous—God or Fate itself. They may be as modern as a powerful society. They may be psychological—an inner, irresistible urge. The tragic hero is one who refuses to allow himself to be drawn along with a current, refuses to be predicted. Instead, he determines to take hold of his own life and so to defy God himself, Fate, or other things in his existence that seem bound to determine what will become of him. Inevitably, in one sense, he is defeated by these forces, but in the struggle, he asserts his nobility as a human being.

The pattern of classic tragedy shows the downfall of a noble man, a man of many virtues and high position, like a king or some other powerful leader. From the heights of worldly fame, fortune, and achievement, along with nonpareil status, he falls to the lowest depths, not through character alone, and not because his motives deserve the end that he comes to; not through a predetermined destiny alone; but through an interplay of Fate and character—Fate working through both his virtues and the fatal flaws in his character.

To understand how Miller has developed a tragedy for a modern audience, it is useful to have a look at what has come to be seen as the prototypical classic tragedy, the great drama *Oedipus the King* by the Greek playwright Sophocles. In this play, the people of Thebes approach King Oedipus for help in ridding the city of a plague under which they are suffering as a curse from the gods, because an evil thing, some unknown, mysterious, and polluted person, has poisoned the air and offended the gods, who will not relent until the polluted thing is driven out. Oedipus vows to curse the pollutant and drive him out, no matter who it turns out to be.

He fearlessly and resolutely pursues his task, even in the face of warnings that he should stop, that terrible harm will come to him if he persists. Oedipus learns at last that he himself is the polluted thing: he had come to Thebes many years before, not knowing that he had been abandoned and adopted as a child. Without realizing it, he had killed his own father, years before, when meeting an angry person at a crossroads. To add horror to horror, Oedipus has married a woman, not knowing that she is his mother. So he carries out his punishment on himself. He tears out his own eyes and banishes himself from the city.

To the ancient Greeks like Sophocles, the author of *Oedipus*, the tragic hero was a noble person like Oedipus, a king, or one who stood above the mass of people, who fought valiantly and, through the hands of Fate plus flaws in his own character, usually met with disaster. In the Middle Ages as well, "tragedy" was the death of a king: a play about a king who died was called tragedy, whether or not the king was admirable.

In the modern world, the era of the "common man," we have long since passed from an idealization of kings. Quite the opposite: in a modern play a king is more likely to be a figure of absurdity, or the subject of fantasy romance, but not the hero of serious tragedy. In a modern tragedy, a "hero" may be "kingly" only in the sense that he possesses qualities that lift him above the ordinary masses. He may be quite an ordinary man, fighting valiantly in the face of overwhelming odds, knowing that in the end he will be defeated. When he does so fight, his very efforts lift him into the realm of the tragic. He is a tragic hero, and his efforts make the play a tragedy.

A few comparisons between the classic tragedy and the modern one by Arthur Miller may be instructive. *Oedipus* ends with the plague removed and the city restored but the hero, a victim of Fate, fallen. *The Crucible* ends with the plague in full swing and the antagonists still in power, all challenges having failed. Goodness is defeated and evil rules triumphant. Also in contrast to *Oedipus*, Fate really has nothing to do with it. Rather, human weakness and human failures determine everything. At the same time, the protagonist, John Proctor, spiritually rises. He gains stature; and in his own world, at least, he regains his sense of goodness and his "name."

Unlike *The Crucible*, there is no real antagonist in *Oedipus*.

There is only a series of revelations, all of which in the end point to the king himself. In *The Crucible*, the leaders themselves are the villains, and the hero is the one who opposes them and loses. In short, this is a *modern* tragedy. It does not concern mythical heroes and legendary cities. It concerns real or realistic people, ordinary people faced with extraordinary circumstances. *The Crucible* is also a play with a *social purpose*: the author intends the viewer or reader to see certain truths about the human situation that affect all people and that, unless tended to, become destructive.

Tragic Heroes in Salem

While John Proctor, in not being a noble leader or a person with great power in Salem, fails to fit the classic form of the tragic hero in many ways, he does fit the pattern that Arthur Miller consciously developed: a modern tragic hero in the form of a common man. In the horror of the Salem hysteria, Proctor achieves some sense of status and courage in the name of goodness and in a cause that is just. In the crucial scene outside the courtroom, when he decides that he will openly admit to all his neighbors that he has committed the crime of lechery, that he has lied, that he has refused to accept responsibility, that he has in fact been guilty of the most serious betrayal of trust, his *motive*, at least, is good: he will risk his own damnation before the community in order to stop the terrible spate of hangings and imprisonment. Even though he knows that they probably will not believe him, he is obligated to do it anyway.

Later he decides to confess, arguing that he is not a good man nor martyr material, and that it is more important that he see that his children are provided for. So he formally admits that he saw the Devil, that he agreed to do the Devil's work, and that he bound himself to the Devil's service. But when he is pressed to name others in league with the Devil, he cannot do it. In the final analysis, when Danforth presses him for names of others, he declares that he will not be used.

Following this exchange, the scene gets to the heart of the matter. He cries out: "I have three children—how may I teach them to walk like men in the world and I sold my friends?!" (Act IV, p. 132). A few lines later, after Danforth has once more pressed as to why, he cries out: "Because it is my *name!* I cannot have another life! Because I *lie* and sign myself to lies! Because I am not worth the dust of the feet of them that hang! How may I live without my name? I have given you my soul, leave me my name!" (Act IV, p. 133). Under Danforth's still-hanging threat, Proctor then deliberately tears up the false confession. His fate is sealed. The weak and pathetic Parris objects in horror, while Hale responds in genuine agony that Proctor will now hang.

The play in fact ends with these two, the chief instigators of the terrible oppression who cannot now face the consequences of their act, crying out in desperation for Rebecca Nurse or Elizabeth Proctor to go to Proctor, to make him change his mind. But his wife knows that this is impossible, for she realizes that "He have his goodness now. God forbid that I take it from him." The stage directions at this point highlight the closing drama of the scene: "(*The drum roll heightens violently. Three seconds and then*) THE CURTAIN FALLS" (Act IV, p. 134).

In fighting overwhelming odds, in this case community insanity, Proctor rises into something that, if not "greatness" in the classical sense, has about it at least a sense of "goodness," facing death in a cause that is noble and just. The terrible hysteria goes on, of course, abetted and inflamed by the leaders of the community, and it drowns him like a tidal wave.

THE SOCIAL PLAYWRIGHT

Whether one considers his second play, *All My Sons*, about war profiteering, or his great *Death of a Salesman*, about a man seduced by shallow materialistic values, Arthur Miller has emphasized that, while any individual must accept responsibility for the consequences of his or her own behavior, society also has responsibilities to accept and consequences to consider. In *The Crucible*, society's sins are to be weighed very solemnly in light of two realities: first, as a group, society itself has far greater power than any single individual. Second, only society, under the control (in this case) of its leaders, can *officially* sanction evil.

While our interest is drawn in *The Crucible* to the way in which individuals perform in the face of chaos and terror, we are, nevertheless, never allowed to forget that it is society's religious and lawful leaders—Putnam, Parris, Hale, Danforth, John Hathorne,

Jonathan Corwin—who, in unison, have created the crucible and continue the chaos despite the timidly and fearfully expressed reservations of the general populace. This is not just the story of a man; it is the story of an entire community that has created and is tested within the red-hot fire of the crucible.

PROJECTS FOR ORAL OR WRITTEN EXPLORATION

1. Write an essay on the idea in *The Crucible* of turning one's conscience over to the group.

2. Write an essay on references in *The Crucible* to religious rites and Holy Scripture. How do these references heighten the irony of the situation?

3. Write an essay on insanity, both individual and collective, in the play.

4. Explore the idea that the accused must confess guilt in order to be found innocent.

5. When Proctor and Hale speak of hypocrisy, they see it somewhat differently from Abby. Explain.

6. Stage a mock trial: Assume that John Proctor is on trial for sexual abuse.

7. Explore the idea of books and "learning" in the play.

8. Explain exactly what Abby means when she says that Proctor has shown her the light.

9. Write an essay on the central figure of Act I, the sick child in the bed. What is the significance of this to the whole play? Explore this as a symbol and a reality. How would this relate to the idea of witchcraft hysteria and contagion?

10. Write an essay on the Reverend Parris's dilemma in Scene 1—his being, so to speak, stranded between concern for his child and fear of being connected with witchcraft.

11. Write an essay on the desire to "save face" in *The Crucible*.

12. Assume that the Reverend Hale has been charged with misconduct during the witch trials, long after they are over. Stage a "church" trial, some students arguing for forgiving him, some for censuring him.

13. Have a debate about the Proctor marriage. Is there proof that Elizabeth is or has been cold? How would your answer to this affect your evaluation of John Proctor's conduct? Would any possible coldness on Elizabeth's part justify his adultery? Why or why not?

14. On the basis of what is revealed about Abby in the play, write an imaginative narrative showing what her life is like after she disappears.

15. Find a good definition of tragedy and make an argument: *The Crucible* is or is not tragedy.

16. Which are the most believable characters in the play? Explain and support your answer.

17. Many of the actions in this play are evil, that is, terribly bad or worthy of condemnation. Write an essay defining evil. How do you tell evil from not-evil? When and under what circumstances must one unquestioningly follow the word of "authority," and when must one automatically defy authority? Explain and support your answer.

SUGGESTED READINGS

Bhatia, Santosh K. *Arthur Miller: Social Drama as Tragedy*. New York: Heinemann, 1985.

Carson, Neil. *Arthur Miller*. New York: Grove Press, 1982.

Corrigan, Robert W. *Arthur Miller: A Collection of Critical Essays*. Englewood Cliffs, N.J.: Prentice-Hall, 1969.

Ferres, John H., ed. *Twentieth Century Interpretations of "The Crucible."* Englewood Cliffs, N.J.: Prentice-Hall, 1972.

Hayman, Ronald. *Arthur Miller*. New York: Ungar, 1972.

Martin, Robert A., ed. *Arthur Miller: New Perspectives*. Englewood Cliffs, N.J.: Prentice-Hall, 1982.

Martine, James J., ed. *Critical Essays on Arthur Miller*. Boston: G. K. Hall, 1979.

Moss, Leonard. *Arthur Miller*. Rev. ed. Boston: Twayne, 1980.

Schlueter, June, and James K. Flanagan. *Arthur Miller*. New York: Ungar, 1987.

Weales, Gerald, ed. *The Crucible: Text and Criticism*. New York: Viking, 1971.

2

Primed for Hysteria

Arthur Miller set his play *The Crucible* in the town of Salem, Massachusetts, in the year 1692, in a community of Puritans. As Miller makes plain in his explanatory notes to the play, even though the belief in witchcraft was widespread throughout the Christian world, New World Puritanism was much harsher than Old World Protestantism because of the Puritans' trials in the wilderness. As we shall see, the disasters that they endured, coupled with their strict theology, led to persecutions, including the Salem witchhunts, that appalled even Old World Puritans. Knowledge of the following tenets of Calvinism is necessary for an understanding of how the Salem witch trials developed:

- All people without exception were evil by nature.
- Satan, the Prince of Darkness, was always just beneath the surface, ready to take control of individuals and communities.
- Satan's last great stronghold on earth was the wilderness of the New World.
- Many emotional outlets like the exercise of the imagination, art, reading, dance, humor, and play were of the Devil.
- A person's actions or deeds were never indicative of the truth of his or her heart.

- God was unceasingly angry at humans and ready to punish both individuals and whole communities for who they were and how they acted.

- The whole community had to be enlisted to ferret out sins.

- Most people in the community were like children who needed to be led by ministerial leaders.

Puritans were regarded as outlaws by the English royalty and the established Church of England. To practice a religion other than the state religion was considered both treasonous and heretical, and persecution of Puritans was especially widespread during the reign of the Stuart kings, James I and Charles I, from 1603 to 1647. They could not meet as congregations; their ministers could not legally preach and were subject to arrest; they were legally forbidden to read Scripture.

These persecutions drove them underground or, in the case of one group of Puritans, to settle in the Netherlands. This last group's fear that their children were leaving the faith as they were assimilated into Dutch society and intermarried with Dutch natives caused them to emigrate to the New World, settling in what is now Plymouth, Massachusetts, in 1620. Conditions were so hard in the settlement that half of them died in the first year.

In 1628, following the settlement at Plymouth, another group of Puritans settled in what is now Boston. Fifteen years later, Boston was the largest city in America. The charter given these settlers allowed them to govern themselves and conduct business without interference from England. In 1649, events in England improved the fortunes of New World Puritans, for in that year a Puritan named Oliver Cromwell became Lord Protector, ruling England until his death in 1658. During Cromwell's rule, the inhabitants of Massachusetts Bay enjoyed their independence, but when, after Cromwell's death, a new king, Charles II, ascended the throne, the Puritans in New England were thwarted in their conduct of their own political affairs and trade. From 1662 to 1696, for example, the English Parliament kept in place Navigation Acts designed to protect English trade, but these acts hampered the colonists' efforts to trade freely with the rest of Europe. During the reign of King James II, who followed Charles, self-government in the Puritan colony was virtually abolished, and royal governors were appointed in place of the governors elected by the people. The royal governors had the power to veto any colonial legislation.

Although the Puritans contributed to the American Revolution, Puritanism virtually disappeared by the end of the eighteenth century. Several circumstances contributed to its decline. For one thing, the clergy lost its immense political power in the new charter forced on the colony by the king in 1692. But ordinary citizens in Massachusetts Bay also began to fall away from a church notorious for tyrannical leaders and harsh intolerance. Many became more interested in worldly rather than spiritual matters. Others moved west to escape the heavy hand of the Puritan church. One interesting way of getting at the character of New World Puritanism is to investigate some of the fallacies that have been perpetuated about the group.

POPULAR ASSUMPTIONS ABOUT PURITANS NEEDING EXAMINATION

- All Puritans left England and settled in America.
- Puritans came to the New World with the intention of making it their permanent home.
- Puritans came to the New World to establish religious freedom.
- Puritans only welcomed into their midst other Protestant dissenters like Baptists and Quakers.
- Unlike the British, the Puritans had no class system.
- Unlike Virginia settlers, the Puritans refused to participate in the slave trade.
- Puritans believed that education posed a danger to their religion.
- Puritans believed that their ministers only had to have "a call" to preach; it was not necessary nor good for them to know Latin, as the Catholic clergy did.
- Puritans wore only black, white, and grey.
- Puritans were more sexually repressive than any of those who followed them, and they believed that sex was shameful.
- The Puritans' only religious holiday was Christmas.
- The Puritans believed that if one's actions were good and one went to church and believed in God (which for them included Jesus), one would go to heaven.
- The Puritans maintained that only babies were pure of heart.

Each of these statements is false. Let us look at each one.

The New World did not corner the market on Puritans. In fact, far fewer Puritans left the mother country than stayed behind in England. The group that threw the king of England off the throne and had control of England for sixteen years was the Puritans. Their leader, who replaced the monarchy, was Oliver Cromwell. What one can say is that the Puritan community in the New World had a much more lasting influence on the culture of the whole country in which they lived than Puritans did in England.

Letters show that most Puritans viewed their stay in the New World as just as temporary as their residence in Holland. What they hoped was that they could live and exercise their religious beliefs in the New World without interference until changes occurred in England that would allow them to return. Many of them did return during Cromwell's reign.

It was never the Puritans' intention to establish in the New World a place where everyone could exercise religion freely. They came to the New World to have religious freedom for themselves, but not for anybody else who differed with them. As a matter of fact, for most leaders, "toleration" was a dirty word, and even English Puritans believed that American Puritans went much too far in their intolerance of other beliefs. Nathaniel Ward, author of a 1647 satire entitled *The Simple Cobler of Aggawam*, wrote after his return to England that nowhere in Scripture does God imply that those whose beliefs are false are to be tolerated, especially if those with the Truth have the power to suppress them.

Nor did Puritans extend any welcome to other Protestants who had rejected the Anglican church. In England, Oliver Cromwell and his followers brutally suppressed some of the dissenting groups (like that called the Levellers). American Puritans were just as bad, if not worse. For example, Baptists who came to the Boston area were persecuted for decades chiefly because they did not approve of infant baptism. (The First Baptist Church of Boston contains a plaque commemorating one of their number who was brutally beaten by the Puritans in the seventeenth century.) Those who wanted to accord importance to "good works" in one's salvation were considered the worst kind of heretic by the Puritans, who persecuted the forerunners of Methodism in their midst. Though Quakerism grew out of Puritanism in England, the Quakers and Puritans became mortal enemies, and Quakers were forbidden to enter the Massachusetts Bay Colony on pain of death. Not only did the Puritans refuse to tolerate other Protestant sects, they refused to tolerate the slightest deviation in thought among their own people, or any criticism of Puritan ministers.

As to their social structure, while the New World Puritans had no rigid inherited class structure, they did maintain a looser system of upper, middle, and lower classes, believing that God placed people at birth in the class he wanted them in and that certain behaviors and occupations were expected of certain classes. For instance, a poor man was not meant to become a legislator.

While slavery never flourished in New England (as much for economic reasons as religious ones), the Puritans were not in principle above participating in the buying and selling of human beings, as witness their decision, noted in their records, to sell the grown children of a Quaker couple in order to pay for the parents' food in prison. The Puritan minister, the Reverend Parris, who figures prominently in the witchcraft trials, brought two slaves with him to Salem, Massachusetts, and one of them was sold again by the Puritan leaders at the time.

While the Puritans would never tolerate teaching children anything that did not agree with their theology, they passionately believed in the teaching of fundamental mathematics, reading, writing, and approved versions of history and natural science. Unlike the Baptists and Methodists of the late eighteenth and nineteenth centuries, the Puritans also insisted on a university-educated clergy, fluent in Latin, Greek, and Hebrew. To this end, one of their first projects was the establishment of Harvard College in a town named for the great place of learning in England where so many Puritan ministers had received their educations, Cambridge.

Regarding their personal habits, Puritans did not restrict their colors to black, white, and grey. They were fond of wearing the many colors favored by those in the Renaissance, with these exceptions: no one was allowed ostentatious ornamentation like gold and expensive lace, a law more rigidly enforced for the lower classes. The second-generation Puritans seem to have assumed a more somber habit of dress than that of the first settlers.

Although the Puritans were brutal in their punishment of sex outside marriage, they believed that sex was a pleasure to be fully enjoyed by both husband and wife in marriage. Failure to fulfill the sexual role in marriage was one of the few grounds for divorce.

In this sense, the Puritans did not consider sex to be as secretive and shameful as their nineteenth-century descendants did.

Nor did Puritans frown on the consumption of alcohol. They drank ale, wine, and hard cider with their meals, allowed the importation of rum and gin, and operated taverns in Massachusetts Bay. However, they also recognized the growing problem of public drunkenness and dealt with it severely, eventually placing restrictions on the operations of taverns in order to control it. However, the Puritans never adopted abstinence from alcohol as a policy.

As to religious beliefs, which we will later investigate in further detail, the Puritans, like other Protestants, had dispensed with many of the rites and religious celebrations of the Roman Catholic church, but had gone even farther than most dissenters in declaring Christmas to be a pagan holiday—actually making it illegal to celebrate Christmas and punishing those who did.

The idea that good deeds and a belief in God got one into heaven was considered a terrible heresy. Puritans believed that neither good deeds nor churchgoing (though it was required) nor faith in God guaranteed a person a place in heaven.

Finally, according to Puritan belief, not even newborn babies were innocent of sin. Because babies had not lived long enough to go through religious self-examination, the Puritans believed that all who died in infancy went to hell, thankfully occupying one of the less horrible rooms in hell.

BASIC PURITAN BELIEFS: THE FIRST COVENANT

To put in perspective particular Puritan characteristics that fostered the witchcraft hysteria, it is useful to look at their particular interpretation of biblical history that formed a basis for their beliefs. Puritans believed that biblical history began with the Garden of Eden when God made a "covenant" or contract with Adam and Eve: In exchange for providing Adam and Eve with a paradise to live in, Adam and Eve were to be obedient. Especially they were to refrain from eating fruit from the tree of the knowledge of good and evil.

But Adam and Eve brought on humankind's great tragedy by breaking their part of the contract: they disobeyed God by eating the forbidden fruit. God's anger at their disobedience became

earth shaking. Anger became his chief characteristic. Puritans believed that from this time on all humans were vile from the time
of their conception and that their minds and wills were too weak
for them to control their own lives or to help them to know God.
Furthermore, men and women remained evil at the core for the
rest of their lives. Nothing changed this. Even though a person
might be outwardly pious and charitable, at heart he remained
sinful and capable of all sins. Because of this, all people were
damned to hell.

Eventually, God made another covenant, but this time with Jesus
who was acting on behalf of humankind. By means of this covenant
a very few people were chosen to be saved in the hereafter. The
rest would still be damned.

Puritan theology tended to divide the populace into two parts:
a few wise, old leaders on the one hand and, on the other, the
rest of the community, who were thought to be deluded children.
The treatment of most citizens as children was accentuated by the
old age of most of the Puritan leaders, who were regarded as "parents" or "fathers" of the whole community. Like parents, church
leaders thought that they knew what was best for everyone and
insisted that their orders were to be followed without question.
To criticize or cross leaders in authority was the same as defying
God. An example can be found in the church trial of accused
heretic Anne Hutchinson, who was scolded from the pulpit for
being a disobedient child who had crossed her parents, meaning
the community leaders.

While the legislators insisted that all citizens should listen to
their own consciences, community leaders nevertheless insisted instead that in practice, the people turn over their consciences to
godly leaders. This can be seen especially in the many laws against
thinking the "wrong" way. An illustration can be found in the
witch hysteria in that many, if not most, people in the community
were appalled by the arrests and the way the trials were being
conducted, but the leaders were able to bully and frighten them
into going along with the proceedings. Having never been in the
habit of thinking for themselves, ordinary citizens were hesitant
about deciding what was right. They may have thought, "Perhaps
there *are* witches among us—the good leaders ought to know
best!"

COMMUNITY MISFORTUNES, 1660–1691

Because community misfortunes in this life were attributable to the everlasting wrath of God, the Puritans had ample reason for believing after 1660 that they were doing something horrendous to incur even greater divine wrath than they had suffered earlier. Misfortunes of great magnitude seemed to be visited on them daily.

The witchcraft trials, which form the subject matter of Arthur Miller's *The Crucible*, have to be studied in the light of this context: the punishments leveled against the community, the community's habit of constant self-scrutiny, and the leaders' insistence that behavior had to change to lessen God's displeasure. The presence of witches in Salem was seen as just one in a sequence of God's punishments. Community leaders' reaction to what seemed to be witchcraft was a characteristic and, to them, rationally justifiable way of quelling God's anger against them by diligently ridding the community of the Devil's agents.

One situation that helped the community justify its extreme actions in the witchcraft trials was the realization that only a comparatively short time away was the millennium—the beginning of a time when it was supposed that the angel Gabriel would blow his horn for judgment day. In light of this, the Puritans believed that Satan was more busily at work than ever in order to garner additional souls for his own kingdom. Thus special vigilance was called for.

It has been supposed that the community reaction might not have been so radical had not other signs of God's wrath surfaced so persistently in the two decades leading up to the trials. As it was, the community was desperate to do everything it could to avoid further pain, even if it meant going to hysterical extremes. What follows is a partial list of events leading up to the trials.

1658	English Puritan leader Oliver Cromwell dies, and the monarchy, publicly favoring the Anglican church, regains the throne.
1660	Church membership begins to fall continuously. The community begins to feel the loss of the older generation, who begin dying.
1660–1661	Appeals made to the Crown to halt Puritan persecution of Quakers, Baptists, and others are received sympathetically

by King Charles II. He pointedly interferes with the Puritans' persecution of Quakers.

1660–1689   A series of shipwrecks results in great monetary losses.

1660–1689   Continual epidemics of smallpox plague the community.

1662   The old charter that allowed Massachusetts Bay freedom to govern itself is revoked.

1675–1676   Puritans find themselves attacked by the Indian chief, King Philip, and his French allies.

1676   The North Church and forty adjacent houses in Boston catch fire and burn to the ground.

1677   The Puritans again perceive an unchecked threat from a new wave of Quakers within their borders.

1677   The Crown appoints a council to examine the laws of Massachusetts and issues objections to same.

1679   A fire spreads through the business district of Boston, burning almost all of the city's businesses to the ground.

1679   Anglicanism is introduced into the Puritan colony.

1684   Increase Mather and other New England ministers and magistrates travel to England to argue that their charter not be revoked, but their efforts fail. One of the most damaging outbreaks of smallpox occurs.

1685   With King James's ascension to the throne, Puritans face even greater losses of liberty with regard to their charter.

1687   Crops are destroyed by locusts and other insects, along with a drought.

1688   An epidemic of measles causes many deaths.

1689   Royal Governor Edmund Andros is sent to the colonies and proves himself to be a tyrant. At Andros's request, construction begins on an Anglican church building in Boston. Andros is kidnapped and jailed by colonists, but William and Mary, the new king and queen, who it was hoped would be sympathetic, refuse to uphold the Puritans' charges of wrongdoing.

1689   A new wave of hostilities with the Indians breaks out. Colonists, especially those in Maine, fear an imminent invasion by the French from Canada.

1689   The colonists suffer another devastating smallpox epidemic.

1690	In an Indian attack, the settlement of Schenectady is completely burned and other outposts are damaged. Several hundred are killed and sixty are taken prisoner.
1691	Despite hopes for restoration of the original charter, reinstituting self-government with a religious purpose, a new charter is issued in which property ownership rather than church membership determines voting rights. In addition, the hated royal governors continue.
1691	Cotton Mather publishes his alarming account of a witchcraft case in Boston.

Throughout the 1670s and 1680s, the Puritans attempted to lessen God's wrath and avoid punishment of the community by enforcing better behavior, rooting out and punishing heretics like the Quakers, and conducting communitywide fasts. The very existence of the fasts and the official language used to inform the public why a fast was necessary graphically illustrate that Puritans felt that they needed to appease God in order to avoid suffering. On March 12, 1684, for example, the colony council ordered a special fast day on the occasion of the end of the First Charter and the subsequent "distressed condition of the people of God." In October 1685, a fast was called "because there is need of our solemn and humble address to God, by reason of 'Rebukes and Threatenings from heaven under which we are at present' by reason of an epidemic sickness." In March 1686, a fast was called because of a smallpox epidemic and the loss of cattle after a severe winter. In the summers of 1687 and 1688, various fasts were called because of plagues of insects, droughts, and an epidemic of measles.

In the documents that follow, one sees various aspects of Puritanism, listed at the beginning of this chapter, that seemed to foster the belief that witchcraft had to be weeded out of the community with a vengeance. These ideas include (1) the depths of mankind's sinfulness; (2) God's wrath and punishment; (3) the necessity of marshalling the whole community to ferret out sin; (4) the reality of Satan, especially in the New World wilderness; (5) the suspicion of joy and art; (6) and the suspicion that good deeds and piety might cover up evil.

Other documents show a community that felt itself to be under siege from many quarters, one whose members believed that their own shortcomings had provoked the wrath of the Almighty and that they needed to find some way to alter the community to lessen God's wrath and their own misfortunes. They include several poems, a funeral address, and a history written at the time.

MANKIND'S EVIL NATURE

The chief result of Adam and Eve's disobedience in the Garden of Eden was that the very nature of human beings changed from being innocently animalic to being utterly evil and depraved. As one Puritan minister wrote, the heart has many rooms and every one is smeared with every crime. But the true evil nature of the heart is usually hidden from everyone. So submerged is this evil that it rarely comes to the surface. But as in a volcano, the hot lava of the "hell" of the earth sometimes erupts onto the surface. This is what happened in the witchcraft trials. According to the Puritans, some evil, that had previously been contained was let loose from the hearts of men to bring havoc on the entire community. The agents of this release of evil were the witches, acting on instructions from Satan. Thus in *The Crucible*, those accused of witchcraft (like John Proctor) were said to be in league with the Devil.

An excerpt showing this belief is from a sermon by John Cotton, one of the earliest settlers in Boston. Cotton was the junior pastor under the senior paster, the Reverend John Wilson, for the first congregation in Boston. He was a prominent, long-lived leader of the Puritan community and was also intimately involved in one of the most famous cases of heresy in Boston when his protégée, Anne Hutchinson, was banished from the community and excommunicated from the church. Cotton argues in his treatise that people fall into several animal-like categories: sheep are the saved and swine and goats are the damned. The swine are unabashedly evil. The goats are just as evil but pretend to be good. His explanation of the unrelieved baseness of human nature was the approved theological opinion in Puritan New England, one that explains the community in *The Crucible*, where it is believed that the weakness and evil at the base of all human beings make them ripe for use by the Devil.

FROM JOHN COTTON, *THE NEW COVENANT*
(London: n.p., 1654)

Swine and Goats

All the men in the world are divided into two ranks, Godly or Ungodly, Righteous or Wicked; of wicked men two sorts, some are notoriously wicked, others are Hypocrites: of Hypocrites two sorts (and you shall find them in the Church of God) some are washed Swine, others are Goats.

1. The *Swine* are those whom our Saviour Christ saith, *That they returne unto their wallowing in the mire*; like unto these are such men who at the hearing of some Sermon have been stomach sick of their sins, and have rejected their wicked courses, but yet the swines heart remaineth in them, as a Swine when he cometh where the puddle is, will readily lye down in it: so will these men wallow in the puddle of uncleanness when their conscience is not pricked for the present: But these are a grosser kind of Hypocrites.

2. There is another sort that go far beyond these, and they are *Goats*, so called, *Math*. 25.32,33. and these are clean Beasts such as chew the cudd, meditate upon Ordinances, and they divide the hoofe; they live both in a general and particular calling, and will not be idle; they are also fit for sacrifice; what then is wanting? Truly they are not *sheep* all this while, they are but *goats*, yet a Goat doth loath that which a Swine will readily break into; but where then doe they fall short of the nature of sheep? A difference there is, which standeth principally in these particulars.

· · ·

2. They are of a Rankish nature all of them, especially the old Goats will have an unsavory relish, far from that pleasant sweetnesse that is in a sheep; and herein Hypocrites are greatly different from the sheep of Christ, as the Prophet speaketh, *Ezek*. 34.21. and they marre the Pastures with their feet, and will be at length mudling the faire waters of the Sanctuary also; and in your best sanctification they fall far short of a sheep-like frame of spirit, diligently to hear the voyce of the Shepheard, this will not be found in the sanctification of the best Hypocrite under Heaven, they may goe far and yet fall away, and this is no Arminianism, but if you search the Scriptures diligently, you will find these things to be true.   (44–47, 69)

THE WRATH OF GOD

The Puritans believed that God's anger toward mankind, because of the disobedience in the Garden of Eden and the resultant depravity of human nature, was unending and horrendous, and that mankind lived constantly under the threat of intense suffering. Puritans believed that God was also angered by the actions of communities and of individuals and that he would vent his anger by punishing both individuals and whole communities. Sometimes, in a funeral sermon, for example, the family of a deceased loved one would be told that their sinful ways had caused God to take their family member's life. Often God was perceived as punishing people by causing them emotional distress. Inevitably, crop failures, famines, disease epidemics, and Indian wars were seen as God's punishment of a community because of its sinful actions.

One thing that angered God, according to the Puritans, was a community's failure to root out and punish wrongdoers and wrong thinkers. To tolerate someone with wrong ideas would surely, they believed, bring down God's wrath on the whole community. Their insistence that toleration was an evil rather than a good developed from their fear of God's wrath toward the community. In imprisoning and then throwing out of the community those suspected of heresy and in imprisoning and even executing Quakers, Puritans felt that they were protecting themselves, not just from polluting ideas, but from actual physical disasters. The same thinking was behind the witchcraft trials. To allow even one "witch" to go unpunished in New England would be to invite God's horrible anger.

The following excerpt showing the Puritan fear of God's mighty wrath and the punishments that might befall the community as a result is from the sermon *Sinners in the Hands of an Angry God* by Jonathan Edwards. While Edwards postdates the Salem witch trials, he is famous for spiritually revitalizing Puritanism in the eighteenth century by returning theology to the foundation on which the Puritan church had been built. *Sinners in the Hands of an Angry God* is Edwards's most famous sermon. He so graphically explained God's anger at mankind for the disobedience in the Garden of Eden and for mankind's resultant odious nature that some of the people who heard him preach reportedly killed themselves from horror and despair. This attitude is seen in *The Crucible* first when Ann and Thomas Putnam seem to feel that others will blame the death of their infants on God's wrath, and in the general feeling that unless witchcraft is rooted out, God will allow the community to be punished.

FROM JONATHAN EDWARDS,
SINNERS IN THE HANDS OF AN ANGRY GOD
(Amherst, Mass.: Printed and Published by Carter and Adams, 1826)

They are now the objects of that very same *anger* and wrath of God, that is expressed in the torments of hell. And the reason why they do not go down to hell at each moment, is not because God, in whose power they are, is not then very angry with them; as he is with many miserable creatures now tormented in hell, who there fell and bear the fierceness of his wrath. Yea, God is a great deal more angry with great numbers that are now on earth: yea, doubtless, with many that are now in this congregation, who it may be are at ease, than he is with many of those who are now in the flames of hell.

So that it is not because God is unmindful of their wickedness, and does not resent it, that he does not let loose his hand and cut them off. God is not altogether such an one as themselves, though they may imagine him to be so. The wrath of God burns against them, their damnation does not slumber.

• • •

There are black clouds of God's wrath now hanging directly over your heads, full of the dreadful storm, and big with thunder; and were it not for the restraining hand of God, it would immediately burst forth upon you. . . . The wrath of God is like great waters that are dammed for the present; they increase more and more, and rise higher and higher, till an outlet is given.

• • •

It is the fierceness of his wrath that you are exposed to. We often read of the fury of God; as in Isaiah lix. 18. . . . And in many other places . . . we read of "the wine press of the fierceness and wrath of Almighty God." The words are exceeding terrible. If it had only been said, "the wrath of God," the words would have implied that which is infinitely dreadful; but it is "the fierceness and wrath of God." The fury of God! the fierceness of Jehovah! Oh, how dreadful must that be! Who can utter or conceive what such expressions carry in them! (1–22)

A COMMUNITY OF INFORMANTS

The great fear that God was always ready and eager to punish the community with disaster because of its toleration of crimes and heresies justified and even necessitated the cooperation of the entire community in searching out misconduct. This behavior was written into law. Not only did citizens break the law of the land in failing to report intolerable behavior, but they risked casting doubts on themselves. These habits naturally helped turn the witch trials into a hysterical competition to name the most names in order to save oneself.

Excerpts from the following laws show how this aspect of the witch trials was prepared for. Ordinary citizens were compelled to turn on people who swore and cursed on threat of being punished themselves if they did not name names. Selectmen were also ordered to turn in families suspected of having unlicensed houses of entertainment and individuals who seemed to be idle. This reportage on one's neighbor was carried to an extreme in the witch trials when it became necessary to inform in order to save one's own life.

FROM *THE COLONIAL LAWS OF MASSACHUSETTS*,
REPRINTED FROM THE EDITION OF 1672
(Boston: Massachusetts Historical Society, 1887)

6. *Whereas there is much Disorder and Rudeness in Youth in many Congregations in some of the worship of God, whereby Sin and Prophaneness is greatly increased; for Reformation whereof*;
It is ordered by this Court; That the Select men do appoint such place or places in the Meeting-House for Children or Youth to sit in, where they may be most together, in publick view; and that the Officers of the Churches or Select men do appoint some Grave and sober Person or Persons to take a particular care of, and inspection over them; who are hearby required to present a list of the Names of such who by their own Observance or the Information of others shall be found Delinquent to the next Magistrate or Court, who are impowered for the first Offence to admonish them, for the second Offence to impose a fine of *five shillings* on their Parents or Governours, or order the said Children to be whipt,

and if Incorrigible, to be whipt with ten stripes, or sent to the House of Correction for three dayes.

7. *Whereas the Name of God is prophaned by Common Swearing and cursing in ordinary Communication, which is a Sin that grows amongst us, and many hear such Oaths and Curses, and Conceals the same from authority, for Reformation whereof;*

It is ordered by this Court, that the laws already in force against this Sin be vigorously prosecuted, and as Addition thereunto;

It is further Ordered, that all such persons who shall at any time hear prophane Oaths and Curses spoken by any person or persons, and shall neglect to disclose the same to some Magistrate, Commissioner, or Constable, such persons shall incurr the same penalty provided in that Law against Swearers, etc.

• • •

And further, It is Ordered, that all private unlicensed houses of Entertainment be diligently searched out, and the penalty in this Law strictly Imposed, and that all such houses may be better discovered, the Select men of every Town shall choose some sober and discreet persons to be Authorized from the County Court, each of whom shall take the Charge of *ten*, or *twelve Families* of his Neighbourhood, and shall diligently inspect them, and present the Names of such persons so transgressing to the Magistrate, Commissioner, or Select men of the Town, who shall return the same to be proceeded with by the next County Court, as the Law directs, and the persons so chosen and Authorized, and attending their duty faithfully therein shall have one third of the Fines allowed them, but if they neglect their Duty, and shall be so Judged by Authority, they shall incurr the same penalty provided against unlicensed houses.

• • •

10. *Whereas the Sin of Idleness (which is a Sin of Sodom) doth greatly Increase, notwithstanding the wholsome Laws in Force against the same. As an Addition to that Law,*

This Court doth Order, that the Constable with such other person or persons, whom the Select men shall Appoint, shall inspect particular Families, and present a list of the Names of all idle persons to the Select men, who are hereby strictly required to proceed with them, as already the Law directs, and in Case of Obstinacy, by charging the Constable with them, who shall Convey them to some Magistrate, by him to be Committed to the house of Correction.   (34–36)

SATAN'S REALITY

To the Puritans, Satan was not just a character in hell or an idea of evil. He was also an active, monstrous, supermanlike presence operating on the earth and in the lives of various people. When a fine sermon against the Devil blew out of Cotton Mather's hand, for example, Mather believed that it was the direct work of Satan, who had grabbed it away so that the people would not hear the warning against the Devil's work.

Puritans believed that the New World was especially close to the workings of the Devil because it was so untouched by Christian civilization. The whole North American continent except for a few miles along the northeast and Virginia coasts was a fearful and unknown wilderness where it was believed that Satan held forth, along with the native Indians, who were regarded as the Devil's disciples by the Puritans. Satan's false promise of ultimate freedom, power, and pleasure to be experienced in the wilderness was always an invitation to the weaker and more naïve settlers and was always threatening to overtake the godly settlements held in place by rigid dogma and severe discipline. In *The Crucible*, the young women and girls whose behavior instigates the witch hysteria alarm the community because it is found that they meet in the forest with Tituba, herself a natural suspect in coming from what was regarded as an uncivilized land.

In the following excerpt, one can see the belief, widely held at that time throughout the world, that Satan operated in individual lives, still vying with God for control of the world and the souls who peopled it. Increase Mather, a prominent New England minister and father of an even more famous clergyman and scholar, Cotton Mather, was, like his son, involved in the Salem witchcraft trials. Both had written extensively on witchcraft before the trials began, but while Cotton Mather was always a central figure in supporting the trials, his father developed serious reservations about how the trials were being conducted.

In response to Increase Mather's early research on evidence of the Devil in New England life, his friend John Higginson passes along stories that he has heard about two men visited by the Devil in human form, accounts that may be useful in Increase's work.

Such widespread convictions made it possible for New Englanders to believe that the Devil could take over Salem and make tools of otherwise decent citizens whose likenesses he could use to create havoc in the community.

FROM JOHN HIGGINSON, "LETTER TO THE REVEREND MR. INCREASE MATHER"
(Salem, August 17, 1683)

Salem, August 17, 1683

For the Reverend Mr. Increase Mather, Teacher of the Church at the North End of Boston.

• • •

Godly Mr. Sharp, who was ruling elder of the church of Salem almost thirty years, often related it of himself, that being bred up to learning till he was eighteen years old, and then taken off and put to be an apprentice to a draper in London, he yet notwithstanding continued a strong inclination and eager affection to books, with a curiosity of hearkening after reading of the strangest and oddest books he could get—spending much of his time that way, to the neglecting of his business. At one time there came a man into the shop and brought a book with him, and said to him, "Here is a book for you; keep this till I call for it again." And so went away.

Mr. Sharp, after his wonted bookish manner, was eagerly affected to look into that book and to read in it, which he did. But as he read it he was seized on by a strange kind of horror, both of body and mind, the hair of his head standing up, et cetera. Finding these effects several times, he acquainted his master with it, who observing the same effects, they concluded it was a conjuring book and resolved to burn it, which they did. He that brought it, in the shape of a man, never coming to call for it, they concluded it was the Devil. He, taking this as a solemn warning from God to take heed what books he did read, was much taken off from his former bookishness, confining himself to reading the Bible and other known good books of divinity which were profitable to his soul.   (1, 2)

THE DANGERS OF ART AND JOY

Many natural, emotional outlets were condemned by the Puritans because it seemed to them that they allowed humankind's baser, evil nature to come to the fore and take over the more pious, controlled, sober side that needed always to be aware of guilt, sin, and misery. To forget God's wrath and one's own despicable state for even a moment in joking or playing or dancing was to get too far from the truth and risk letting Satan take over one's heart.

In this category of forbidden activities were play-acting, joking, novel reading, and participating in various sports and games. These things were forbidden not only because they were thought to let the dangerous imagination have free rein, but because they kept people from everlasting work that they were supposed to attend to constantly. This is largely why the Puritans made the celebration of Christmas illegal. In the first place, all the merry singing and dining associated with celebrating Christmas was considered paganish, and in the second place, celebrating Christmas gave people a day off from work.

Dancing was especially dangerous because it allowed the wildness and exuberance deep in nature to frolic on the surface. It was of the Devil. Laws were enacted against it. Of course, it is to cover up their dancing in the forest that the girls in *The Crucible* first begin to deceive the community.

The 1672 *Colonial Laws of Massachusetts* reveal that the commonwealth made it illegal for citizens to engage in bowling, playing cards, shuffleboard, or any other games in entertainment establishments. Gambling, dancing, and celebrating Christmas and other festivals were also forbidden by law. Those who broke these laws were subject to fines.

In 1684, New England clergyman Increase Mather, at the height of his career before the Salem witch trials, wrote a book against dancing, especially "mixed" dancing. Dancing, he contends, is immoral and is forbidden by Scripture.

FROM INCREASE MATHER, *AN ARROW AGAINST*
PROFANE AND PROMISCUOUS DANCING
(Boston: Published by the Author, 1684)

But our question is concerning *Gynecandrical Dancing*, or that which is
commonly called *Mixt* or *Promiscuous Dancing, viz.* of Men and Women
(be they elder or younger persons) together: Now this we affirm to be
utterly unlawful, and that it cannot be tollerated in such a place as *New-
England*, without great Sin. And that it may appear, that we are not trans-
ported by Affection without Judgment, let the following Arguments be
weighed in the Ballance of the Sanctuary.

Arg. 1. *That which the Scripture condemns is sinful*. None but Atheists
will deny this *Proposition*: But the Scripture condemns *Promiscuous
Dancing*. This *Assumption* is proved, 1. *from the Seventh Commandment*. It is an Eternal Truth to be observed in expounding the Commandments, that whenever any sin is forbidden, not only the highest acts
of that sin, but all degrees thereof, and all occasions leading thereto are
prohibited. Now we cannot find one Orthodox and Judicious Divine, that
writeth on the Commandments, but mentions *Promiscuous Dancing*, as
a breach of the seventh Commandment, as being an occasion, and an
incentive to that which is evil in the sight of God. Yea, this is so manifest
as that the *Assembly* in the *larger Catechism*, do expresly take notice of
Dancing as a violation of the Commandments. It is sad, that when in
times of Reformation, Children have been taught in their C[a]techism,
that such *Dancing* is against the Commandment of God, that now in *New-
England* they should practically be learned the contrary. The unchast
Touches and Gesticulations used by *Dancers*, have a palpable tendency
to that which is evil.   (1–3)

THE DECEPTIVENESS OF GOOD DEEDS

One habit of mind that allowed the witchcraft trials to happen was the underlying idea, deeply embedded in the Puritan system of belief, that the actions or deeds of an individual are deceptive and reveal little of the more important heart that lies beneath. This idea operates in Puritan religion in the following way: since the fall from the Garden of Eden, all people, without exception, have sinful hearts. This is what damns them, and only God's grace saves a very few, despite their evil natures.

But being weak minded and easily self-deceived, people think that they can still be good at heart by acting holy and pious and doing good deeds. Many think that they can "buy" their way into heaven with good deeds. Yet wise ministers knew that good actions (while they are necessary to hold the community together) do not really reveal what a person is like inside. As a consequence, when the witchcraft hysteria broke out, people were easily convinced that citizens who lived decent lives and even devoted themselves to charity (like Rebecca Nurse) could really be hiding their devotion to the Devil.

Furthermore, this long-standing tendency to insist on the reality of the invisible world and the inner life and to doubt the sincerity of those actions that one could see made it possible to convict on "spectral evidence," to be discussed in Chapter Three in greater detail. Basically, spectral evidence meant that while a person's body could be sitting in church for all to see, her spectre or spirit could be out killing a cow. If someone accused you of killing his cow on Sunday morning, you could not vindicate yourself by saying that a hundred witnesses could testify that you were in church at the time. The Puritan dogma is reflected in *The Crucible*, where we see the community leaders regarding good and charitable people as witches, covering up their true evil identity with good actions. But in *The Crucible*, even the Reverend Hale cannot with confidence convince himself that Rebecca Nurse's prayerfulness and good works are just a deceptive cover-up for an evil heart intent on bewitching the village girls.

Michael Wigglesworth, a Puritan minister, Harvard professor, and the most widely read poet of his day, wrote a poem called *The*

Day of Doom about judgment day. Many of the damned appear before the throne of God to argue that it is unfair that they be damned. One such group is the "civil honest men," whose behavior has always been exemplary. But in Wigglesworth's poem, God tells them that God looks at the heart, not the actions, and that their hearts are found wanting; they have just been doing good deeds, not from good hearts, but selfishly as a way to climb into heaven.

FROM MICHAEL WIGGLESWORTH, *THE DAY OF DOOM*
(Cambridge, Mass.: Samuel Green, 1666)

92

Then were brought nigh a Company
  of Civil honest Men,
That lov'd true dealing and hated stealing,
  ne'er wron'd their Brethren;
Who pleaded thus: "Thou knowest us
  that we were blameless livers; . . .

94

"We hated vice and set great price,
  by virtuous conversation;
And by the same we got a name,
  and no small commendation. . . ."

99

"God looks upon th' affection
  and temper of the heart;
Not only on the action,
  and the external part.
Whatever end vain men pretend,
  God knows the verity,
And by the end which they intend
  their words and deeds doth try.

100

. . .

"In all you do you have show'd your intent:
You thought to scale Heav'ns Lofty Walls
    By ladders of your own."

THE SUFFERINGS VISITED UPON GOD'S CHOSEN PEOPLE

Michael Wigglesworth, Harvard professor, poet, and one of the older generation of ministers, wrote a poetic "jeremiad" in 1662, warning the people of New England that their troubles, both literal and figurative droughts, were the result of God's unhappiness with the colony. He reminds his readers of their happier days as God's chosen people in a new land, when there were no Indian wars and no foreign interference in their affairs, and when the Puritans could elect their own rulers. But he also reminds them that they enjoyed spiritual abundance as well as physical abundance. By line 217, however, the poet chides the members of the Puritan community for their too-great love of the world and its luxuries and their own greediness, hypocrisy, and spiritual sloth; as a result, he notes by line 262, God has determined to punish the community. They have become a generation "ripe for God's vengeance." By line 357, we see that part of this vengeance will be sickness.

FROM MICHAEL WIGGLESWORTH,
GOD'S CONTROVERSY WITH NEW-ENGLAND
WRITTEN IN THE TIME OF THE GREAT DROUGHT
ANNO 1662
BY A LOVER OF NEW-ENGLAND'S PROSPERITY
(Boston: Proceedings of the Massachusetts Historical Society,
1871–1873)

Isaiah 5.4

. . .

From that day forward hath the Lord
  Apparently contended
With us in Anger, and in wrath;
  But we have not amended.

. . .

Our healthful dayes are at an end,
  And sicknesses come on

From yeer to yeer, becaus our hearts
   Away from God are gone.

. . .

One wave another followeth,
   And one disease begins
Before another cease, becaus
   We turn not from our sins.

. . .

Our fruitful seasons have turnd
   Of late to barrenness,
Sometimes through great & parching drought,
   Sometimes through rain's excess.

. . .

We have been also threatened
   With worser things than these:
And God can bring them on us still,
   To morrow if he please.

• • •

A Concluding Hortatory

To those that are, or hereafter may be in Affliction.

Oh let *New-England* turn,
  When gentler Warning's given:
Lest by our sins the Lord to use
  Severity be driven.
  It will be to our cost
  To put him thereupon:
Oh therefore let's repent in time,
  Before we be undone.   (83–93)

GOD'S PUNISHMENTS: THE INDIAN WARS

In 1676, at the end of King Philip's War (the "king" in this instance was a Native American chief), the Reverend William Hubbard, who had seen the devastation firsthand, recorded a meticulous history of the terrible year. In destroying so much of the colony, the Indians had the support of the French, whose aim was to claim much of the area. The following is Hubbard's account of events as they occurred, first, in April 1675, in the areas of Sudbury, Concord, Lancaster, and Brookfield; and second, in May 1676, around Plymouth, Middleborough, Chelmsford, Woburn, Concord, and Lancaster. In this instance, the colonists were attacked by the Wameset Indians, who had been friendly until they were mistakenly fired on by the English. The final selection is part of his conclusion about the meaning of this war to the colony: God's wrath and punishment of the colony for its sins.

FROM THE REVEREND WILLIAM HUBBARD, *THE HISTORY OF THE INDIAN WARS IN NEW ENGLAND FROM THE ORIGINAL WORK, CAREFULLY REVISED, AND ACCOMPANIED WITH AN HISTORICAL PREFACE, LIFE, AND PEDIGREE OF THE AUTHOR, AND EXTENSIVE NOTES,* BY SAMUEL G. DRAKE, VOL. 1
(Roxbury, Mass.: Printed for W. Elliot Woodward, 1865)

April 17, the next Day they set upon *Sudbury* all their might, to do there, as they had done at the Towns next beyond it: They did at the first prevail so far as to consume several Houses, and Barns, and kill several Persons, ten or twelve of the English, that came from *Concord* to assist their Neighbours at *Sudbury*, a town distant five Miles from them, at the first hearing of the Alarm, tho unaware were surprised near a Garison House, in Hope of getting some advantage upon a small Party of the Enemy that presented themselves in a Meadow; a great Number of *Indians* that lay unseen in the Bushes, suddenly rose up, and intercepting the Passage to the Garison-house, killed and took them all. (5)

• • •

When on the sudden a great Body of the Enemy appeared, about five hundred as was thought, who compassing them in round, forced them

at the top of an Hill, where they made very stout Resistance a considerable while; but the Night drawing on, and some of the Company beginning to scatter from the rest, their Fellows were forced to follow them,
so as the Enemy taking the Chase, persued them on every Side, as they
made too hasty a Retreat, by which Accident, being so much overpowered
by the Enemies numbers, they were most of them lost. (8)

• • •

But if Enquiry be made into the moral and procuring Causes, whereby
God hath been provoked to let loose the Rage of the Heathen thus against
us, it is not hard to give an Answer. The Sovereign Ruler of the World
need never pick a Quarrel with any Sort of Men (the best of his Servants
at all Times giving him too just Occasion of Controversy with them) or
be to seek of a Ground why to bring a Scourge upon them, having also
the other holy Ends why he contends with his People, of which he is not
bound to render the World an Account: It may be Reason enough to
work in them a Sympathy for the Sufferings and Calamities of others; or
to keep them from being *exalted above Measure;* or to humble and prove
them, that they should by their long Peace, and Prosperity be ready to
look upon themselves as less Sinners than others, who have drunk deep
of the Cup of Trembling before them: To prevent what Evil may, as well
as reform what is ready grown upon amongst them. Standing Waters are
most apt to corrupt. Gods Dispensations of this Nature in the World,
are usually observed to be for Correction of the Vices, as well as for
the Tryal of the Virtues found in his Servants. . . . Nor need HE be instructed by Men, what Instruments to make use of, in the chastening of
his People. (9)

GOD'S PUNISHMENT: THE DEATH OF VALUED LEADERS

A constant refrain in many a funeral sermon was that the grand old ministers of the older generation were dying because of the sins of the community. These deaths were especially alarming because it was felt that such holy men protected the community from God's anger. With such men gone, the members of the community would be exposed to the punishments they deserved because of their failure to attend to their spiritual lives.

The Reverend Thomas Shepard was one of those grand old men who had come from England in the early days of settlement to lead the colonies. In 1677, Urian Oakes, a minister of the church in Cambridge and president of Harvard College, wrote a poem on the death of Thomas Shepard. Shepard is seen as a great man in his own right, but also as a representative of the passing generation of leaders who protected the people from God's wrath. Oakes sees that without Shepard and his kind, New England would be exposed to angry, divine punishment. Moreover, he sees that the sins of the community have caused God to punish the community by allowing Shepard to die: "Our sins have slain our Shepard!"

FROM URIAN OAKES, *ELEGY UPON THE DEATH OF
MR. THOMAS SHEPARD*
(Cambridge, Mass.: Printed by Samuel Green, 1677)

46

Ah! could not Prayers and tears prevail with God!
Was there no warding off that dreadful Blow!
And was there no averting of that Rod!
Must Shepard die! and that good Angel go!
  Alas! Our heinous sins (more than our hates)
  It seems, were louder, and outcried our Prayers.

47

See what our sins have done! what Ruins wrought
And how they have pluck'd out our very eyes!
Our sins have slain our Shepard! we have bought,

And dearly paid for, our Enormities.
   Ah Cursed sins! that strike at God, and kill
   His servants, and the Blood of Prophets spill.

48

As you would loathe the Sword that's warm and red,
As you would hate the hands that are embru'd
I' th' Heart's blood of your dearest Friends: so dread,
And hate your sins; Oh! let them be pursu'd:
   Revenges take on bloody sins: for there's
   No refuge-City for these Murders.

49

In vain we build the Prophet's Sepulchers.
In vain bedew their Tombs with Tears, when Dead;
In vain bewail the Deaths of Ministers,
Whilst Prophet-killing sins are harbored.
   Those that these Murderous Traitors favor, hide;
   Are with the blood of Prophets deeply dyed.

50

New England! know thy heart-plague: feel this blow;
A blow that sorely wounds both Head and Heart,
A blow that reaches All, both high and low,
A blow that may be felt in every part.
   Mourn that this Great Man's fallen in Israel:
   Lest it be said, with him New England fell! (14–16)

ATTEMPTS TO LESSEN GOD'S ANGER BY GOOD BEHAVIOR AND REFUSAL TO TOLERATE EVIL

In 1679, the Massachusetts General Court completed painstaking deliberations to come up with ways of lessening God's anger. Its work was published as "The Result" of the Synod—new guidelines of behavior, meaning less individual freedoms and less toleration of any kind of behavior or dogma that it believed angered God.

"THE SYNOD'S WORK: THE RESULT OF 1679,"
MASSACHUSETTS GENERAL COURT
(Boston: Printed by John Foster, 1679)

The Synod's Work

A. THE RESULT OF 1679

THE NECESSITY OF REFORMATION / With the Expedient subservient / thereunto, asserted; / in Answer to two / QUESTIONS / 1. *What are the Evils that have provoked the Lord to bring his Judgments on New-England?* / II. *What is to be done that so these Evils may be Reformed?* / *Agreed upon by the* / *ELDERS and MESSENGERS* / *of the Churches assembled in the* / *SYNOD* / *At Boston in New-England,* / *Sept. 10. 1679.* / — / *Mat. 3.7* Even from the dayes of your Fathers yee are gone away from mine Ordinances, and have not kept them; Return unto me and I will return unto you, saith the Lord of Hosts: but ye said, Wherein shall we return? *Rev. 2.4, 5.* Nevertheless I have somewhat against thee, because thou hast left thy first love. Remember therefore from whence thou art fallen, and Repent, and doe thy first works; or else I will come unto thee quickly and will remove thy Candlestick out of his place, except thou Repent.—

TO THE MUCH HONOURED General Court
Of the *Massachusetts Colony* now sitting at *Boston*
in NEW-ENGLAND
RIGHT WORSHIPFUL, WORSHIPFUL,
AND MUCH HONOURED IN OUR LORD
JESUS!

The wayes of God towards this his People, have in many respects been like unto his dealings of Israel of old: It was a great and high undertaking of our Fathers, when they ventured themselves and their little ones upon the rude waves of the vast Ocean, that so they might follow the Lord unto this land.

• • •

[A]nd therefore the Lord is righteous in all the evil that has befallen us. And it is high time for us to be earnest, as to an impartial *Scrutiny* concerning the causes of his holy displeasure against us, together with the proper Remedyes or Scripture expedients, for Reformation, that so the Lord, who hath said, Return unto me, and I will return unto you, may be at peace with us.

• • •

What are the Evils that have provoked the Lord to bring his Judgments on New-England

Answ. That sometimes God hath had, and pleaded a Controversy with his People, is clear from the Scripture, Hos. 4.1. and 12.2. Mic. 6.1, 2. Where God doth plainly and fully propose, state and plead his Controversy, in all the parts and Causes of it, wherein he doth justifie himself, by the Declaration of his own infinite Mercy, Grace, Goodness, Justice, Righteousness, Truth and Faithfulness in all his proceedings with them; And judge his People, charging them with all those provoking Evils which had been the causes of that Controversy, and that with the most high, and heavy aggravation of their Sins, and exaggeration of the guilt and punishment, whence he should have been most just, in pleading out his Controversy with them, unto the utmost extremity of Justice and Judgement.

That God hath a Controversy with his New-England People is undeniable, the Lord having written his displeasure in dismal characters against us. Though Personal afflictions do oftentimes come only or chiefly for Probation, yet as to publick Judgements it is not wont to be so; especially when by a continued Series of Providence, the Lord doth appear and plead against his People. 2 Sam. 21.1 As with us it hath been from year to year. Would the Lord have whetted his glittering Sword, and his hand have taken hold on judgement? would he have sent such a mortal Contagion like a Beesom of Destruction in the midst of us? Would he have said, Sword! Goe through the Land, and cut off man and Beast? Or would he have kindled such devouring Fires, and made such fearfull Desolations in the Earth, if he had not been angry? It is not for nothing that the merciful God, who doth not willingly afflict nor grieve the Children of men, hath done all these things unto us; yea and sometimes with a cloud hath covered himself, that our Prayer should not pass through. And although it is possible that the Lord may Contend with us partly on account of secret unobserved Sins, Josh. 7.11, 12. 2 Kings. 17.9. Psal. 90.8. In which respect, a deep and most serious enquiry into the Causes of his Controversy ought to be attended. Nevertheless, it is sadly evident that there are visible, manifest Evils, which without doubt the Lord is provoked by. (419–423)

PROJECTS FOR ORAL OR WRITTEN EXPLORATION

1. Explore the idea of the Devil in *The Crucible* by looking carefully at all mentions of the Devil in dialogue and then at any suggestive, indirect references to the Devil. What things are considered devilish by these Puritans?

2. History has suggested that the Devil was in the accusers rather than the victims. Write a paper on this irony of the witch trials.

3. Explore the metaphoric meaning of the Devil in contemporary life. What are referred to as modern-day devils, and where do they reside?

4. Does the play suggest that the Puritans believed that the Devil lurked in everyone's heart? Explain.

5. Have a major debate on this proposition: that human beings are born depraved and evil.

6. Have a major debate on this proposition: that the wilderness, or nature untouched by man, is innocent.

7. Note some of the forbidden pastimes in *The Crucible*. Using your own research as well as your own speculation, write a paper on why the Puritans identified these activities as tools of the Devil.

8. Research newspapers in the last several decades (some newspaper indexes may be keys) for similar instances of churches that have banned such things as dancing, certain kinds of music, movies, and kinds of dress in general. Write a report on what you have found.

9. Debate the following proposition: As Benjamin Franklin wrote, a good person is one who does good deeds. (This, of course, is diametrically opposed to the Puritan view.)

10. Discuss the idea of why "bad" things happen to "good" people.

11. Write a paper tracing the origins of your own philosophy. How did it evolve? Did you come up with it yourself, or did you inherit it?

12. In getting at the Puritan habit of mind concerning absolute deference to authority, explore your own definition of authority with examples and your attitude toward various manifestations of authority. What, if anything, assumes authority in your own life? What figures of authority do you admire?

13. Write an essay on "authority" in *The Crucible*.

14. In what ways, if any, do the government, church, and educational institutions treat adults as children? What are the possible results of this kind of treatment on a society?

15. Throughout history, groups of individuals—like the Quakers and

then the witches of New England—have been blamed for the disasters that befall the community. Write a comprehensive definition of the term *scapegoating*.

16. One such instance of scapegoating occurred during the reign of Adolf Hitler. Write a research paper on Hitler's rise to power and his attempt to blame Germany's troubles on the Jews.

17. Coming closer to the subject of *The Crucible* (the "Red Scare" of the 1950s), do some research on the scapegoating of labor unions in the 1930s and 1940s—that is, blaming our national ills on labor unions. You may want to interview some older members of your community who were involved in labor unions at this time.

18. Write a research paper on an instance of scapegoating of your own choosing, perhaps involving members of a particular race, religious group, political party, or nationality.

19. As a major project, discuss the human need to explain why troubles happen to us—the need to find some reason why we suffer. Write a brief essay on how the Puritans explained their troubles.

20. What reasons do people today give for why they suffer? For example, how do they explain the untimely death of a child? How does one explain death to a child? (The Puritans often blamed such deaths on the sins of family members.) It is often assumed that it would be less hard to believe that some terrible suffering (think of something like a drive-by shooting of a child) was caused by one's own failures or by God's will than to think that one suffered for no reason at all, that one's suffering is, in effect, chance or just a roll of the dice. Debate this proposition, perhaps drawing on your own knowledge or experience. You may want to approach this question by writing out a script in which you explain to a child why another child has died. Then let your classmates comment on what you have said.

21. Review the Puritan laws in the documents in this chapter that limit human behavior in order to protect the community. Make a list of current laws that limit human behavior in order to protect the community.

22. One often hears the pronouncement that "morals cannot be legislated." What exactly does this mean? To what extent is it true? To what extent is it fallacious? Consider a tricky question like the marketing of pornography or the legalization of marijuana. You might consider having a debate on these questions.

SUGGESTED READINGS

Andrew, Charles M. *The Colonial Period of American History*. 4 vols. New Haven: Yale University Press, 1934–1938.

Bremer, Francis J. *The Puritan Experiment: New England Society from Bradford to Edwards*. Rev. ed. Hanover, N.H.: University Press of New England, 1995.

Clark, Charles E. *The Eastern Frontier: The Settlement of Northern New England, 1610–1763*. New York: Knopf, 1970.

Craven, Wesley Frank. *The Colonies in Transition, 1660–1713*. New York: Harper & Row, 1968.

Foster, Stephen. *The Long Argument: English Puritanism and the Shaping of New England Culture, 1570–1700*. Chapel Hill: University of North Carolina Press, 1991.

Friedman, Lawrence M. *Crime and Punishment in American History*. New York: Basic Books, 1993.

Heimert, Alan, and Andrew Delbanco, eds. *The Puritans in America: A Narrative Anthology*. Cambridge, Mass.: Harvard University Press, 1985.

Hill, Douglas Arthur. *The English to New England*. London: Gentry Books, 1975.

Hutchinson, Thomas. *The History of the Colony of Massachuset's Bay*. London: Printed for M. Richardson, 1760–1828.

Kences, James E. *Some Unexplored Relationships of Essex County Witchcraft to the Indian Wars of 1675 and 1689*. Salem, Mass.: Essex Institute Historical Collections, 1984.

Knight, Janice. *Orthodoxies in Massachusetts: Rereading American Puritanism*. Cambridge, Mass.: Harvard University Press, 1994.

Miller, Perry. *The New England Mind: From Colony to Province*. Cambridge, Mass.: Harvard University Press, 1953.

Rutman, Darrett Bruce. *American Puritanism: Faith and Practice*. Philadelphia: Lippincott, 1970.

Shurtleff, Nathaniel, ed. *Records of the Governor and Company of the Massachusetts Bay in New England*. 5 vols. Boston: Massachusetts Historical Society, 1853–1854.

Stavely, Keith. *Puritan Legacies: Paradise Lost and the New England Tradition, 1630–1890*. Ithaca: Cornell University Press, 1987.

Vaughan, Alden T. *New England Frontier: Puritans and Indians, 1620–1675*. Boston: Little, Brown, 1965.

The courtroom in hysterics at the trial of George Jacobs. From a painting by T. H. Matteson. Courtesy, Peabody Essex Museum, Salem, Mass.

3

Witchcraft in Salem

CHRONOLOGY

1689	Samuel Parris arrives in Salem Village and is ordained as minister of the newly formed Salem Church.
1692 January	Young girls in Parris's household begin acting strangely.
February	Parris's servants bake witch cake to heal girls. Other girls in community become involved, and first charges of witchcraft are made. Aggressive interrogations begin.
March	Three women are sent to prison and others are charged. Afflictions prompt day of prayer. Reverend Deodat Lawson and Parris deliver sermons that stir up the populace. Martha Corey, Rebecca Nurse, and Sarah Good's four-year-old daughter are examined and sent to prison.
April	John and Elizabeth Proctor, Giles Corey, and George Burroughs are among the twenty-three more people jailed.
May	Governor William Phips appoints panel of judges to hear cases as arrests mount.

June	Bridget Bishop is the first one hanged. A group of ministers in Boston convey their alarm to the governor. Five more persons are sentenced to death.
July	Rebecca Nurse is among those hanged on Gallows Hill.
August	John Proctor is among those brought to trial and executed.
September	Giles Corey is pressed to death and Martha, his wife, is among the last people, a group of eight, hanged.
October	The governor forbids any more arrests and dissolves the witchcraft court, but another is appointed and some trials go on.
1693 May	The governor orders the release of all accused witches upon payment of their fees.
1697 January	Fast Day is held in Massachusetts in penance for witch trials. Judge Samuel Sewall apologizes. Jurors apologize.
1706	Ann Putnam, the younger, apologizes.
1711	Disgrace is officially removed from those accused, and compensation is ordered.

CHARACTERS

Those Executed:

June 10, 1692	Bridget Bishop
July 19, 1692	Sarah Good, Sarah Wildes, Elizabeth How, Susanna Martin, Rebecca Nurse
August 19, 1692	George Burroughs, John Proctor, George Jacobs, John Willard, Martha Carrier
September 19, 1692	Giles Corey
September 22, 1692	Martha Corey, Mary Esty, Alice Parker, Ann Pudeator, Margaret Scott, Wilmot Reed, Samuel Warwell, Mary Parker

Panel of Judges:
William Stoughton, Chief Justice
Samuel Sewall, John Hathorne, Jonathan Corwin, Bartholomew Sergeant

Chief Accusers:
Elizabeth Parris, Abigail Williams, Ann Putnam and her daughter, also named Ann, Mercy Lewis, Thomas Putnam, Mary Walcott, Mary Warren, Elizabeth Hubbard, Tituba and John Indian

Other Supporters of the Proceedings:
The Reverends Samuel Parris, Deodat Lawson, John Hale, and Cotton Mather

Chief Critics of the Proceedings:
Thomas Brattle, Francis Nurse, Robert Calef, and the Reverends Increase Mather and Samuel Willard

The historical events on which Arthur Miller based his play *The Crucible* were some of the most shameful in the nation's history, leaving twenty innocent people executed and dumped without ceremony in mass graves on Gallows Hill and over two hundred imprisoned, one a little girl who, like the rest, was chained to the wall. Most of them were subjected to the most intrusive indignities on their bodies and stripped of their earthly belongings, not to mention their reputations.

The horror of the events between June 10 and September 22 of 1692 is that they were perpetrated by religious men, most of whom were among the most prominent ministers of their time, and that those holy men who were aware of how abominable the proceedings were did little to courageously and effectively call a halt to the suffering until the public as a whole had withdrawn support of the witch trials. Furthermore, as documents in previous chapters have shown, this injustice was, on the surface, done in the name of the Lord for religious reasons: God had visited punishment after punishment on New England for its sins; Satan was working overtime to convert souls to his allegiance before the coming millennium; and, to prevent further disasters, the people needed to bring all their strength to the task of ridding their community of those who had signed pacts with the Devil.

This was the ostensible reason, the openly declared reason, for encouraging members of the community to turn against each other hysterically. The murder, torture, and thievery that resulted can only be described as community insanity. As will be obvious, however, there were ugly, hidden reasons for the trials that were later seen to have more validity than the need, claimed by the New

England leaders who urged on the hunt, for some kind of religious purgation.

THE BEGINNING OF THE SALEM WITCH HUNT

Arthur Miller's play about seventeenth-century trials held in the name of religion, with parallels to twentieth-century trials held in the name of patriotism, is fundamentally true to the historical record. In February 1692, the Reverend Samuel Parris of Salem Village, north of Boston, became alarmed at the condition of his eleven-year-old daughter Elizabeth and his twelve-year-old niece Abigail Williams, who was living in the house with Parris's immediate family. Both girls, but especially Elizabeth, began to be subject to some strange nervous disorders somewhat like convulsions. Parris and a physician he consulted began to suspect that witchcraft was involved. Discovering that the girls had spent time with Parris's servant from Barbados and played games with palm readings and similar activities (very likely somewhat like Ouija-board games), Parris and his friends were convinced that witchcraft was involved. The witchcraft diagnosis was lent credence by cases in nearby Boston made public by the leading scholar and minister of the colony, the Reverend Cotton Mather.

When Parris's servants Tituba and her husband heard of the rumor, they tried to make matters better by making a "witch cake" of the girls' urine to cure them. This had the opposite effect of worsening the situation when Parris and Thomas Putnam heard of it because it convinced them that Satan was on the move in Salem.

The two girls, joined by several others who were their companions in all this, began to divert attention from their own forbidden activities by claiming that various women in the village were witches and had caused their sickness. From this moment on, the witch hysteria was under way.

THE SPREADING HYSTERIA THROUGHOUT
THE SUMMER

Before the winter had ended, the girls, joined by others of their playmates and, most prominently, one young matron named Ann Putnam, had begun to accuse others of bewitching them: Tituba, the household servant, Sarah Good, a cantankerous and destitute old woman whom we might describe today as a mentally unstable bag lady, and Sarah Osborne, an eccentric who had displeased the church by failing to attend services and by living with a man before marrying him. On February 29, 1692, the sheriff served the first warrants for the three women to appear before magistrates John Hathorne (a direct ancestor of Nathaniel Hawthorne, author of *The Scarlet Letter*) and Jonathan Corwin, who in a completely extra-legal fashion heard testimony and imprisoned the women.

The arrest of Tituba and the two Sarahs was only the beginning. The ailments of the "bewitched" girls—always under the spotlight now and the center of attention—continued unabated, as did their accusations. In an atmosphere of mounting hysteria, Tituba, likely under fear of death or torture, confessed her own guilt and implicated others. In the intense spotlight, the young girls and Ann Putnam, senior, who continued as the prime movers in this frenzied episode, would claim to have been bitten or burned or in some other way attacked by whoever was accused and would almost in unison begin screaming, rolling their eyes, and babbling whenever they saw an accused person. Eventually, the accusations by the girls were reinforced by the testimony of others who claimed suddenly to have seen the accused fly through the air or to have had his or her "spectre" or spirit lie on top of them like a demon. Suddenly all of New England, but especially Salem, was in a state of satanic siege. Witches appeared behind every bush; accusations followed every faltering step, dead cow, or failed crop. In the hysteria that ensued, charges and arrests multiplied, each one inflaming the situation further.

A little more than a month after the young girls were first found to be afflicted, on March 1, 1692, the Reverend Parris held a day of prayer to combat the evil, and another minister, Parris's friend Deodat Lawson, came to town to add his support (some said to "excite"). One of the women in Salem, Martha Corey, had criticized the officials and ridiculed the witch-hunt from the first. On March 21, she was thrown into jail on charges of witchcraft. Her eighty-year-old husband Giles had actually supported the officials until his wife was arrested. When this quarrelsome old man objected, he was also arrested. At this point, anything that could not be explained was presumed to be caused by witchcraft—the illnesses of people or animals and even deaths that had happened years before.

Little Dorcas, Sarah Good's four-year-old daughter, was arrested for witchcraft on March 23. For nine months she lay in shackles in prison. On March 24, Rebecca Nurse, long and widely known as a sister of charity in the community, was arrested on charges of witchcraft. Shortly afterward, her two sisters were also arrested when they came to their sister's defense. John Hathorne arrogantly presided over the quasi-legal trials, entrapping, threatening, and terrifying those accused and assuming that anyone accused was then automatically guilty. No evidence other than accusations was deemed necessary.

CONFESSING AND NAMING NAMES

Those accused of witchcraft would, in the terror of the moment and at the urging of loved ones, confess and name other "witches" in order to escape the hangman. Those newly accused would be arrested, and the cycle would continue. Robert Calef, a business-man of the time who failed to be taken in by the proceedings, wrote facetiously of who the Devil really was in this situation and showed that the peak of community madness was in the naming of names, accusing others in order to escape:

If this be the true state of the Afflictions of this Country, it is very deplorable, and beyond all other outward Calamities miserable. But, if on the other side, the Matter be as others do understand it, That the Devil has been too hard for us by his Temptations, signs, and lying Wonders, with the help of pernicious notions, formerly im-bibed and professed; together with the Accusations of a parcel of possessed, distracted, or lying Wenches, accusing their Innocent Neighbors, pretending they see their Spectres (i.e.) Devils in their likeness Afflicting of them, and that God in righteous Judgment (af-ter Men had ascribed his Power to Witches, of commissioning Devils to do these things) may have given them over to strong delusions to believe lyes, etc. And to let loose the Devils of Envy, Hatred, Pride, Cruelty, and Malice against each other; yet still disguised un-der the Mask of Zeal for God, and left them to the branding one another with the odious Name of Witch; and upon the Accusation of those above mentioned, Brother to Accuse and Prosecute Brother, Children their Parents, Pastors and Teachers their imme-

diate Flock unto death; Shepherds becoming Wolves, Wise Men in-
fatuated; People hauled to Prisons. (*More Wonders of the Invisible World*, 298–299)

ARRESTS CONTINUE

The Salem and Boston jails were full of those accused by April 1, but on April 21 an arrest occurred that rocked the area clergy, that of the Reverend George Burroughs of Maine, a man of almost superhuman physical strength. By this time a few people, including two Boston ministers, Samuel Willard and Increase Mather, Cotton Mather's father, had begun to work quietly to bring the situation under control and to insist that the panel of judges and a jury be lawfully constituted. In response, the newly appointed royal governor, William Phips, as one of his first official acts, established such a council on May 29.

On June 2, the official hearings before the court began. The panel of judges included Chief Justice William Stoughton and Associate Judges Samuel Sewall, John Hathorne, Bartholomew Sergeant, and Nathaniel Saltonstall, who resigned after the first trial and was replaced by Jonathan Corwin. On the first day of court, Bridget Bishop was found guilty. Some of the evidence against her, typical of all the testimony, seemed to be a vicious interpretation placed upon natural events, as, for example, when John Bly testified that he had had a disagreement with Bishop over a payment he owed her for a hog he had bought from her. Bly testified that the strange fits to which the hog was subject were a result of its being bewitched by Bishop, as is shown in the following court records, quoted in Charles Upham's *Salem Witchcraft* (Boston: Wiggin & Lunt, 1867):

> [The hog] grew better; and then, for the space of near two hours together, she, getting into the street, did set off, jumping and running between the house of said deponents and said Bishop's, as if she were stark mad, and, after that, was well again: And we did then apprehend or judge, and do still, that said Bishop bewitched said sow. (262–263)

Other evidence against her was "spectral," as when John Louder, who had also had a quarrel with Bishop, testified that he had seen her "likeness" sitting on his stomach. On June 10, Bridget Bishop was the first to be hanged.

FAULTY EVIDENCE

On June 15, a group of citizens from the Boston area, including businessman Thomas Brattle and ministers Increase Mather and Samuel Willard, conveyed their alarm about the conduct of the trials to Governor Phips. What alarmed them as much as anything else was what the court accepted as evidence. Two kinds of "evidence" assumed great importance in these trials. One was the presence on the body of what the examiner called "a witch's teat." Often a mole, a wart, an old scar, or a fold of skin would be reported to the court as a witch's teat—clear proof that the defendant was a witch. In addition, the court readily admitted what was called spectral evidence. It was well known, of course, that witches could be in several places at the same time, that one's neighbor, for example, might be in his kitchen eating dinner while his spectre or another embodiment of an evil spirit was out riding a broom. "Alibi" had no meaning at all. Accusers often reported that they had seen the spectre of the accused do witchcraft, and the court admitted this as evidence.

Five additional cases came to trial on June 29, and there was no abatement in arrests. The executions by hanging of Sarah Good, Sarah Wildes, Elizabeth How, Susanna Martin, and Rebecca Nurse took place on Gallows Hill on July 19. They were not buried decently but only dumped there in crevices in the rocks, their limbs protruding above ground.

THE PUBLIC MOOD CHANGES

The trials continued throughout the summer. On August 19, the next executions occurred when the Reverend George Burroughs, John Proctor, George Jacobs, John Willard, and Martha Carrier were all hanged on Gallows Hill. By this time, many of Salem's citizens had begun to object boldly to the proceedings, and some area ministers were appalled at the conviction of the Reverend Burroughs. Just before the August 19 executions, word began to circulate that there would be an attempt to stop them. On the day of the executions, the mood of citizens in attendance at Gallows

Hill turned rebellious after they heard George Burroughs's eloquent defense of himself, but the attempt to halt the hangings was stopped by the Reverend Cotton Mather. Mather, a Boston minister who had written extensively on witchcraft, had become a close advisor to the Salem officials and strongly supported the trials. Upon hearing rumors that a mob might interfere with the executions on August 19, he galloped frantically from Boston to Salem, appearing on the scene just in time to intimidate the rebellious crowd members and send them cowering back to their acquiescent places.

The court was stymied in its attempt to try old Giles Corey because he would not enter a plea. As he well knew, if his case went to court, his property could and would have been confiscated by the state; since he entered no plea—neither guilty nor not guilty—the state's hands were tied at first. So without benefit of trial, heavy stones were piled on Corey's body as a way of forcing him to enter a plea. He refused and eventually was tortured to death on September 19. Giles Corey's wife Martha was among the eight people hanged on September 22—the last of Salem's citizens to be executed for witchcraft. Still, however, people continued to be arrested and jailed on the charge.

On October 3, Increase Mather for the first time publicly objected to what was transpiring in Salem, declaring that the evidence on which people were being found guilty was faulty. He declared that it was better for ten witches to go free than for one innocent person to be punished. On October 12, Governor Phips officially called a halt to any further arrests.

In the winter of 1692, those first accused had generally been paupers or mentally disturbed women who were easy targets. But as members of the privileged class began to be charged, public opinion began to turn against the courts and valuable support in high places was lost, as, for example, when the Reverend Hale's wife was charged.

In May 1693, when Sir William Phips ordered all those who had been charged to be released, 150 persons jailed for witchcraft left the jails. It is estimated that the total number jailed was several hundred. In addition to the twenty who had been executed, at least two—some accounts claim more than this—had died in jail.

Even many of those who were acquitted or released on order of Governor Phips were held in jail long after their names were cleared because each prisoner was required to repay the common-wealth for food, board, travel to and from prison, jailer's fees, court fees, executioner's fees, and the paper on which any court business was conducted involving them; they were even charged for their chains and handcuffs. Those who were poor when they were arrested languished in prison for as much as a year as friends and relatives made appeals for their release. Those who had some means were completely impoverished by their stay in jail. The irony is that the state had already seized at the time of their imprisonment property that the prisoners could have used to pay the debts to the state that they had incurred in prison. Those who were fortunate enough to find sponsors to pay their bonds were in debt for years to those who had gotten them out of jail.

THE WITCH-HUNTS END

Members of the general public, many of whom had been wary of the trials from the beginning, were openly critical of the judges by the fall of 1692. Over the next four years, several of those involved in the trials expressed public remorse for what they had done as judges. Despite the Puritans' vigilance in rooting out witchcraft, God's wrath seemed to be stronger than ever, and ordinary people began to suspect that rather than being appeased by the Salem trials, God had been angered even more by what had happened. On December 17, 1696, a proclamation was issued, written by Samuel Sewall, expressing the sentiments of most of the members of the government, asking God's help and forgiveness for anything they might have done wrong with regard to the trials and ordering a day of fasting and prayer. Over the years, the government issued small amounts of money in restitution to the families of those who had been executed or had had their property taken by the courts. Those condemned remained under an official "taint" of dishonor until October 17, 1711, when the "several convictions Judgments and Attainders" against the Salem "witches" were "reversed" and a total of 578 pounds and 12 shillings was paid to the families in compensation. Damages in the amount of 21 pounds were paid to the family of Giles Corey and his wife and 150 pounds to the family of John Proctor and his wife. Amazingly, as late as August 28, 1957, largely as a result of Arthur Miller's *The Crucible*, a judicial resolution was passed that deplored the convictions of the condemned witches not covered in the 1711 reversal, but failed to repeal them.

REASONS FOR THE WITCH-HUNTS

All the human suffering was perpetrated in the name of religion—fighting the Devil in a holy cause to cleanse the community of the worst manifestations of evil in order to lessen God's wrath and ease his punishment of his "Chosen People." But as many people knew even at the time, there were other, more persuasive reasons for the hysteria. Some of the impetus for the witch trials came from very basic human psychology, so puzzling and frightening to a community that believed in the manifestation of the Devil—a kind of supermagician—in their daily lives. Many of the other compelling forces were less psychological and more crass, coming as they did from less mysterious forms of evil: plain human greed, ambition, self-preservation, and revenge.

On what one might term the psychological level, the witch-hunts seem to have arisen more from the mental disturbance of one grown woman (Ann Putnam) and several adolescent girls under emotional stress. This was a group of girls just entering what for them especially was a time of terrifying physical and emotional awakening with little useful adult direction or support and a great deal of guilt and repression. On top of this, they had few approved emotional outlets; the issue of their dancing in the forest is a vivid case in point. Metaphorically, they constituted a pressure cooker that finally exploded.

To cover up what they believed (with good cause) was behavior for which they would be punished, they began to divert blame elsewhere. Almost immediately, they attracted attention and gained respect by accusing people of witchcraft. The most important citizens in the area hung on the girls' every word. The Reverend Cotton Mather and others sought them out for advice. Moreover, the girls found that they had the power to affect the lives of those who had had authority over them. They literally had the power over life and death.

THE DANGER OF "DIFFERENCE"

What the girls seemed to have picked up on immediately in their naming of Tituba and the two Sarahs was that "difference" and "powerlessness" were convenient, safe targets. Tituba was for all intents and purposes a slave from Barbados, brought with her husband by Parris to a place where she had no friends or family except her husband to come to her defense. She later testified that Parris had misused her consistently during her employment and that he had beat her unmercifully and threatened her in other ways to force her to confess. With no one to come to her defense, she remained in prison far longer than others who confessed—for well over a year—and then was sold as a slave to pay for her expenses in prison.

The great majority of the others accused at first fit a similar pattern: they were old, poverty-stricken, mentally disturbed women. These accused women were vulnerable, were disliked by most of the community, and had few defenders. Moreover, their eccentricities, often coupled with cantankerousness and physical deformity, made them frightening and strange in the eyes of a community that understood little or nothing of mental disorders. Robert Calef described Sarah Good as having "long been counted a Melancholy or distracted Woman," and Sarah Osborne as an "Old Bed-rid Woman," both of whom were "ill thought of" (343). Anyone who has seen homeless men and women, especially aggressive ones, has some notion of the response they elicit from most observers. Such people have universally been labeled as witches. Arthur Miller himself writes that the community's hysteria arose largely from its fear of those who were different from them.

LAND GRABS AND REVENGE

These were some of the psychological undercurrents at work in the Salem witch trials. But also involved from the beginning were calculated evils: taking advantage of an opportunity to grab someone else's land by accusing him or her of witchcraft; the exacting of vengeance against one with whom an accuser had been feuding; and, once the trials had gone too far, the accusation of those who disapproved in order to justify the accuser's actions to save a job or a reputation or have influence within the community (Parris being a case in point).

Many of those accused had valuable land and other possessions that their accuser coveted. One case involved two families developed as characters in *The Crucible*: Thomas Putnam and his family,

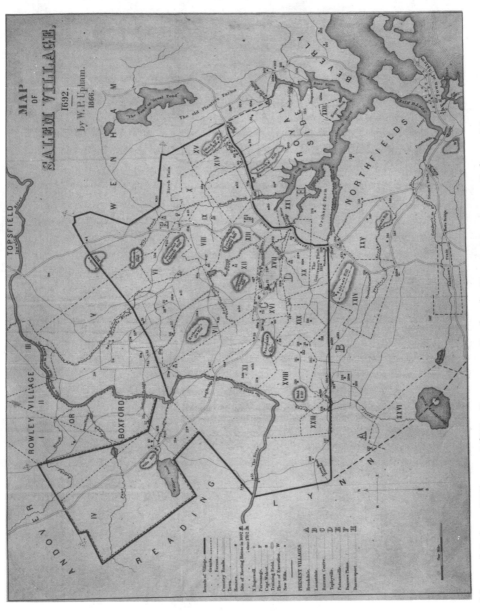

Map of Salem Village, 1692. Courtesy, Peabody Essex Museum, Salem, Mass.

the principal accusers in the witchcraft trials, were involved in a fierce battle with Rebecca and Francis Nurse over some land that lay between their two properties. Earlier the two families had had a two-day battle over the land. In a move that was neither subtle nor sanctified, Thomas Putnam's brothers, his wife Ann, and his daughter were the first to bring charges against Rebecca Nurse, who was subsequently executed.

Robert Calef in *More Wonders of the Invisible World* recorded several instances in which the property of the accused was confiscated, including the invasion of John and Elizabeth Proctor's house and the taking of everything they owned. Calef reported that the sheriff and other officers "came and seized" the Jacobs family estate—all they had, including the wife's wedding ring (364). Those who escaped death by fleeing Salem, like the Edward Bishops and Philip English and his wife, also lost everything they had.

The motive to take someone else's land was often coupled with a desire for vengeance. Documented feuds were behind many of the accusations, especially involving Thomas Putnam and his family and the Reverend Samuel Parris, all of whom seemed to control the accusations of the young girls. Many of the warring factions seemed to involve Parris himself. One group had fought against the appointment of Parris as minister. Some in this group even refused to attend services at Parris's church after he was brought there. Thomas Putnam, one of the wealthiest men in the area, was Parris's chief supporter. Among Parris's most outspoken opponents (whom he thought responsible for his not receiving the pay he wanted) were the Proctors and the Nurses. They were also among the first to be accused.

Putnam also held a grudge against various parishioners for other reasons. Long before the trials began, Putnam's brother-in-law James Bayley had been rejected as minister by a faction in the Salem Church, and another man, George Burroughs, had gotten the post instead. When Burroughs went bankrupt trying to pay for his wife's funeral on an inadequate minister's salary, the Putnams, from sheer maliciousness, had him arrested for debts he did not owe. In the summer of 1692, George Burroughs, then a minister in Maine, was hunted down and arrested on charges of witchcraft, brought back to Salem for trial, and executed alongside John Proctor.

Two groups of documents follow, most of them produced during the trials or within a few years of the trials. The first group consists of documents directly related to historical characters who appear in Arthur Miller's *The Crucible*: the Reverend Samuel Parris, Abigail Williams, Thomas and Ann Putnam, Giles Corey, Rebecca Nurse, John and Elizabeth Proctor, and the Reverend John Hale. In the case of most of these characters, we have actual documents that they wrote themselves in addition to firsthand observations of their behavior. The final group is made up of excerpts from documents that sought in some way to counter the damage done by the trials.

SAMUEL PARRIS

The witch hysteria began in the household of the Reverend Samuel Parris, a failed businessman fairly recently arrived from Barbados whom many felt ill qualified to be minister in Salem Village, despite his Harvard education. Because of factional objections to his appointment, his quarrelsome personality, and his unreasonable demands, he continued to be a controversial figure who divided the community.

He seemed to immediately see witchcraft in his household both as a possible threat to his position (something his enemies could use against him) and as an opportunity to get back at his enemies. The same objections to Parris that were at the root of the witchcraft trials continued after the trials were over.

The conflict between Parris and his church, which had been apparent even before the trials, broke out in a very public way afterward. Most of the members of the parish joined together to be rid of Parris, and he in response filed a legal grievance against his own church. The heated war between Parris, who was supported by the courts, and his congregation went on for five years after the trials were over. At one point Parris noted that more people went to the funeral of one of his enemies than came to church to hear the sermon. Finally, in 1697, arbitrators recommended that the congregation buy Parris off and send him on his way. He spent the rest of his life in poverty, until 1720, going as pastor from one tiny church in New England to another. The following is an excerpt from a complaint against the Reverend Parris by his parishioners on April 21, 1693. Some of the complaints, going back to earlier years, were that he only preached about depravity and damnation. Most had to do with his behavior in fomenting the witch trials that had ruined the lives of so many citizens of Salem. Note that one of the signers is a kinsman of accuser Thomas Putnam with whom he had been feuding for years, and one is the son of Rebecca Nurse.

FROM "AN ACCOUNT OF THE DIFFERENCES IN SALEM
VILLAGE," IN *NARRATIVES OF THE WITCHCRAFT CASES, 1648–
1706.* ED. GEORGE LINCOLN BURR
(New York: Charles Scribner's Sons, 1914)

The Reasons why we withdraw from Communion with the Church of
Salem Village, both as to hearing the word Preached, and from partaking
with them at the Lord's Table, are as followeth.

Why we attend not on publick Prayer, and preaching the word, there
are,

1. The Distracting, and Disturbing tumults and noises made by the
persons under Diabolical Power and delusions: preventing sometimes
our hearing, understanding, and profiting by the Word preached. We
having after many Trials, and Experiences found no redress in this matter,
account ourselves under a necessity to go where we might hear the word
in quiet.

2. The apprehension of danger of ourselves, being accused as the
Devil's Instruments, to assist the persons complaining, we seeing those
that we have reason to esteem better than ourselves thus accused, blem-
ished, and of their lives bereaved: for seeing this, thought it our prudence
to withdraw.

3. We found so frequent and positive preaching up some Principles
and Practices by Mr. Parris, referring to the dark and dismal mystery of
Iniquity working among us, was not profitable, but offensive.

4. Neither could we in Conscience join with Mr. Parris, in many of the
Requests which he made in Prayer, referring to the trouble then among
us and upon us; therefore thought it our most safe and peaceable way
to withdraw.

The Reasons why we hold not Communion with them at the Lord's
Table, are because we find ourselves justly aggrieved, and offended with
the Officer, who does administer, for the Reasons following.

1. From his declared and published Principles, referring to our moles-
tations from the Invisible World: Differing from the Opinion of the gen-
erality of the Orthodox Ministers of the Country.

2. His easie and strong Faith and Belief of the before-mentioned accusations, made by those called the Afflicted.

3. His laying aside that grace (which above all we are to put on,) viz.
Charity towards his Neighbours, and especially those of his Church, when
there is no apparent reason, but for the contrary.

4. His approving and practicing unwarrantable and ungrounded meth-
ods, for discovering what he was desirous to know, referring to the bewitched, or possessed persons, as in bringing some to others, and by

them pretending to inform himself and others, who were the Devil's instruments to afflict the sick and maimed.

5. His unsafe unaccountable Oath, given by him against sundry of the accused.

6. His not rendering to the World so fair (if so true) account of what he wrote on Examination of the afflicted.

7. Sundry unsafe (if sound points of Doctrine delivered in his Preaching) which we find not warrantable (if Christian.)

8. His persisting in these Principles, and justifying his Practice; not rendering any satisfaction to us, when regularly desired, but rather offending and dissatisfying ourselves.

We whose Names are under written heard this Paper read to our Paster, Mr. Samuel Parris, the 21st of April, 1693.

Nathaniel Ingersol	Peter Cloyce, Seniour
Edward Putnam	Samuel Nurse
Aaron Way	John Tarboll
William Way	Thomas Wilkins (140–143)

ABIGAIL WILLIAMS

Abigail Williams, Parris's niece, though she is about sixteen in Arthur Miller's play, is thought to have actually been only about eleven or twelve years old. Still, young as she was, she was seemingly extraordinarily sophisticated and calculating and became a leader of the young girls who first made the accusations. She, above the others, was the figure who seemed to provoke the hysteria in the first few days of its outbreak and was consulted by people of prominence throughout most of the trials. From being a young miscreant who dared to dance in the forest and play fortune-telling games with Tituba, she became labeled as one of the "afflicted." With the other girls and some older married women, she began "proving" her charges by going into hysterics, claiming that the spirit of the accused was biting or otherwise hurting her.

She and the others became extremely powerful during the trials. In the fall of 1692, when public support for the trials was dwindling, she disappeared from Salem. Although no one knows with any certitude what happened to her, one rumor was that she lived her life as a prostitute in Boston. The following is the Reverend Deodat Lawson's account of what he saw and recorded of her behavior in March 1692.

FROM DEODAT LAWSON, *A BRIEF AND TRUE NARRATIVE OF SOME REMARKABLE PASSAGES RELATING TO SUNDRY PERSONS AFFLICTED BY WITCHCRAFT, AT SALEM VILLAGE WHICH HAPPENED FROM THE NINETEENTH OF MARCH, TO THE FIFTH OF APRIL, 1692,* IN *NARRATIVES OF THE WITCHCRAFT CASES, 1648–1706,* ED. GEORGE LINCOLN BURR
(New York: Charles Scribner's Sons, 1914)

In the beginning of the Evening, I went to give Mr. P.[arris] a visit. When I was there, his Kins-woman, Abigail Williams, (about 12 years of age) had a grievous fit; she was at first hurryed with Violence to and fro in the room, (though Mrs. Ingersol endeavoured to hold her,) sometimes making as if she would fly, stretching up her arms as high as she could, and crying "Whish, Whish, Whish!" several times; Presently after she said there was Goodw. N.[urse] and said, "Do you not see her? Why there she stands!" And the said Goodw. N. offered her The Book, but she was resolved she would not take it, saying Often, "I wont, I wont, I wont, take it, I do not know what Book it is: I am sure it is none of Gods Book, it is the Divels Book, for ought I know." After that, she run to the Fire, and begun to throw Fire Brands, about the house; and run against the Back, as if she would run up Chimney, and, as they said, she had attempted to go into the Fire in other Fits.

• • •

In Sermon time when Goodw. C[orey] was present in the Meetinghouse Ab. W[illiams] called out, "Look where Goodw. C sits on the Beam suckling her Yellow bird betwixt her fingers!"

• • •

The 31 of March there was a Publick Fast kept at Salem on account of these Afflicted Persons. And Abigail Williams said, that the Witches had a Sacrament that day at an house in the Village, and that they had Red Bread and Red Drink. (153–160)

THOMAS AND ANN PUTNAM

Thomas Putnam, one of the largest landholders in the area, was central in the Salem witch trials in being Samuel Parris's chief supporter, in holding many grudges against Salem residents who had interfered with him in the past, and in being the moving force behind most of the accusations. His brothers, his wife Ann, and his daughter, also named Ann, were the most active accusers in bringing complaints against others.

The following comments by Deodat Lawson, a sympathetic observer, and by a more critical observer, Robert Calef, show the Putnams to have been avid accusers. Accounts of the "affliction" of Putnam's wife Ann clearly reveal her instability, which made her a convenient tool to be used by her husband and Parris for their vengeful, greedy purposes. Ann Putnam, who was known to be as deeply engaged in spiritualism as Tituba (who was considered a barbarian), revealed her instability in her own depositions to the court, in which she claimed that apparitions of Rebecca Nurse and Martha Corey tried to choke her. The final Putnam document is a confession made by Ann Putnam, the daughter of Thomas and Ann, in August 1706.

FROM DEODAT LAWSON, *A BRIEF AND TRUE NARRATIVE OF SOME REMARKABLE PASSAGES RELATING TO SUNDRY PERSONS AFFLICTED BY WITCHCRAFT, AT SALEM VILLAGE WHICH HAPPENED FROM THE NINETEENTH OF MARCH, TO THE FIFTH OF APRIL, 1692*, IN *NARRATIVES OF THE WITCHCRAFT CASES, 1648–1706*, ED. GEORGE LINCOLN BURR
(New York: Charles Scribner's Sons, 1914)

The Number of Afflicted Persons were about that time Ten, *viz*, Four married Women, Mrs. Pope, Mrs. Putnam, Goodw. Bibber, and an Ancient Woman, named Goodall, three Maids, Mary Walcut, Mercy Lewes, at Thomas Putnam's and a Maid at Dr. Griggs's, there were three Girls from 9–12 Years of Age, each of them, or thereabouts, *viz*, Elizabeth Parris, Abigail Williams and Ann Putnam.

• • •

[About Martha Corey's trial] [T]hese are most of them at Corey's examination, and did vehemently accuse her in the Assembly of afflicting them,
by Biting, Pinching, Strangling, etc. And that they did in their Fit see her
Likeness coming to them, and bringing a Book to them, she said, she
had no Book; they affirmed, she had a Yellow-Bird, that used to suck
betwixt her Fingers, and being asked about it, if she had any Familiar
Spirit, that attended her, she said, She had no Familiarity with any such
thing. She was a Gospel Woman: which Title she called her self by; and
the Afflicted Persons told her, ah! She was, A Gospel Witch. Ann Putnam
did there affirm, that one day when Lieutenant Fuller was at Prayer at
her Fathers House, she saw the shape of Goodw. C. and she thought
Goodw. N. Praying at the same time to the Devil, she was not sure it was
Goodw. N. she thought it was;

· · ·

   On Wednesday the 23 of March, I went to Thomas Putnam's, on purpose to see his Wife: I found her lying on the Bed, having had a sore fit
a little before. She spake to me, and said, she was glad to see me; her
Husband and she both desired me to pray with her, while she was sensible; which I did, though the Apparition said, I should not go to Prayer.
At the beginning she attended; but after a little time, was taken with a
fit: yet continued silent, and seemed to be Asleep: when Prayer was done,
her Husband going to her, found her in a fit; he took her off the Bed, to
set her on his Knees; but at first she was so stiff, she could not be bended;
but she afterwards set down; but quickly began to strive violently with
her Arms and leggs; she then began to Complain of, and as it were to
Converse personally with, Goodw. N., saying "Goodw. N. Be gone! Be
gone! Be gone! are you not ashamed, a Woman of your Profession, to
afflict a poor Creature so? what hurt did I ever do you in my life! you
have but two years to live, and then the Devil will torment your Soul, for
this your Name is blotted out of Gods Book, and it shall never be put in
Gods Book again, be gone for shame, are you not afraid of that which is
coming upon you? I Know, I know, what will make you afraid; the wrath
of an Angry God, I am sure that will make you afraid; be gone, do not
torment me, I know what you would have (we judged she meant, her
Soul) but it is out of your reach; it is Clothed with the white Robes of
Christs Righteousness." After this, she seemed to dispute with the Apparition about a particular Text of Scripture. The Apparition seemed to
deny it, (the Womans eyes being fast closed all this time); she said, She
was sure there was such a Text; and she would tell it: and then the Shape
would be gone, for said she, "I am sure you cannot stand before that
Text!" then she was sorely Afflicted; her mouth drawn on one side, and
her body strained for about a minute, and then said, "I will tell, I will

tell; it is, it is, it is!" three or four times, and then was afflicted to hinder her from telling, at last she broke forth and said, "It is the third Chapter of the Revelations." I did something scruple the reading it, and did let my scruple appear, lest Satan should make any Superstitious lie to improve the Word of the Eternal God. However, tho' not versed in these things, I judged I might do it this once for an Experiment. I began to read, and before I had near read through the first verse, she opened her eyes, and was well; this fit continued near half an hour. Her Husband and the Spectators told me, she had often been so relieved by reading Texts that she named, something pertinent to her Case.

• • •

[About Rebecca Nurse's trial] Thomas Putnam's wife had a grievous Fit, in the time of Examination, to the very great Impairing of her strength, and wasting of her spirits, insomuch as she could hardly move hand, or foot, when she was carryed out. . . . After the commitment of Goodw. N., Tho. Putnam's wife was much better, and had no violent fits at all from that 24th of March to the 5th of April.   (155–162)

A WARRANT FOR ARREST

In his critical history of the Salem witch trials, Robert Calef reproduces a warrant issued by John Hathorne and Jonathan Corwin for the arrest of eight citizens on charges of witchcraft. Two members of the Putnam family are mentioned in the warrant as being involved in the accusations. Understand that "Gaol" in this warrant means "Jail." Also, Calef's description of a scene in the courthouse, when Rebecca Nurse is brought in for examination, is revealing of the elder Ann Putnam's state of mind.

FROM ROBERT CALEF, *MORE WONDERS OF THE INVISIBLE WORLD, 1692*, IN *THE WITCHCRAFT DELUSION IN NEW ENGLAND*, ED. SAMUEL G. DRAKE
(Roxbury, Mass.: W. Elliot Woodward, 1865)

To their Majesties Gaol-Keeper in Salem

You are in Their Majesties Names hereby required to take into your care, and safe custody, the Bodies of William Hobs, and Deborah his Wife, Mary Easty, the wife of Isaac Easty, and Sarah Wild, the Wife of John Wild, all of Topsfield; and Edward Bishop of Salem-Village, Husbandman, and Sarah his Wife, and Mary Black, a Negro of Lieutenant Nathaniel Putnams of Salem-Village; also Mary English, the Wife of Philip English, Merchant in Salem; who stand charged with High Suspicion of Sundry Acts of Witchcraft, done or committed by them lately upon the Bodies of Ann Putnam, Mercy Lewis and Abigail Williams, of Salem-Village, whereby great Hurt and Damage hath been done to the Bodies of the said Persons, as according to the complaint of Thomas Putnam and John Buxton of Salem-Village, Exhibited Salem, Apr 21 1692, appears, whom you are to secure in order to their further Examination. Fail not.

John Hathorne,
Jona. Corwin

Dated Salem, April 22, 1692 (347)

• • •

March the 24th, Goodwife Nurse was brought before Mr. Hathorn and Mr. Curwin (Magistrates) in the Meeting House. Mr. Hale, Minister of Beverly, began with Prayer, after which she being Accus'd of much the same Crimes made the like answers, asserting her own Innocence with earnestness. The Accusers were mostly the same, Tho. Putnam's Wife, etc., complaining much. The dreadful Shrieking from her and others, was very amazing, which was heard at a great distance. (345)

THE DEPOSITION OF ANN PUTNAM

Ann Putnam, wife of Thomas Putnam, was the chief accuser of both Martha Corey and Rebecca Nurse at an early stage in the witch-hunt in the spring of 1692, shortly after the hysteria had gotten under way. Putnam, who, as much as any one person, represented the insanity of the accusers, was (as *The Crucible* makes clear) obsessed with the deaths of her infants. In the quotation here, she sees infants in winding-sheets—clothing placed around the dead.

FROM "THE DEPOSITION OF ANN PUTNAM," IN CHARLES
UPHAM, *SALEM WITCHCRAFT*
(Boston: Wiggin and Lunt, 1867)

THE DEPOSITION OF ANN PUTNAM, the wife of Thomas Putnam, aged about thirty years, who testifieth and saith that, on the 18th March, 1692, I being wearied out in helping to tend my poor afflicted child and maid, about the middle of the afternoon I lay me down on the bed to take a little rest; and immediately I was almost pressed and choked to death, that, had it not been for the mercy of a gracious God and the help of those that were with me, I could not have lived many moments: and presently I saw the apparition of Martha Corey, who did torture me so as I cannot express, ready to tear me all to pieces, and then departed from me a little while; but, before I could recover strength or well take breath, the apparition of Martha Corey fell upon me again with dreadful tortures, and hellish temptation to go along with her. And she also brought to me a little red book in her hand and a black pen, urging me vehemently to write in her book; and several times that day she did most grievously torture me, almost ready to kill me. . . . 24th March, being the day of the examination of Rebecca Nurse, I was several times afflicted in the morning by the apparition of Rebecca Nurse, but most dreadfully tortured by her in the time of her examination, insomuch that the honored magistrates gave my honored husband leave to carry me out of the meeting-house.

• • •

Immediately there did appear to me six children in winding-sheets, which called me aunt, which did most grievously affright me; and they told me that they were my sister Baker's children of Boston; and that

Goody Nurse and Mistress Carey of Charlestown, and an old deaf woman
at Boston, had murdered them, and charged me to go and tell these
things to the magistrates, or else they would tear me to pieces, for their
blood did cry for vengeance. Also there appeared to me my own sister
Bayley and three of her children in winding-sheets, and told me that
Goody Nurse had murdered them.   (Vol. 2: 278–282)

THE CONFESSION OF ANN PUTNAM, THE YOUNGER, 1706

In 1706, seven years after the death of her parents, Thomas and Ann Putnam, the younger Ann Putnam was taken into the church of Salem Village. On August 25 of that year, she stood in the church congregation while the Reverend Joseph Green, who succeeded Samuel Parris, read aloud her confession. Among the hearers in the church were the children and grandchildren of Rebecca Nurse. As nineteenth-century historian Charles Upham observes, however, beliefs at the time allowed her to escape full responsibility for her actions in that she could blame what she did on Satan.

"THE CONFESSION OF ANNE PUTNAM, WHEN SHE WAS RECEIVED TO COMMUNION, 1706" IN CHARLES UPHAM, *SALEM WITCHCRAFT*
(Boston: Wiggin and Lunt, 1867)

I desire to be humbled before God for that sad and humbling providence that befell my father's family in the year about '92; that I, then being in my childhood, should, by such a providence of God, be made an instrument for the accusing of several persons of a grievous crime, whereby their lives were taken away from them, whom now I have just grounds and good reason to believe they were innocent persons; and that it was a great delusion of Satan that deceived me in that sad time, whereby I justly fear I have been instrumental, with others, though ignorantly and unwittingly, to bring upon myself and this land the guilt of innocent blood; though what was said or done by me against any person I can truly and uprightly say, before God and man, I did it not out of any anger, malice, or ill-will to any person, for I had no such thing against one of them; but what I did was ignorantly, being deluded by Satan. And particularly, as I was chief instrument of accusing of Goodwife Nurse and her two sisters, I desire to lie in the dust, and to be humbled for it, in that I was a cause, with others, of so sad a calamity to them and their families; for which cause I desire to lie in the dust, and earnestly beg forgiveness of God, and from all those unto whom I have given just cause of sorrow and offence, whose relations were taken away or accused.

    [Signed]   Anne Putnam

This confession was read before the congregation, together with her relation, Aug. 25, 1706; and she acknowledged it.

J. Green, Pastor   (510)

GILES COREY

Giles Corey had a typical profile for a man who was accused. He was up in years, was fond of suing his neighbors, had a history of personal feuding with various people, and often seemed to be a bit confused by what was going on around him in this troubled time.

But when the critical moment arrived, he acted with amazing clarity and courage. When any accused man was arrested, as Corey was after his wife's arrest, the government could seize his property, but only after he entered a plea of "guilty" or "not guilty." So Giles Corey, who had all his life worked hard to accumulate property and saw the estates of his neighbors being confiscated by the officials, refused to enter a plea, thereby legally prohibiting the state from taking his property immediately.

However, to force an accused person to enter a plea, English law allowed the state to use torture, the piling up of boulders upon anyone who was charged with a crime and refused to plead. These were the circumstances under which Giles Corey died. His only response to his persecutors' questions was "More weight." The gruesomeness of Corey's punishment is indicated by Robert Calef, who writes that when Corey's tongue was pressed out of his mouth, the sheriff forced it back into his mouth with his cane as Corey was dying.

The following document is what remains of the transcript of the examination of Corey. It did not appear in the transcripts first published by Cotton Mather, but only a century later in Samuel G. Drake's nineteenth-century book *The Witchcraft Delusion in New England*. As Drake suspects, this testimony may have been carefully overlooked by Mather because it does not put the court's proceedings in a very good light.

The second document is an unsigned nineteenth-century ballad from the *Salem Observer* (reprinted by Drake) illustrating the extent to which Corey and his wife had became mythic, if not heroic, figures. The writer of the ballad still considers that Corey and his wife were witches and that the godly folks of Salem were doing their duty by getting rid of them.

TRANSCRIPT OF THE EXAMINATION OF GILES COREY

This transcript only came to light in 1832. Samuel Drake could only guess the reason that Cotton Mather, who was so intimately involved in the witchcraft trials and would certainly have known of Corey's testimony, failed to include it in his account. Drake suspected one reason: "It may have been thought not sufficiently damning to the Accused" (169).

In the original document, no differentiation is made between the questions posed by Hathorne and Corwin, the inquisitors, and Giles Corey's responses. For clarity, Hathorne and Corwin's words will be identified as "I" and Corey's as "C."

FROM "EXAMINATION OF GILES COREY," IN *THE WITCHCRAFT DELUSION IN NEW ENGLAND*, ED. SAMUEL G. DRAKE
(Roxbury, Mass.: W. Elliot Woodward, 1865)

The Examination of Giles Corey, at a Court at Salem Village, held by John Hathorne and Jonathan Corwin, Esqrs., April 19, 1692.

I: Giles Corey, you are brought before Authority upon high Suspicion of sundry Acts of Witchcraft. Now tell us the Truth in this Matter.

C: I hope, through the Goodness of God, I shall; for that Matter I never had no Hand in, in my Life.

I: Which of you have seen this Man hurt you?

(Mary Wolcott, Mercy Lewis, Ann Putnam, Jr., and Abigail Williams affirmed he had hurt them.)

I: Hath he hurt you too? (speaking to Elizabeth Hubbard. She going to answer was prevented by a Fit.)

I: Benjamin Gold, Hath he hurt you?

Gold: I have seen him several Times, and been hurt after it, but cannot affirm that it was he.

I: Hath he brought the Book to any of you?

(Mary Wolcott and Abigail Williams and others affirmed he had brought the Book to them.)

I: Giles Corey, they accuse you, or your Appearance, of hurting them, and bringing the Book to them. What do you say? Why do you hurt them? Tell us the Truth.

C: I never did hurt them.

I: It is your Appearance hurts them, they charge you; tell us. What have you done?

C: I have done nothing to damage them.

I: Have you never entered into Contract with the Devil?

C: I never did.

I: What Temptations have you had?

C: I never had Temptations in my Life.

I: What! have you done it without Temptations?

Goodwife Bibber: What was the Reason that you were frighted in the Cow-house? (And then the questionist was suddenly seized with a violent Fit.)

(Samuel Braybrook, Goodman Bibber, and his Daughter, testified that he had told them this Morning that he was frighted in the Cow-house. Corey denied it.)

I: This was not your Appearance but your Person, and you told them so this Morning. Why do you deny it?

I: What did you see in the Cow-house?

C: I never saw nothing but my Cattle.

(Divers witnessed that he told them he was frighted.)

I: Well, what do you say to these Witnesses?

C: I do not know that ever I spoke the word in my Life.

I: Tell the Truth. What was it frighted you?

C: I do not know any Thing that frighted me.

(All the Afflicted were seized now with Fits, and troubled with Pinches. Then the Court ordered his Hands to be tied.)

I: What! Is it not enough to act Witchcraft at other Times, but must you do it now in Face of Authority?

C: I am a poor Creature and cannot help it.

(Upon the Motion of his Head again, they had their Heads and Necks afflicted.)

I: Why do you tell such wicked Lies against Witnesses, that heard you speak after this Manner, this very Morning?

C: I never saw anything but a black Hog.

I: You said that you were stopped once in Prayer; what stopt you?

C: I cannot tell. My Wife came towards me and found Fault with me for saying living to God and dying to Sin.

I: What was it frighted you in the Barn?

C: I know nothing frighted me there.

I: Why there are three Witnesses that heard you say so to-day.

C: I do not remember it.

(Thomas Gold testified that he heard him say, that he knew enough against his Wife, that would do her Business.)

I: What was that you knew against your Wife?

C: Why, that of living to God, and dying to Sin.

(The Marshal and Bibber's Daughter confirmed the same; that he said he could say that that would do his Wife's Business.)

C: I have said what I can say to that.

I: What was that about your Ox?

C: I thought he was hipt.

I: What Ointment was that your Wife had when she was seized. You said it was Ointment she made by Major Gidney's Direction.

(He denied it, and said she had it of Goody Bibber, or from her Direction)

I: Goody Bibber said it is not like that Ointment.

I: You said you knew upon your own Knowledge, that she had it of Major Gidney.

(He denied it)

I: Did you not say, when you went to the Ferry with your Wife, you would not go over to Boston now, for you should come yourself next Week?

C: I would not go over because I had not Money.

(The Marshal testified he said as before.)

(One of his hands was let go, and several were afflicted. He held his Head on one Side, and then the Heads of several of the Afflicted were held on one Side. He drew in his Cheeks, and the Cheeks of some of the Afflicted were suckt in.)

(John Bibber and his Wife gave in Testimony concerning some Temptations he had to make away with himself)

I: How doth this agree with what you said, that you had no Temptations?

C: I meant Temptations to Witchcraft.

I: If you can give way to self murder, that will make way to Temptation to Witchcraft.

Note.—There was Witness by several, that he said he would make away with himself, and charge his Death upon his Son.

(Goody Bibber testified that the said Corey called said Bibber's Husband, Damned Devilish Rogue.)

(Other vile Expressions testified to in open Court by several others.)

Salem Village, April 19, 1692. Mr. Samuel Parris being desired to take in Writing the Examination of Giles Corey, delivered it in; and upon hearing the same, and seeing what we did see at the Time of his Examination, together with the Charge of the afflicted Persons against him, we committed him to their Majesties Gaol.

John Hathorne   (169–173)

BALLAD OF GILES COREY

The author of the following ballad on Giles Corey and his wife is unknown. It was given by a reader for publication in the *Salem Observer* around 1808 and was included in Samuel G. Drake's 1865 edition of *The Witchcraft Delusion in New England* but is assumed to be much older than its first nineteenth-century publication.

"GILES COREY AND GOODWYFE COREY," A BALLAD OF 1692,
IN *THE WITCHCRAFT DELUSION IN NEW ENGLAND*,
ED. SAMUEL G. DRAKE
(Roxbury, Mass.: W. Elliot Woodward, 1865)

Come all New-England Men
    And harken unto me,
And I will tell what did befalle
    Upon ye Gallows Tree.

In Salem Village was the Place
    As I did heare them saye,
And Goodwyfe Corey was her Name
    Upon that Paynfull Daye:

This Goody Corey was a Witch
    The People did believe,
Afflicting of the Godly Ones
    Did make them sadly Greave.

There were two pyous Matron Dames
    And goodly Maidens Three,

That cryed upon this heynous Witch
  As you shall quicklie see.

Goodwyfe Bibber, she was one,
  And goodwyfe Goodall two
These were the sore afflicted ones
  By Fyts and Pynchings too:

And those Three Damsels fair
  She worried them full sore,
As all could see upon their Arms
  The divers Marks they bore.

And when before the Magistrates
  For Tryall she did stand,
This Wicked Witch did lye to them
  While holding up her Hand;

"I pray you all Good Gentlemen
  Come listen unto me,
I never harmed those two Goodwyfes
  Nor yet these Children Three:"

"I call upon my Saviour Lord"
  (Blasphemously she sayed)
"As Witness of my Innocence
  In this my hour of Need."

The Godly Ministers were shockt
  This Witch-prayer for to hear,
And some did see the Black Man there
  A whispering in her Eare.

The Magistrates did saye to her
  Most surely thou doth lye,
Confess thou here thy hellish Deeds
  Or ill Death thou must dye.

She rent her Cloaths, she tore her Haire,
  And lowdly she did crye,
"May Christe forgive mine Enimies
  When I am called to dye."

This Goodwyfe had a Goodman too,
  Giles Corey was his Name,
In Salem Gaol they shut him in
  With his Blasphemous Dame.

Giles Corey was a Wizzard strong,
　　A Stubborn Wretch was he,
And fit was he to hang on high
　　Upon the Locust Tree:

So when before the Magistrates
　　For tryall he did come,
He would no true Confession make
　　But was compleatlie dumbe.

"Giles Corey," said the Magistrate,
　　"What hast thou hear to pleade
To these who now accuse thy foule
　　Of Crymes and horrid Deed?"

Giles Corey—he sayd not a Word,
　　No single Word spake he:
"Giles Corey," sayth the Magistrate,
　　"We'll press it out of thee."

They got them then a *heavy Beam*,
　　They layde it on his Breast,
They loaded it with heavy Stones,
　　and hard upon him prest.

"More weight," now sayd this wretched Man,
　　"More weight," again he cryed,
And he did no Confession make
　　But wickedlie he Dyed.

Dame Corey lived but six Dayes more,
　　But six Day's more lived she,
For she was hung at Gallows Hill
　　Upon the Locust Tree.

Rejoice all true New-England Men,
　　let Grace still more abounde,
Go search the Land with myght and maine
　　Till all these Imps be founde:

And that will be a glorious Daye,
　　A goodlie Sight to see,
When you shall hang these Brands of Fyre
　　Upon the Gallows Tree.   (174–177)

REBECCA NURSE

Rebecca Nurse was known as an outspoken person (as was her litigious husband Francis), but also for her many charities throughout the community. Above all others, she was known as "a good Christian woman" whose behavior and life of good works attested to her faith. In this atmosphere and given the Puritans' doctrinal distrust of good works as only a cover for an evil heart, what she did amounted to nothing.

Even under intense pressure from Putnam, Parris, Hathorne, and other powerful people involved, the jury initially returned a "not guilty" verdict, sending the "afflicted" accusers into hysterical screeches and fits. The judges prevailed, however, and she was convicted and hanged. The following documents were generated during her trial: one court record and one testimonial from her neighbors.

ROBERT CALEF'S ACCOUNT OF REBECCA NURSE'S COURT CASE

Rebecca Nurse's case was exceptional even among many exceptional cases in a bizarre time. Calef's account shows that the jury that heard her case at first brought in a verdict of not guilty but was bullied by the magistrates to reconsider and change its decision. The jury was informed that Rebecca Nurse had said that two of the witches who had confessed were "one of us" or something to that effect. When she was asked to explain the remark, she did not answer and was thus found "guilty." Afterward, she explained that her remark "one of us" was meant to indicate that they were all accused and prisoners—not witches—together, and that she had not heard or understood the question put to her by the jury as it reconsidered its "not guilty" verdict. But it was too late. The governor himself at first granted her a reprieve, but then, under pressure, reversed himself, and she was hanged.

House of Rebecca Nurse, in Danvers, Massachusetts. Photo by the author.

FROM ROBERT CALEF, *MORE WONDERS OF THE INVISIBLE
WORLD, 1692*, IN *THE WITCHCRAFT DELUSION IN NEW
ENGLAND*, ED. SAMUEL G. DRAKE
(Roxbury, Mass.: W. Elliot Woodward, 1865)

At the Tryal of Rebecka Nurse, this was remarkable that when the Jury brought in their Verdict not Guilty, immediately all the accusers in the Court, and suddenly after all the afflicted out of Court, made an hideous out-cry, to the amazement, not only of the spectators, but the Court also seemed strangely surprised. One of the Judges exprest himself not satisfied, another of them as he was going off the Bench, said they would have her Indicted anew. The chief Judge said he would not Impose upon the Jury; but intimated, as if they had not well considered one Expression of the Prisoners, when she was upon Tryal, *viz*. That when one Hobbs, who had confessed her self to be a Witch, was brought into the Court to witness against her, the Prisoner turning her head to her, said, "What, do you bring her? she is one of us," or to that effect; this together with the Clamours of the Accusers, induced the Jury to go out again, after their Verdict, not Guilty. But not agreeing, they came into the Court, and she being then at the Bar, her words were repeated to her, in order to have had her explanation of them, and she making no Reply to them, they found the Bill, and brought her in Guilty; these words being the Inducement to it, as the Foreman has signified in writing, as follows:

July 4, 1692. I Thomas Fisk, the Subscriber hereof, being one of them that were of the Jury the last week at Salem-Court, upon the Tryal of Rebecka Nurse, etc., being desired by some of the Relations to give a Reason why the Jury brought her in Guilty, after her Verdict not Guilty; I do hereby give my Reasons to be as follows, *viz.*

When the Verdict not Guilty was, the honoured Court was pleased to object to it, saying to them, that they think they let slip the words, which the Prisoner at the Bar spake against her self, which were spoken in reply to Goodwife Hobbs and her Daughter, who had been faulty in setting their hands to the Devils Book as they have confessed formerly; the words were "What, do these persons give in Evidence against me now, they used to come among us." After the honoured Court had manifested their dissatisfaction of the Verdict, several of the Jury declared themselves desirous to go out again, and thereupon the honoured Court gave leave; but when we came to consider of the Case, I could not tell how to take her words, as an Evidence against her, till she had a further opportunity to put her Sense upon them, if she would take it; and then going into Court, I mentioned the words aforesaid, which by one of the Court were affirmed to have been spoken by her, she being then at the Bar, but made no reply, nor interpretation of them; whereupon these words were to me a principal Evidence against her.

Thomas Fisk.

When Goodwife Nurse was informed what use was made of these words, she put in this following Declaration into the Court.

These presents do humbly shew, to the honoured Court and Jury, that I being informed, that the Jury brought me in Guilty, upon my saying that Goodwife Hobbs and her Daughter were of our Company; but I intended no otherways, than as they were Prisoners with us, and therefore did then, and yet do judge them not legal Evidence against their fellow Prisoners. And I being something hard of hearing, and full of grief, none informing me how the Court took up my words, and therefore had not opportunity to declare what I intended, when I said they were of our company.

Rebecka Nurse   (358–359)

PETITION IN SUPPORT OF REBECCA NURSE

When one considers the extreme danger at this time of coming forward to defend a relative or neighbor, the petition signed by thirty-five citizens of Salem in defense of Rebecca Nurse is an extraordinary testimonial to a good woman as well as to the bravery of her friends.

"PETITION FOR REBECCA NURSE," IN CHARLES W. UPHAM, *SALEM WITCHCRAFT*
(Boston: Wiggin and Lunt, 1867)

We whose names are hereunto subscribed, being desired by Goodman Nurse to declare what we know concerning his wife's conversation for time past,—we can testify, to all whom it may concern, that we have known her for many years; and, according to our observation, her life and conversation were according to her profession, and we never had any cause or grounds to suspect her of any such thing as she is now accused of.

Israel Porter	Samuel Abbey
Elizabeth Porter	Hepzibah Rea
Edward Bishop, Sr.	Daniel Andrew
Hannah Bishop	Sarah Andrew
Joshua Rea	Daniel Rea
Sarah Rea	Sarah Putnam
Sarah Leach	Jonathan Putnam
John Putnam	Lydia Putnam
Rebecca Putnam	Walter Phillips, Sr.
Joseph Hutchinson	Margaret Phillips
William Osburn	Joseph Houlton, Jr.
Joseph Holton, Sr.	Samuel Endicott
Sarah Holton	Elizabeth Buxton

Benjamin Putnam

Sarah Putnam

Job Swinnerton

Esther Swinnerton

Joseph Herrick, Sr.

Samuel Aborn, Sr.

Isaac Cook

Elizabeth Cook

Joseph Putnam

(Vol. 2: 272)

JOHN AND ELIZABETH PROCTOR

John Proctor, also very outspoken and a longtime adversary of the Putnams and Parris, continued to defy the judges to the end. His wife Elizabeth was able to escape execution because she was pregnant. By the time the child was born, the hysteria had passed, and her life was spared. The following documents include a letter written by Proctor to the court, the account of witness Robert Calef, a petition on behalf of the Proctors, and Thomas Brattle's brief comment on Proctor's death.

LETTER OF JOHN PROCTOR

The following letter was written by John Proctor on behalf of those accused of witchcraft to several ministers in Boston known to be unhappy with the proceedings in Salem. "Mather" is not Cotton Mather but Increase, his father, who was not, like his son, cooperating with the Salem magistrates. Willard was Samuel Willard, minister of the South Church in Boston, who was one of the most vocal critics of the Salem proceedings and who had assisted in the escape of several of those about to be accused. Parson Moody's own wife had been accused of witchcraft, and the Reverend Allen, when he had been a landowner in Salem, had been a friend of Rebecca and Francis Nurse and had likely been associated with Proctor and others of the accused. The Reverend Bailey was his assistant at the First Church of Boston. Proctor indicates how ridiculous some of the evidence is—charging people for committing crimes while they were locked up in prison—and how heinous some of the torture is.

JOHN PROCTOR, "LETTER OF JOHN PROCTOR," FROM ROBERT
CALEF'S *MORE WONDERS OF THE INVISIBLE WORLD, 1692,* IN
THE WITCHCRAFT DELUSION IN NEW ENGLAND,
ED. SAMUEL G. DRAKE
(Roxbury, Mass.: W. Elliot Woodward, 1865)

Salem-Prison, July 23, 1692

Mr. Mather, Mr. Allen,
Mr. Moody, Mr. Willard, and
Mr. Bailey.
Reverend Gentlemen.

The innocency of our Case with the Enmity of our Accusers and our
Judges, and Jury, whom nothing but our Innocent Blood will serve their
turn, having Condemned us already before our Tryals, being so much
incensed and engaged against us by the Devil, makes us bold to Beg and
Implore your Favourable Assistance of this our Humble Petition to his
Excellency, That if it be possible our Innocent Blood may be spared,
which undoubtedly otherwise will be shed, if the Lord doth not mercifully
step in. The Magistrates, Ministers, Jewries, and all the People in general,
being so much enraged and incensed against us by the Delusion of the
Devil, which we can term no other, by reason we know in our own
Consciences, we are all Innocent Persons. Here are five Persons who have
lately confessed themselves to be Witches, and do accuse some of us, of
being along with them at a Sacrament, since we were committed into
close Prison, which we know to be Lies. Two of the 5 are (Carriers Sons)
Young-men, who would not confess any thing till they tyed them Neck
and Heels till the Blood was ready to come out of their Noses, and 'tis
credibly believed and reported this was the occasion of making them
confess that they never did, by reason they said one had been a Witch a
Month, and another five Weeks, and that their Mother had made them
so, who had been confined here this nine Weeks. My son William Proctor,
when he was examin'd, because he would not confess that he was Guilty,
when he was Innocent, they tyed him Neck and Heels till the Blood
gushed out at his Nose, and would have kept him so 24 Hours, if one
more Merciful than the rest, had not taken pity on him, and caused him
to be unbound. These actions are very like the Popish Cruelties. They
have already undone us in our Estates, and that will not serve their turns,
without our Innocent Bloods. If it cannot be granted that we can have
our Trials at Boston, we humbly beg that you would endeavour to have
these Magistrates changed, and others in their rooms, begging also and
beseeching you would be pleased to be here, if not all, some of you at

our Trials, hoping thereby you may be the means of saving the shedding
our Innocent Bloods, desiring your Prayers to the Lord in our behalf, we
rest your Poor Afflicted Servants,

                                        John Proctor, etc.   (362–364)

ROBERT CALEF'S ACCOUNT

  Despite Proctor's well-argued letter, the trials continued in August. Robert Calef records the trials of the Proctors and the seizure
of their property, which left their young children without parents
or home.

FROM ROBERT CALEF, *MORE WONDERS OF THE INVISIBLE
WORLD, 1692*, IN *THE WITCHCRAFT DELUSION IN NEW
ENGLAND*, ED. SAMUEL G. DRAKE
(Roxbury, Mass.: W. Elliot Woodward, 1865)

  August 5. The Court again sitting, six more were tried on the same
Account, *viz.* Mr. George Burroughs, sometimes minister of Wells, John
Proctor, and Elizabeth Proctor his Wife, and John Willard of Salem-Village,
George Jacobs Senior, of Salem, and Martha Carryer of Andover; these
were all brought in Guilty and Condemned; and were all Executed Aug.
19, except Proctor's Wife, who pleaded Pregnancy.

                              • • •

  John Proctor and his Wife being in Prison, the Sheriff came to his
House and seized all the Goods, Provisions, and Cattle that he could
come at, and sold some of the Cattle at half price, and killed others, and
put them up for the West-Indies; threw out the Beer out of a Barrel, and
carried away the Barrel; emptied a Pot of Broath, and took away the Pot,
and left nothing in the House for the support of the Children: No part
of the said Goods are known to be returned. Proctor earnestly requested
Mr. Noyes to pray with and for him, but It was wholly denied, because
he [that is, Proctor] would not own himself to be a Witch.   (360, 361)

PETITION ENTERED ON BEHALF OF THE PROCTORS

As in the case of Rebecca Nurse, neighbors and friends of the Proctors, at great danger to themselves, signed petitions to the court attesting to their good character. What follows is one of two petitions on their behalf. Thirty-two citizens signed this petition.

"THE HUMBLE AND SINCERE DECLARATION OF US,
SUBSCRIBERS, INHABITANTS IN IPSWICH, ON THE BEHALF OF
OUR NEIGHBORS, JOHN PROCTOR AND HIS WIFE, NOW IN
TROUBLE AND UNDER SUSPICION OF WITCHCRAFT,"
IN CHARLES UPHAM,
SALEM WITCHCRAFT
(Boston: Wiggin and Lunt, 1867)

"To the Honorable Court of Assistants Now Sitting in Boston" Honored and Right Worshipful,—The aforesaid John Proctor may have great reason to justify the Divine Sovereignty of God under these severe remarks of Providence upon his peace and honor, under a due reflection upon his life past; and so the best of us have reason to adore the great pity and indulgence of God's providence, that we are not exposed to the utmost shame that the Devil can invent, under the permissions of sovereignty, though not for that sin forenamed, yet for our many transgressions. . . . [B]eing smitten with the notice of what hath happened, we reckon it within the duties of our charity, that teacheth us to do as we would be done by, to offer thus much for the clearing of our neighbor's innocency; *viz.*, that we never had the least knowledge of such a nefandous wickedness in our said neighbors, since they have been within our acquaintance. Neither do we remember any such thoughts in us concerning them, or any action by them or either of them, directly tending that way, no more than might be in the lives of any other persons of the clearest reputation as to any such evils. What God may have left them to, we cannot go into God's pavilion clothed with clouds of darkness round about; but, as to what we have ever seen or heard of them, upon our consciences we judge them innocent of the crime objected. His breeding hath been amongst us, and was of religious parents in our place, and, by reason of relations and properties within our town, hath had constant [interaction] with us. We speak upon our personal acquaintance and observation; and so leave our neighbors, and this our testimony on their behalf, to the wise thoughts of Your Honors.   (305, 306)

THOMAS BRATTLE'S ACCOUNT OF PROCTOR'S DEATH

Cambridge businessman Thomas Brattle was one of the first to point out the insanity of the witchcraft trials. In his letter to the magistrates, he documents Proctor's last hours.

FROM THOMAS BRATTLE, "LETTER OF THOMAS BRATTLE,
OCTOBER 8, 1692,"
COLLECTIONS OF THE MASSACHUSETTS HISTORICAL SOCIETY,
IN *NARRATIVES OF THE WITCHCRAFT CASES, 1648–1706,*
ED. GEORGE LINCOLN BURR
(New York: Charles Scribner's Sons, 1914)

As to the late executions, I shall only tell you, that in the opinion of many unprejudiced, considerate and considerable spectatours, some of the condemned went out of the world not only with as great protestations, but also with as good shews of innocency, as men could do.

They protested their innocency as in the presence of the great God, whom forthwith they were to appear before: they wished, and declared their wish, that their blood might be the last innocent blood shed upon that account. With great affection [emotion] they entreated Mr. C. M. [Cotton Mather] to pray with them: they prayed that God would discover what witchcrafts were among us; they forgave their accusers; they spake without reflection on Jury and Judges, for bringing them in guilty, and condemning them: they prayed earnestly for pardon for all other sins, and for an interest in the precious blood of our dear Redeemer; and seemed to be very sincere, upright, and sensible of their circumstances on all accounts; especially Proctor and Willard, whose whole management of themselves, from the Gaol to the Gallows, and whilst at the Gallows, was very affecting and melting to the hearts of some considerable Spectatours, whom I could mention to you.   (177)

THE REVEREND JOHN HALE

The Reverend John Hale, pastor of the church in the nearby town of Beverly, was initially a fairly avid supporter of the witch trials. In fact, his participation in the proceedings included testifying as a witness against several of the accused in the beginning. But something happened along the way to disillusion him: his wife was accused.

After the trials, he wanted to leave a record of the events and consulted with several others who had also become disillusioned, like trial judge Samuel Sewall (who believed that Hale had gone too far in his condemnation of officials at the trials). Support in many official circles for what had happened in Salem was still so strong that ministers, especially, were hesitant to take on giants of the day like Cotton Mather, so it is not surprising that Hale's account was not published until 1702, after he had died. Still, to the modern reader, Hale's *Enquiry* is scarcely enlightened. Obviously Hale's own complicity in the executions and arrests lies heavily on his conscience, but while acknowledging that the lives of some innocent people may have been destroyed, he still urges his readers to be alert to "real" witches among them and to learn enough to destroy them properly. His record of the events he observed follows.

FROM JOHN HALE, *A MODEST ENQUIRY INTO THE NATURE OF
WITCHCRAFT*
(Boston: B. Green and J. Allen, 1702)

I have been present at several Examinations and Tryals, and knew sundry of those that Suffered upon that account in former years, and in this last affair, and so have more advantages than a stranger, to give account of these Proceedings.

I have been from my Youth trained up in the knowledge and belief of most of those principles I here question as unsafe to be used. The first person that suffered on this account in New-England, about Fifty years since, was my Neighbour, and I heard much of what was charged upon her, and others in those times; and the reverence I bore to aged, learned and judicious persons, caused me to drink in their principles in these things, with a kind of Implicit Faith.

• • •

But observing the Events of that sad Catastrophe, Anno 1692, I was brought to a more strict scanning of the principles I had imbibed, and by scanning, to question, and by questioning at length to reject many of them, upon the reasons shewed in the ensuing Discourse.

• • •

I have had a deep sense of the sad consequence of mistakes in matters Capital; and their impossibility of recovering when compleated. And what grief of heart it brings to a tender conscience, to have been unwittingly encouraging of the Sufferings of the innocent. And I hope a zeal to prevent for the future such sufferings is pardonable, although there should be much weakness, and some errors in the pursuit thereof.

• • •

But that which chiefly carried on this matter to such an height, was the increasing of confessors till they amounted to near about Fifty: and four or six of them upon their tryals owned their guilt of this crime, and were condemned for the same, but not Executed. And many of the confessors confirmed their confessions with very strong circumstances.

• • •

By these things you see how this matter was carried on, *viz.*, chiefly by the complaints and accusations of the Afflicted, Bewitched ones, as it was supposed, and then by the Confessions of the Accused, condemning themselves, and others. Yet experience shewed that the more there were apprehended, the more were still Afflicted by Satan, and the number of Confessors increasing, did but increase the number of the Accused, and the Executing some, made way for the apprehending of others; for still the Afflicted complained of being tormented by new objects as the former were removed. . . . And at last it was evidently seen that there must be a stop put, or the Generation of the Children of God would fall under that condemnation.

• • •

Here was generally acknowledged to be an error (at least on the one hand) but the Querie is, Wherein? . . .

I have heard it said, That the Precedents in England were not so exactly followed, because in those there had been previous quarrels and threatnings of the Afflicted by those that were Condemned for Witchcraft; but here, say they, not so. To which I answer.

1. In many of these cases there had been antecedent personal quarrels,

and so occasions of revenge; for some of those Condemned, had been suspected by their Neighbours several years, because after quarrelling with their Neighbours, evil had befallen those Neighbours.

• • •

4. It was considerable [deserving of consideration] that Nineteen were Executed, and all denyed the Crime to the Death, and some of them were knowing persons, and had before this been accounted blameless livers. And it is not to be imagined, but that if all had been guilty, some would have had so much tenderness as to seek Mercy for their Souls in the way of Confession and sorrow for such a Sin.

• • •

I shall conclude this Discourse with some Application of the whole.
1. We may hence see ground to fear, that there hath been a great deal of innocent blood shed in the Christian World, by proceeding upon unsafe principles, in condemning persons for Malefick Witchcraft.

• • •

I am abundantly satisfyed that those who were most concerned to act and judge in those matters, did not willingly depart from the rules of righteousness. But such was the darkness of that day, the tortures and lamentations of the afflicted, and the power of former precedents, that we calked in the clouds, and could not see our way. And we have most cause to be humbled for error on that hand, which cannot be retrieved. So that we must beseech the Lord, that if any innocent blood hath been shed, in the hour of temptation, the Lord will not lay it to our charge . . . , but blot it out, and wash it away with the blood of Jesus Christ.   (1–34)

THE PROCLAMATION BY THE ASSEMBLY OF MASSACHUSETTS BAY

In the four years following the witch trials, the New England community and especially many of the people directly involved in prosecution during the trials underwent many personal disasters—deaths, illnesses, and economic hardships. As a result of these misfortunes, they began to suspect that God was displeased with their conduct in 1692 and was punishing them for their persecution of witches. One of the most prominent cases was Judge Samuel Sewall, who had suffered many reversals after the trials. Finally, in 1696, he felt that he had to make some attempt to reach God with a community apology for the trials, so he drafted a proclamation for the ruling body of the commonwealth to make public. Cotton Mather, who had been such an avid supporter of the witch-hunt, wanted the Assembly to adopt his less apologetic version, but it was rejected, and Sewall's was passed.

"PROCLAMATION OF 1696," FROM ROBERT CALEF, *MORE WONDERS OF THE INVISIBLE WORLD, 1692*, IN *THE WITCHCRAFT DELUSION IN NEW ENGLAND*, ED. SAMUEL G. DRAKE
(Roxbury, Mass.: W. Elliot Woodward, 1865)

By the Honorable the Lieutenant Governour, Council and Assembly of his Majesties Province of the Massachusetts Bay, in General Court Assembled.

Whereas the Anger of God is not yet turned away, but his Hand is still stretched out against his People in manifold Judgments, particularly in drawing out to such a length the troubles of Europe, by a perplexing War; and more especially, respecting ourselves in this Province, in that God is pleased still to go on in diminishing our Substance, cutting short our Harvest, blasting our most promising undertakings more ways than one, unsettling of us, and by his more Immediate hand, snatching away many out of our Embraces, by sudden and violent Deaths, even at this time when the Sword is devouring so many both at home and abroad, and that after many days of publick and Solemn addressing of him, And altho considering the many Sins prevailing in the midst of us, we cannot but wonder at the Patience and Mercy moderating these Rebukes; yet we cannot but also fear that there is something still wanting to accompany our Supplications. And doubtless there are some particular Sins, which God is Angry with our Israel for, that have not been duly seen and repented by us, about which God expects to be sought, if ever he turn against our Captivity.

Wherefore it is Commanded and Appointed, that Thursday the Fourteenth of January next be observed as a Day of Prayer, with Fasting throughout this Province, strictly forbidding all Servile labour thereon; that so all Gods People may offer up fervent Supplications unto him, for the Preservation, and Prosperity of his Majesty's Royal Person and Government, and Success to attend his Affairs both at home and abroad; that all iniquity may be put away which hath stirred God's Holy Jealousie against this Land; that he would shew us what we know not, and help us wherein we have done amiss to do so no more; and especially that whatever mistakes on either hand have been fallen into, either by the body of this People, or any orders of men, referring to the late Tragedy, raised among us by Satan and his Instruments, thro the awful Judgment of God, he would humble us therefore and pardon all the Errors of his Servants and People, that desire to love his Name and be atoned to his Land; that he would remove the Rod of the wicked from off the Lot of the Righteous; that he would bring the American Heathen, and cause them to hear and obey his Voice.

Given at Boston, Decemb. 17, 1696, in the 8th Year of his Majesties Reign.

Isaac Addington, Secretary   (385–386)

SAMUEL SEWALL'S PERSONAL ATONEMENT

Samuel Sewall, who drafted the public proclamation in which the state itself entertained the possibility that the magistrates had erred during the witch hysteria, issued his own apology for his actions as a judge in Salem. As Sewall described it in his *Diary*, he went to the South Church of Boston on the fast day set up by the proclamation. This was the church presided over by the Reverend Samuel Willard, who had been vehemently opposed to the witchcraft trials. As he entered the church, Sewall gave Willard a piece of paper, which he called a "Copy of the Bill." At the end of the service, Sewall walked down to the front of the church where the paupers generally sat. As Willard began to read Sewall's paper, Sewall got to his feet, remaining standing throughout and then bowing when Willard finished the reading. The following is the paper Sewall gave Willard to read.

FROM SAMUEL SEWALL, "COPY OF THE BILL," IN HIS *DIARY,*
1674–1700
(Boston: Collections of the Massachusetts Historical Society, 1878)

Samuel Sewall, sensible of the reiterated strokes of God upon himself and family; and being sensible, that as to the Guilt contracted upon the opening of the late Commission of Oyer and Terminer at Salem (to which the order for this Day relates) he is, upon many accounts, more concerned than any that he knows of, Desires to take the Blame and shame of it, Asking pardon of men, And especially desiring prayers that God, who has an Unlimited Authority, would pardon that sin and all other his sins, personal and Relative: And according to his infinite Benignity, and Sovereignty, Not Visit the sin of him, or of any other, upon himself or any of his, nor upon the Land: But that He would powerfully defend him against all Temptations to Sin, for the future; and vouchsafe him the efficacious, saving Conduct of His Word and Spirit. (Vol. I: 445)

THE APOLOGY OF THE JURORS IN THE WITCHCRAFT TRIALS

In the year 1696, twelve of the men who served as jurors in the Salem witchcraft trials asked forgiveness for their part in the hysteria. Their statement follows.

"THE APOLOGY OF THE JURORS," FROM ROBERT CALEF, *MORE WONDERS OF THE INVISIBLE WORLD, 1692*, IN *THE WITCHCRAFT DELUSION IN NEW ENGLAND*, ED. SAMUEL G. DRAKE
(Roxbury, Mass.: W. Elliot Woodward, 1865)

Some that had been of several Jewries, have given forth a Paper, Sign'd with their own hands in these words

We whose names are under written, being in the Year 1692 called to serve as Jurors, in Court at Salem, on Tryal of many, who were by some suspected Guilty of doing Acts of Witchcraft upon the Bodies of sundry Persons:

We confess that we our selves were not capable to understand, nor able to withstand the mysterious delusions of the Powers of Darkness, and Prince of the Air; but were for want of Knowledge in our selves, and better Information from others, prevailed with to take up with such Evidence against the Accused, as on further consideration, and better Information, we justly fear was insufficient for the touching the Lives of any, Deut. 17.6 whereby we fear we have been instrumental with others, tho Ignorantly and unwittingly, to bring upon our selves, and this People of the Lord, the Guilt of Innocent Blood; which Sin the Lord saith in Scripture, he would not pardon, 2 Kings 24.4, that is we suppose in regard of his temporal Judgments. We do therefore hereby signifie to all in general (and to the surviving Sufferers in especial) our deep sense of, and sorrow for our Errors, in acting on such Evidence to the condemning of any person.

And do hereby declare that we justly fear that we were sadly deluded and mistaken, for which we are much disquieted and distressed in our minds; and do therefore humbly beg forgiveness, first of God for Christ's sake for this our Error; And pray that God would not impute the guilt of it to our selves, nor others; and we also pray that we may be considered candidly, and aright by the living Sufferers as being then under the power of a strong and general Delusion, utterly unacquainted with, and not experienced in matters of that Nature.

We do heartily ask forgiveness of you all, whom we have justly offended, and do declare according to our present minds, we would none of us do such things again on such grounds for the whole World; praying you to accept of this in way of Satisfaction for our Offence; and that you would bless the Inheritance of the Lord, that he may be entreated for the Land.

Foreman, Thomas Fisk,	Thomas Perly, *Senior*,
William Fisk,	John Pebody,
John Batcheler,	Thomas Perkins,
Thomas Fisk, *Junior*,	Samuel Sayer,
John Dane,	Andrew Elliott,
Joseph Evelith,	Henry Herrick, *Senior* (387–388)

THE REVERSAL OF ATTAINDER OF 1711

Despite the immediate reversal of attitudes with regard to the witchcraft trials, even on the part of those who had actively participated in them, it took almost twenty years for the Province of the Massachusetts Bay to make official partial amends for the execution and persecution of New England citizens. On October 17, 1711, the government issued a Reversal of Attainder that, in effect, was a declaration that many of those executed should no longer be considered tainted with the dishonor of witchcraft and should have their civil rights restored, reversing any attempts to seize their property and awarding damages to some of their heirs.

"REVERSAL OF ATTAINDER, OCTOBER 17, 1711," IN *RECORDS OF SALEM WITCHCRAFT*, ED. W. E. WOODWARD
(Roxbury, Mass.: Privately Printed, 1864)

Province of the Massachusetts Bay: Anno Regni Anna Reginae Decimo.

An Act to reverse the attainders of George Burroughs and others for Witchcraft

Forasmuch as in the year of our Lord one Thousand six hundred ninety-two several Towns within this Province were Infested with a horrible Witchcraft or possession of devils: And at a Special Court of Oyer and Terminer holden at Salem in the County of Essex in the same year 1692. George Burroughs of Wells, John Proctor, George Jacobs, John Willard, Giles Corey, and Martha his wife, Rebecca Nurse and Sarah Good all of Salem aforesaid Elizabeth How of Ipswich, Mary Eastey, Sarah Wildes and Abigail Hobbs all of Topsfield, Samuel Wardwell, Mary Parker, Martha Carrier, Abigail Faulkner, Anne Foster, Rebecca Eames, Mary Post and Mary Lacey all of Andover, Mary Bradbury of Salesbury, and Dorcas Hoar of Beverly were severally Indicted convicted and attainted of Witchcraft, and some of them put to death. Others lying still under the like sentence of the said Court, and liable to have the same Executed upon them.

The Influence and Energy of the Evil Spirits so great at that time acting in and upon those who were the principal accusers and Witnesses proceeding so far as to cause a Prosecution to be had of persons of known and good reputation, which caused a great dissatisfaction and a stop to be put thereunto until their Majesties' pleasure should be known therein:

And upon a Representation thereof accordingly made her late Majesty Queen Mary the second of blessed memory by Her Royal Letter given at her Court at Whitehall the fifteenth of April 1693 was Graciously pleased to approve the care and Circumspection therein; and to Will and require that in all proceedings against persons accused for Witchcraft, or being possessed by the devil, the great Moderation and all due Circumspection be used, so far as the same may be without Impediment to the Ordinary course of Justice.

And some of the principal Accusers and Witnesses in those dark and severe prosecutions have since discovered themselves to be persons of profligate and vicious conversation.

Upon the humble Petition and suit of several of the said persons and of the children of others of them whose Parents were Executed. Be it Declared and Enacted by his Excellency the Governor Council and Representatives in General Court assembled, and by the authority of the same That the several convictions Judgments and Attainders against the said George Burroughs, John Proctor, George Jacobs, John Willard, Giles Corey and Martha Corey, Rebecca Nurse, Sarah Good, Elizabeth How, Mary Eastey, Sarah Wildes, Abigail Hobbs, Samuel Wardwell, Mary Parker, Martha Carrier, Abigail Faulkner, Anne Foster, Rebecca Eames, Mary Post, Mary Lacey, Mary Bradbury, and Dorcas Hoar, and every of them Be and hereby are reversed made and declared to be null and void to all Intents, Constructions and purposes whatsoever, as if no such convictions Judgments, or Attainders had ever been had or given. And that no penalties or Forfeitures of Goods or Chattels be by the said Judgments and attainders or either of them had or Incurred. Any Law Usage or Custom to the contrary notwithstanding. And that no Sheriff, Constable, Jailer or other officer shall be Liable to any prosecution in the Law for anything they then Legally did in the execution of their respective offices.

Made and passed by the Great and General Court or
Assembly of Her Majesty's Province of the Massachusetts Bay
in New England held at Boston the 17th day of October, 1711.
Order of Compensation

By his Excellency the Governor

Whereas the General Assembly in their last session accepted the report of their committee appointed to consider of the Damages sustained by Sundry persons prosecuted for witchcraft in the year 1692 viz

	pds	s	d		pds	s	d
To Elizabeth How	12	0	0	John Proctor & wife	150	0	0
George Jacobs	79	0	0	Sarah Wildes	14	0	0
Mary Eastey	20	0	0	Mary Bradbury	20	0	0

	pds	s	d		pds	s	d
Mary Parker	8	0	0	Abigail Faulkner	20	0	0
Gge. Burroughs	50	0	0	Abigail Hobbs	10	0	0
Giles Corey & wife	21	0	0	Anne Foster	6	10	0
Rebecca Nurse	25	0	0	Rebecca Eames	10	0	0
John Willard	20	0	0	Dorcas Hoar	21	17	0
Sarah Good	30	0	0	Mary Post	8	14	0
Martha Carrier	7	6	0	Mary Lacey	8	10	0
Samuel Wardwell & wife	36	15	0				

• • •

The whole amounting unto Five hundred seventy eight pounds and Twelve shillings.

I do by and with the advice and consent of her Majesty's council hereby order you to pay the above sum of five hundred seventy eight pounds and twelve shillings to Stephen Sewall Esquire who together with the gentlemen of the Committee that estimated and Reported the said damages are desired and directed to distribute the same in proportion as above to such of the said persons as are Living and to those that legally represent them that are dead according as the law directs and for which this shall be your Warrant.

Given under my hand at Boston the 17 Day of December 1711.

J. Dudley   (Vol. II: 216–221)

MASSACHUSETTS RESOLVE OF 1957

A number of those convicted of witchcraft, even some of those executed, remained on the records among the guilty, still legally witches. It was not until 1957, after the appearance of Arthur Miller's *The Crucible* as well as a nationally televised drama of Ann Pudeator's trial, that interest was generated in clearing the names of the remaining people accused of witchcraft, especially those who had not been mentioned in the 1711 Reversal of Attainder.

Curiously, the resolve merely says that the proceedings were "shocking" and that "no disgrace or cause for distress attaches to the said descendants." It expressly refuses to reverse the convictions. The second part of the two-part resolve states that no one can now be sued for what was done, and that the descendants are not entitled to any rights that they did not have before the resolution.

RESOLVE OF THE MASSACHUSETTS GENERAL COURT, BOSTON, AUGUST 28, 1957

RESOLVE RELATIVE TO THE INDICTMENT, TRIAL CONVICTION AND EXECUTION OF ANN PUDEATOR AND CERTAIN OTHER PERSONS FOR "WITCHCRAFT" IN THE YEAR SIXTEEN HUNDRED AND NINETY-TWO

Whereas, One Ann Pudeator and certain other persons were indicted, tried, found guilty, sentenced to death and executed in the year sixteen hundred and ninety-two for "Witchcraft"; and

Whereas, Said persons may have been illegally tried, convicted and sentenced by a possibly illegal court of oyer and terminer created by the then governor of the Province without authority under the Province Charter of Massachusetts Bay; and

Whereas, Although there was a public repentance by Judge Sewall, one of the judges of the so-called "Witchcraft Court," and by all the members of the "Witchcraft" jury, and a public Fast Day proclaimed and observed in repentance for the proceedings, but no other action taken in regard to them; and

Whereas, The General Court of Massachusetts is informed that certain descendants of said Ann Pudeator and said other persons are still distressed by the record of said proceedings; therefore be it

Resolved, That in order to alleviate such distress and although the facts of such proceedings cannot be obliterated, the General Court of Massachusetts declares its belief that such proceedings, even if lawful under the Province Charter and the law of Massachusetts as it then was, were and are shocking, and the result of a wave of popular hysterical fear of the Devil in the community, and further declares that, as all the laws under which said proceedings, even if then legally conducted, have been long since abandoned and superseded by our more civilized laws no disgrace or cause for distress attaches to the said descendants or any of them by reason of said proceedings; and be it further

Resolved, That the passage of this resolve shall not bestow on the commonwealth, or any of its subdivisions, or on any persons any right which did not exist prior to said passage, shall not authorize any suit or other proceeding nor deprive any party to a suit or other proceeding of any defense which he hitherto had, shall not affect in any way whatever the title to, or rights in any real or personal property, nor shall it require or permit the remission of any penalty, fine or forfeiture hitherto imposed or incurred.

Approved August 28, 1957

PROJECTS FOR ORAL OR WRITTEN EXPLORATION

1. Write a paper defining and exploring spectral evidence. What exactly makes this kind of evidence so dangerous?

2. Do some research on the subject of presently constituted "rules of evidence," especially as they regard damning testimony. Write a legal decision, as if you were a judge, on the admissibility of the evidence reported in these documents and *The Crucible*.

3. Discuss the motives that each of the following people had in the witch trials: Abigail Williams, Samuel Parris, and Thomas Putnam. Write a paper on one of the three.

4. Have a debate on which character seems to deserve most of the blame in the witchcraft hysteria.

5. Construct and produce a drama of the examination of Giles Corey. You will have many choices to make: Are the questions by the inquisitors to be delivered in a fatherly fashion or an adversarial one? Is Corey to be a strong and defiant old man or a stumbling and confused one? What body language and tone of voice will the characters have? What pace will the piece have? Will there be any changes in the delivery of the characters? Be prepared to justify your interpretation.

6. Based on Miller's characterization of Abigail Williams and what you see of her in the documents provided here, write a vivid but imaginative account of what happened to Abigail Williams after she disappeared from Salem. Be prepared to justify your speculation.

7. Write and produce a dramatic monologue, delivered by Abigail Williams as an old woman, in which she explains what was going through her mind in 1692 and how she regards her past actions now, looking back from old age.

8. Write a paper on witch-trial confession using both documents and play. Consider the extent of it, as well as the motive and effects of it. How does John Proctor's report of torture affect our judgment of the "confessors" and of those who refused to confess? What is the difference between these two groups of people? Work in an analysis of Act IV in which the subject of confession is paramount.

9. Consider Miller's contention that the first ones accused were those who in some essential way were "different" and therefore to be scorned and sometimes feared. Write a paper on the accused people who were different in some way from ordinary citizens. What kinds of people today does society regard as "different," and how do we continue to marginalize and persecute "difference"?

10. How does our modern-day reaction to the aberrant homeless person compare with the 1692 community's reaction? What specific physical characteristics of such people would have been interpreted as witch-like?

11. History has shown us that women, especially old women, have been disproportionately among those accused of witchcraft. Write an essay investigating this fact in the 1692 trials and offering speculation as to why this happens.

12. Write a major paper on the similarities between Hitler's Germany and 1692 Salem.

13. Do some research on one other period of witch hysteria in history. What similarities do you find between it and 1692 Salem?

14. Construct a talk show/panel on which the guests are John Proctor, Samuel Parris, and John Hale and the topic is the danger of witches. The audience should be free to ask questions and also to challenge a character's response as historically uncharacteristic.

15. Examine the activities in 1692 of Ann Putnam, the younger, and then her confession. Write a paper or have a debate on the interpretation of her confession. Is she to be admired or pitied? Or are you critical of her confession?

16. If you were Rebecca Nurse's son Samuel, would you forgive fellow church member Ann Putnam after her confession? Explain. This can either be debated or actually staged.

17. Ann Putnam, the younger, blames her actions on the Devil's deception. On what might other characters blame their behavior as they look back?

18. What in your society is often blamed for an individual's behavior? For example, what extenuating circumstances might a defense attorney claim in representing a murderer? To the extent that you can document with actual cases, your paper will be more convincing.

19. Do an analysis of John Proctor's argument in his letter. What are its strengths? How do you suppose his arguments were answered by the prosecution?

20. Do a careful analysis of the statements of Samuel Sewall—the proclamation he penned and his personal statement read in church. Include in your analysis the statement of the Salem jurors. How would you judge them? Are they sincerely repentant? Are they assuming responsibility for their actions? What are their expressed motives for apologizing? Do these motives diminish the genuineness and the credit due their apology?

21. Do some research on the following: what exactly does a "pardon" consist of? What is legally required for a person convicted of a crime to be pardoned? Have all of those found guilty of witchcraft been pardoned? Why do you suppose the Massachusetts General Court of 1957 failed to pardon them?

22. Write an essay on Arthur Miller's creation of the character of John Proctor. What in the historical documentation shows that characteristics of the historical Proctor are consistent with those of the fictional one?

SUGGESTED READINGS

Boyer, Paul, and Stephen Nissenbaum. *Salem Possessed: The Social Origins of Witchcraft*. Cambridge, Mass.: Harvard University Press, 1974.

Demos, John Putnam. *Entertaining Satan: Witchcraft and the Culture of Early New England*. New York: Oxford University Press, 1982.

Hill, Frances. *A Delusion of Satan*. New York: Doubleday, 1995.

Karlsen, Carol F. *The Devil in the Shape of a Woman: Witchcraft in Colonial New England*. New York: Norton, 1987.

Nevins, Winfield S. *Witchcraft in Salem Village in 1692*. Salem: North Shore Publishing Co., 1892.

Starkey, Marion. *The Devil in Massachusetts*. New York: Doubleday, 1949.

Trask, Richard B. *The Devil Hath Been Raised*. West Kennebunk, Maine: Published for Danvers Historical Society, 1992.

4

Witch-Hunts in the 1950s

In the Preface we noted that many critics referred to the parallels drawn by *The Crucible* to the political situation of the early 1950s when the play appeared. Arthur Miller, though he wrote his play about the Salem witch-hunts, a subject that had interested him for a long time, was admittedly and specifically drawn to his subject by the events of the late 1940s and early 1950s. It was as if the circumstances of 1692 gave him a way of understanding the troubling times of his own day. The political climate that had developed in the wake of World War II involved an anti-Communist hysteria referred to by commentators as witch-hunts, with remarkable similarities to the events of Salem in 1692. In the 1930s, 1940s, and 1950s, instead of seeing witches everywhere, the government saw "subversives"—people involved in an international conspiracy to overthrow the country. At first the target was the Communist Party, but it grew to include those who expressed opinions critical of the government.

VALID PARALLELS

Did Miller draw a *false* parallel between 1692 and 1952? Critics who claimed that it was false argued that while witches did not exist in Salem in 1692, Communists *did* exist in the United States in 1952. This, of course, is true: communism did exist in the United States in the 1950s. However, parallels drawn in other ways are justifiable on a number of levels. First, Miller explains in his autobiography, *Timebends*, that the parallels in which he was interested involved the extralegal way in which those in power, for political and economic reasons, provoked hysteria and fear—fear even of expressing an opinion and of making the wrong friends.

Second, there were parallels between the governments' tenuous holds on reality and the actual community situations in both cases: there were a few souls like Tituba practicing a form of what Salemites would call witchcraft (fortune-telling, cooking up home remedies, making voodoo dolls, and even inventing things were all considered forms of witchcraft), and in the 1950s a very small percentage of the American population (the estimate is that it was less than 1 percent) were members of the Communist Party. Certain parallels are also valid in that while in 1692 there was no evidence of significant numbers of people being supernaturally in league with the Devil to undermine the Christian community, in 1952 there was no evidence of significant numbers of people acting to overthrow the U.S. government. Even members of the American Communist Party had no interest, by and large, in turning America over to the Russians. Of course, it would be inaccurate to say that no spies for Russia ever got into the U.S. State Department or the CIA (we cannot even say that about the 1990s), but historical evidence does not support a significant or alarming infiltration of Russian spies into the U.S. government in the decades after World War II. Yet at that time citizens in every level of government work, in every level of teaching, in journalism, and especially, for some unaccountable reason, in show business were hounded, terrorized, financially ruined, and deprived of their reputations and basic liberties because of the government's fear that there was a widespread conspiracy to turn the United States over to the Russians. So while some might argue that the parallel drawn between the hunt for witches and the hunt for Communists is weak since many of those targeted initially actually were Communist Party members, the parallel between the hunt for witches and the hunt for traitors has definite validity.

THE TARGETS OF THE WITCH-HUNT

In considering the parallels drawn between the two periods, it is important to realize as well that many citizens were put in the same class with Communists: to have once been a member of the Communist Party was considered just as bad as being a member unless, as with the Salem witch-hunts, one confessed, was repentant, and named others. It is instructive to remember that membership in the Communist Party was a perfectly legal act at the time. As time went on, however, other political behavior was classed as just as despicable as membership in the Communist Party: to have been associated with Franklin Roosevelt, to be a radical member of the Democratic Party, to speak too strongly about civil liberties, to be involved in any peace movement, to criticize elected officials or big business, to feel too sorry for the poor, to mention communism in any objective way in teaching students about systems of government, or to be seen in the company of people considered to be troublemakers.

Similarly, the phrase "conspiring to overthrow the U.S. government" was broadly interpreted. This did not mean only plotting to turn the United States over to the Russians; some legislators even interpreted this to mean overthrowing in fair and honest elections the politicians then in the U.S. government. It was interpreted to mean working to change the way that big business in America treated its workers, or making the tax system more equitable, or providing social services, or creating a minimum wage, or opening up higher education without regard to economic status, social status, race, or gender. Many people regarded capitalism as it was enjoyed by big business as a sacred, patriotic system that was *the* American way. To opine that it needed some alteration was to advocate the overthrow of America.

EVENTS CONTRIBUTING TO THE HYSTERIA

Communism

Communism was the powerful political philosophy articulated by Karl Marx that gained ground in the late nineteenth century, finding a stronghold in Russia and spreading to China and other parts of Asia, other parts of Europe, Africa, and South America.

Those who governed and controlled the United States viewed it from the beginning as antithetical to everything they saw represented by this country. Whereas the United States was founded on the idea that the pursuit of capital was the cornerstone of democracy and must be restricted as little as possible, communism was posited on government ownership of such property in order to take from the "haves" and distribute to the "have-nots." Since the settlement of the United States in the sixteenth century, the country has been based on private ownership of land, unfettered private initiative, private development of industry, and private holdings of capital, and a class system had developed based on economic holdings and sanctioned by religion.

The reason communism made such inroads in countries where for centuries the poor had been driven into the dirt was that, ideally, power and property were taken out of the hands of the very wealthy and controlled by the state for the use of all of the people, not just a few. Private property and, theoretically, the old class divisions between rich and poor, peasant and ruling class, were abolished. It is little wonder that communism, even from its beginnings, would be seen as dangerous, especially by those with economic power, those who felt that any limit placed on money making in the United States was a danger to the very foundation of the country. They also believed that U.S. capitalism had been undermined even as early as the 1920s by communism and by the chief Communist country in the world, the Soviet Union.

The Economic Depression of the 1930s and Roosevelt's New Deal

Many of the reasons for the Red Scare and "witch-hunts" of the 1940s and 1950s—the belief that the country and particularly its economic freedoms were falling apart—can be traced to the Great Depression of the 1930s. Rampant, uncontrolled capitalism, as it had prevailed in the first part of the century, had brought the country to the edge of ruin. Overspeculation and greed had caused financial institutions and industry to collapse, leaving millions of people out of work and starving, with no programs of federal assistance. As a result, labor unions became more active. Working people banded together to secure decent wages and working conditions from factory owners who saw the unions as threats to American capitalism and the American way of life.

The efforts by the Roosevelt administration not only alleviated much individual suffering, but drew the country back from the edge of collapse or revolution. However, this was done at the expense of unbridled capitalism. Private individuals lost some of their opportunities to make money without restraint when the government itself took on the power to regulate business and to modify the pursuit of wealth by individual companies, as, for example, in levying taxes on industry to help alleviate the suffering of the poor.

While their numbers were small, some Communists were involved in the unionizing efforts of the 1940s, contributing to the fear that a Communist conspiracy was aimed at overthrowing the American way of life. By the late 1940s and early 1950s, many Americans, especially those who wielded economic and political power and had much to lose in any social revision, regarded union members and New Deal Democrats as the dupes of Communists and the pawns of the Soviet Union. Many Americans felt it necessary to root out sources of further trouble during what came to be known as the Red Scare.

Another reason for the great fear of communism in the 1940s and 1950s can be found in the communistic Soviet Union's continued tyranny and aggression during that period. American fear of communism was heightened not only by events in Russia, surrounded by its Iron Curtain, but by events in China, a country with one of the largest land masses and greatest populations in the world, which fell to communism in 1949 under the leadership of Mao Zedong. The threat of world communism grew with the outbreak of the Korean War, which erupted when North Korean soldiers, abetted by the Communist Chinese, poured across the 38th parallel into South Korea. As Edward Pessen writes in *Losing Our Souls: The American Experience in the Cold War* (Chicago: Ivan, R. Dee, 1995) it was believed "that any insurrection or radical political movement was aided, abetted, and directed by the Kremlin" that is, the Soviet Union.

In summary, for a variety of reasons, the fear of communism in the United States was very real and very widespread: the social unrest in the American Great Depression, the New Deal restrictions on capitalism, the Republican Party's attempt to disempower the long-reigning Democratic Party, the general threat that Communist philosophy posed for capitalism, and the aggression and tyranny of international communism in the Soviet Union and China. Americans believed that their basic liberties and the survival of their country were hanging in the balance (88).

ANTI-COMMUNIST MEASURES TAKEN AT HOME

Having looked at some of the reasons why communism was feared, let us go back to examine the ways in which the country responded to communism in the 1930s, 1940s, and 1950s. In 1936, President Roosevelt responded to fear that the American Communist Party was growing by lifting prohibitions from federal policing organizations like the FBI, which could then freely pursue those with radical leftist views. This allowed FBI director J. Edgar Hoover to go full speed ahead in his investigation of communism and other left-wing organizations.

Establishment of the House Committee on Un-American Activities

Official investigations into communism in the United States go back to Congress's establishment in 1938, well before American involvement in World War II, of the House Committee on Un-American Activities, known as HUAC. Ostensibly, to be legal, these hearings could be held only in preparation for formulating legislation. The committee, led by Texas conservative Martin Dies, contended that Roosevelt and New Deal supporters were little more than the tools of Communists.

Dies and his committee could not have functioned without the widespread support they enjoyed throughout the country. There was little question that the great majority of Americans, both those on the right and on the left, felt uncomfortable with what they perceived as the growing threat of international communism's possible impact on the United States. It is also true that a few Americans were already going to the extreme in opposing communism. A prime example was radio commentator Father Charles E. Coughlin, who advocated a fascist world order. After 1939, unhappiness with the Communist Party in America skyrocketed on both the political right and left, not only because of the activity of the Dies committee but because of the actions of the Soviet Union in signing a nonaggression pact with Hitler and because it had started on its own path of expansion, overrunning parts of Poland, Finland, and Romania.

The Smith Act

In 1940, the Smith Act was passed, requiring aliens to register with the government, but also allowing the government to bring to trial anyone perceived as advocating the violent overthrow of the government, a charge that could be (and was) easily brought against many non-Communists, including union organizers.

Revival of HUAC

In 1947, Richard M. Nixon was responsible for the revitalization of the old Dies House Committee on Un-American Activities, which had been operating in disrepute under the leadership of Mississippi representative John Rankin, Martin Dies's successor. Probably because of its publicity potential, the primary target of the committee was Hollywood and ten writers who were known to be Communists or had been Communists. These men refused to plead the Fifth Amendment; that is, they refused what then seemed a sure way out of trouble with the committee: all they had to do was to say that they refused to testify on the grounds that it might incriminate them. This they would not do even though they were led to believe that doing so would keep them out of jail. Instead, they turned to the First Amendment, which guaranteed them freedom of speech. All ten were cited for contempt of Congress, many of them were jailed, and all were blacklisted by Hollywood, unable to work again.

Little HUACs spun off to operate at every local level. Two of the most active were the Southern one under the vigorous leadership of Senator James Eastland and the California one under the leadership of Jack Tenney, which continued to focus on the entertainment business with the wholehearted cooperation of movie moguls.

Young people first learned of the far-reaching hand of HUAC and the loyalty boards when teachers disappeared from the schools they were attending. In most cases, they were fired for trying to give their students some objective idea of what this ideology called communism was. To speak of communism in a way that was intellectual rather than purely emotional was grounds for immediate firing. In *Un-American Activities* (New York: HarperCollins, 1994), a book about the period, when she was a girl in high school, Sally Belrage remembers favorite teachers disappearing from her school in New York City: "Then one fine day in April 1953, Dr. Julius Hlavaty, chairman of the math department, was gone. Dr. Hlavaty was not just respected, he was revered; he was considered the best mathematics teacher in the country" (175).

The Taft-Hartley Act

In June 1947, Republicans passed the Taft-Hartley Act over President Truman's veto. This act made it illegal for union officials to be members of the Communist Party. In order to determine party members, a further vast level of investigations was put in place, aimed at rooting Communists out of the unions. Workers were informed on, hauled before review boards to be quizzed, and often bereft of their trades. Union leaders were required to file affidavits declaring that they were not Communists, but because neither management nor government wanted unions, they refused to accept the validity of the affidavits because, they argued, Communists would lie to the board to keep their jobs. This attitude intensified investigations, creating jobs for paid informers whose testimony could send a worker to jail.

Loyalty Review Boards

Responding largely to pressures beyond his control, President Truman in 1947 introduced Executive Order 9835. The purpose of this order was to forbid anyone judged to be "subversive" from working at a government job. The order was intended to quiet the nation's fears over communism by checking its spread in sensitive government jobs. But Truman soon regretted putting Executive Order 9835 in place. It turned into a national nightmare in the hands of FBI director Hoover. Eventually Executive Order 9835 empowered a Republican senator, Joseph McCarthy, whose first act was to turn the power given him by that order against Truman himself, calling the president subversive and the years of Roosevelt's and Truman's administrations "twenty years of treason." By means of Executive Order 9835, boards were set up to seek out disloyal public employees and dismiss them from government service. Review boards spread to state and local levels as well as to the private sector. No citizen in public service was exempt from scrutiny, from the lowliest clerk to the nuclear scientist. Most of those who were accused did not have security-sensitive jobs. Citizens were usually accused by informers, sometimes paid informers, who fed the committee involved with damaging information about their associations, private lives, and political opinions. They would be quizzed about who their friends were, what meetings they had attended, what causes they had supported, what books they had read, what associations their families and in-laws had, whom they criticized, whom they admired—every aspect of their personal lives.

Many people were charged, were interrogated repeatedly, were forced to spend money on lawyers to present their cases, were publicly humiliated and discredited, and watched as their families were torn apart and their livelihoods dissolved. They found it difficult if not impossible to find other jobs. They were, in effect, blacklisted. Those who were eventually cleared ended up frequently too demoralized and destroyed by the process to continue in their jobs.

The boards who summoned public employees had the rights of courts to try individuals and could solicit information, buy information, hold hearings, and render judgments. But those who were summoned had no legal rights. They were not allowed to face their accusers and could not examine the information on which they were being accused. Almost none of the hundreds and hundreds brought before these boards were Communists. Frequently they were completely unpolitical. Often their crimes consisted of going to dinner at the house of someone suspected of having radical ideas.

In 1948, fears of widespread Communist conspiracies heated up when twelve leaders of the Communist Party of the United States were arrested and investigations of Alger Hiss, a former State Department official of the 1940s, got under way. He was accused by Whittaker Chambers, a former Communist, of passing secrets to the Soviet Union. (The trial of Hiss, who maintained his innocence to the end, has remained controversial.)

Two international events in 1949 contributed to the general hysteria: the exploding of an atomic bomb by the Soviet Union and the takeover of China by Communists. In February 1950, a little-known senator named Joseph McCarthy of Wisconsin began making speeches calculated to inflame the public about the Communist menace. Because of his subsequent actions at the height of his influence, between 1951 and 1954, his name would be given to some of the most shameful years in the history of the U.S. government. McCarthy began his rise to fame with a speech in Wheeling, West Virginia, where he waved a list of names that he claimed proved that the Truman administration was riddled with Communists and Communist sympathizers. In the next several weeks after his first speech in February 1950, he traveled around the country making the same speech but gradually increasing his numbers and making his other supporting evidence more sensational. Before the year was out, he was a key figure in Senate committee anti-Communist attacks on government personnel, including what he called the "treasonous" Truman administration, his fellow congressmen on both the Democratic and Republican sides, and even the Department of the Army, the case that finally brought him down. In 1953, when he assumed the chairmanship of the Senate Committee on Government Operations, he began his highly publicized campaign to attack not only self-proclaimed radicals but moderate Republicans, along with high-ranking government officials, including President Truman, World War II general George Marshall, Dean Acheson, and Adlai Stevenson. He denounced them as "fellow travellers," meaning that while they might not actually be Communist Party members, they revealed through their associations and opinions that they were Communist sympathizers.

In June 1950, three former FBI agents published the first of several lists of citizens they considered dangerous subversives in a book called *Red Channels*. Among those listed at one time or another were Arthur Miller, author of *The Crucible*, actor Will Geer, who later appeared as the grandfather in television's "The Waltons," and Sophie Smith, a woman who is interviewed along with her husband in this chapter. The book was ongoing—regularly updated—and used by employers and financiers to determine who would be hired, fired, or supported with grants or loans. For many people, to be listed in *Red Channels* was a death sentence.

In July of the same year, Julius Rosenberg, and later his wife

Ethel, were arrested on charges of spying for the Russians and giving them atomic-bomb secrets, even though President Truman contended that there was no atomic-bomb "secret" to pass on at that time. Julius and Ethel Rosenberg were tried in 1951 and sentenced to die, contending to the end that they were innocent.

In September 1950, Congress passed the Internal Security Act, also called the McCarran Act, which made it legal for the government to withhold passports and government jobs from those who had been associated with Communists and in essence made joining the Communist Party a crime. President Truman vetoed the legislation, but it was passed by Congress over his veto. In 1952, Congress passed another act over Truman's veto that made immigrants who had been associated with Communists subject to arrest and deportation. In the years of the Red Scare, Congress proposed fifty anti-Communist bills. In summing up the far-reaching negative effects of a time when so many citizens were innocent victims of the anti-Communist witch-hunts, historian Edward Pessen writes:

> In suggesting that criticism of capitalism was a communist game, the Red Scare effectively insulated our economic system and its inequities from the challenges that had been leveled against it by populist reformers for generations. . . . It was an atmosphere, too, in which patriotism was misdefined as uncritical approval of government foreign policy actions, no matter how unjustified, illegal, or brutal the actions. (*Losing Our Souls* 161–162)

ARTHUR MILLER AND THE 1950S WITCH-HUNT

Arthur Miller, author of *The Crucible*, was deeply engaged in the events that scarred the United States in the late 1940s and 1950s. Even from the time of his graduation from the University of Michigan, he had dedicated himself to progressive causes, becoming involved in a number of activist political organizations that the government regarded as "pinko"—sympathetic to the Communist cause. Although he went several times to meetings with Communists and had hoped in the 1930s that the Soviet Union would be a positive experiment, he never joined the Communist Party and, in fact, came to regard the "party line" to be at variance with what he stood for as a writer.

The Crucible, produced in 1953, was his fourth Broadway play.

Arthur Miller on May 14, 1959 as he arrives at Federal District Court to face charges of Contempt of Congress for refusing to give the House Un-American Activities Committee names of people he saw attending radical meetings. Photo courtesy AP/Wide World Photos.

The first, *The Man Who Had All the Luck*, played briefly in 1944; the second, *All My Sons*, about war profiteering in World War II, opened in 1947 and won the New York Drama Critics' Circle Award and the Tony Award for Best Play of the Year; his third, *Death of a Salesman* (1949), a criticism of the empty values fostered by a materialistic society, won a Pulitzer Prize.

Both Miller's plays and his political activity made him a predictable target for the various boards and committees bent on uncovering what they regarded as subversives. *Death of a Salesman* was not to be tolerated because it indirectly criticized business values and the plight of those like the salesman, Willy, who are used up by society and then thrown away. Despite the play's high popularity, in the early 1950s, it was denounced and sometimes picketed by patriotic and business groups wherever it played. When Columbia Pictures decided to make a film of *Salesman*, the studio, fearing reactions from government and businesses, tried to pressure Miller to publicly denounce his radical views. It also proposed introducing the movie with a lengthy film in the way of an apology, saying that the shameful conditions under which Willy is tossed out after he is old and no longer useful to the business world did not exist anymore. Miller angered the studio and the government by storming out of the screening and telling them candidly and in no uncertain terms why he flatly refused to go along with either plan.

Miller also realized that he would have difficulty working in Hollywood when, after being hired to write a play on mob corruption on the waterfront, an area that he knew intimately, he was asked to turn the Mafia thugs into "Communist thugs," a change that would totally distort the reality of the situation. Miller refused to do this and removed himself from the picture.

In 1949, only two years after writers in Hollywood had been called before HUAC and arrested for failing to cooperate, Miller was asked to chair a panel for the Cultural and Scientific Conference for World Government. At the time, he realized that, given the climate in the United States, this would be a dangerous thing to do, but he agreed because, while he made it clear at the conference that he had his differences with the American Communist Party, he strongly supported the idea of trying to establish harmonious relations with the Soviet Union, in large measure to avoid a catastrophic nuclear war. Because of this and other activities, he was listed in *Red Channels* as a man so dangerous he needed to be monitored.

Though Miller was not himself called at this time to testify, he had become dismayed at the actions of the HUAC and the review boards because of the damage they were causing in the lives of innocent people and the general climate of fear they had generated. This came home to him when in the early 1950s, Louis Untermeyer, a personal friend, a genial scholar and poet in his sixties who had been appearing on a famous television panel show called "What's My Line?," was summarily fired just for having been one of many sponsors of a world peace conference. Untermeyer, humiliated and destroyed, did not leave his apartment for a year and a half. Another friend, actress Pert Kelton, who played Jackie Gleason's wife in what was then the country's most successful television show, was also fired, to her utter amazement. She found out many years later that it was because her husband had once many years before been an actor in a May Day parade, not even realizing that it had something to do with a celebration of the Russian Revolution.

In *Timebends* Miller indicates his memory of those days:

> It bothered me much more that with each passing week it became harder to simply and clearly say why the whole procedure was vile. Almost to a man, for example, the accused in 1950 and 1951 had not a political connection since the late thirties or early forties, when in their perfectly legitimate idealism they had embraced the Russian Revolution as an advance for humanity. Yet the Committee had succeeded in creating the impression that they were pursuing an on-going conspiracy. (329)

Miller saw what the climate of terror and fear was doing to basically decent people. Most traumatic for him were the actions of Elia Kazan, his friend and the director of his plays, who was called before HUAC in 1952 and decided to give the committee names of people who had been Communists or whom he thought had been Communists. It was the parting of the ways of two men who had worked closely and well with one another. Kazan called Miller to his home in Connecticut in April 1952 to tell him what he had decided to do. After Miller left Kazan's home, extremely depressed about his friend's inability to stand up to the committee, Miller drove north to Salem, Massachusetts, to begin research on *The Crucible*, which would be about another community rocked by hysteria, the betrayal of friends under pressure, and one man's refusal to name names in order to save his own skin. The great irony is that Kazan would not again direct a Miller play until 1964, when they teamed up for *After the Fall*, a play about Miller's own trouble with HUAC because of his refusal to name names as Kazan had done.

The Crucible's obvious assault on HUAC and the loyalty review committees had much to do with Miller's being snubbed by acquaintances in the lobby on the night the play opened and much to do with some of the bad reviews the play received. In the eyes of many, the play seemed to confirm his reputation as a dangerous man. His first indication that he himself might be in trouble with the government came when he was denied a passport to see a production of one of his plays in Europe. The only reason given was that his going abroad was not in the national interest.

In 1955, when he was approached to write a film on juvenile delinquency and gangs in New York City, he was called on the carpet by the New York City Youth Board, a group that included the head of city sanitation. One member of the board rose at one point to accuse him personally of killing American boys in Korea. By a narrow margin, the board voted to deny the funds necessary to produce the film. In the same year, his two one-act plays, *A View from the Bridge* and *Memory of Two Mondays*, had miserable receptions in New York City, and a New York newspaper condemned him for his left-wing activities. One of the plays, *A View from the Bridge*, turned to the question of the informant, still a timely issue in 1955, and also to the plight of the European immigrant to an America in the throes of paranoia about the importation of communism from Europe.

The year 1956 was a critical year in Arthur Miller's life. In the spring of that year, he received an honorary doctorate from his alma mater, the University of Michigan. On June 21, 1956, while on location for the filming of his movie *The Misfits*, starring Marilyn Monroe, whom he married on June 27 of that year, he received a dreaded subpoena from the House Committee on Un-American Activities. The night before the first day of his hearing, the chairman of the committee, Representative Francis E. Walter of Pennsylvania, sent a message to Miller's lawyer telling him that he, the chairman, would see that the whole committee hearing was called off if Marilyn Monroe would agree to be photographed with him. Miller and Monroe declined this way out of his difficulties while at the same time they appreciated the comic relief provided by Walter's ridiculous request.

During the very hostile and confrontational hearing on the committee's part, Miller was asked if he had signed various petitions that seemed to number in the hundreds, and he was queried about other opinions. He did not refuse to answer questions about himself and his own opinions, but when asked about the activity of others, he refused to answer. As a result, he was cited for contempt of Congress by a vote of 373 to 9. In February 1957, he was indicted on two charges of contempt of Congress for refusing to answer and was tried in court. On May 23 he was found guilty, fined $500, and given a one-month suspended jail sentence. In 1958, this sentence was reversed by a U.S. court of appeals.

In 1964, Miller wrote another dramatic chapter in his history of the witch-hunts of the 1940s and 1950s. His autobiographical play *After the Fall* chronicles his personal and professional anguish during the early period, much of it having to do with his living through a reign of terror created by the government.

COMPARISONS OF THE WITCH-HUNTS OF 1692 TO THOSE OF THE 1950S

Miller was able to draw on many parallels between the Salem witch-hunts of 1692 and the McCarthy hearings of 1952. The points that follow are among them:

- Both sets of "trials" occurred outside the bounds of legal practice. The Salem trials were at first conducted as extralegal hearings by Nathaniel Hawthorne's ancestor John Hathorne. Citizens were arrested solely on the accusations of others and were found guilty on the accusations of others. It was not mandatory to follow legal rules of evidence. Similarly, the congressional hearings were not court trials. Yet citizens were hauled before Congress on the secret accusations of others. Furthermore, the accused had none of the legal rights expected in a regular trial (for example, being able to confront their accusers), while the committee had the powers of subpoena and investigation usually given to the courts.

- People were forced to appear and defend themselves in extralegal trials of both the seventeenth and twentieth centuries against charges based almost solely on two kinds of evidence: first, accusations that were patently unreliable and, second, their associations. Accusations in Salem were made chiefly and at first by young women and girls who protected themselves from charges of witchcraft and lewdness by accusing others; later accusations were made by those who themselves had been accused and confessed to witchcraft in order to save themselves from the gallows. In the 1940s and 1950s, the charges were initially brought by ex-Communists who wanted to prove their "loyalty." In both cases, people were accused on the basis of their associations. In Salem, these often had to do with familial and clan connections. In 1952, they had to do with one's friends and causes.

- At the root of both trials were ulterior motives having little to do with witchcraft or communism. In Salem of 1692, the base motives seem to have been feuds, vengeance, and land grabs. In Washington in 1952, the base motives seem to have been Republican resentment of Democratic presidencies and vote grabs.

- In both cases, the accused were guilty until proven innocent, rather than the other way around. Furthermore, the trials had as a basic assumption the idea that the accused were naturally liars and that any arguments or evidence the accused could muster in their own defense were faked. The arguments went as follows: witches can distort reality and manufacture evidence in their defense, and Communists naturally lie and put up a false front in society to further their cause. An accused man claims that he is a churchgoer to the committee; the committee response is that Communists deliberately put up a false front by going to church to throw the government off and conceal their true identities.

- Confession and the naming of names were required in both cases in order to save oneself. Just as in the witchcraft trials, the committee required that those accused confess their past political activity, make a grand show of penitence, and name others who were Communists.

By studying the following excerpts from documents from the 1940s and 1950s, the student can find other parallels between the two periods. These documents consist of (1) an excerpt from Executive Order 9835; (2) excerpts from a pamphlet distributed by HUAC, defining its own purpose; (3) excerpts from President Truman's veto of the Internal Security Act of 1950; (4) excerpts from

Red Channels, compiled by FBI agents; (5) excerpts from a Mc-Carthy interrogation of a State Department official named Theodore Kaghan; (6) case studies of government employees caught in inquisitions mandated by various executive orders; and (7) an interview with two people, committed to social action, who were repeatedly fired from their jobs because of their political activity.

EXECUTIVE ORDER 9835

Executive Order 9835, otherwise known as the National Security Act, was signed by President Truman in 1947, against his best judgment, as a way to appease the Red baiters in Congress in order to get them to support his program for social action. Nevertheless, the order was the means by which many people's lives were turned into tragedies. Note the potential here for violating very basic rights in a democratic society and the potential for acting on misinformation.

George Orwell, in his anti-Communist novel *1984*, coined a new term, "Big Brother." In his futuristic society, there were reminders everywhere that Big Brother, that is, the government, "is watching you!" There were even television cameras in every person's home to allow Big Brother to literally watch what went on there.

Ironically, this order contains many of the elements of Big Brotherism, a concept coined to deride communism. Yet here it is being used to violate basic freedoms and privacy, supposedly to combat communism. Note that the government in the provisions of this order can use "any other appropriate source" to get information on citizens working in civil service jobs. This meant acting solely on uncorroborated accusations, as was done in Salem during the witch-hunts, and it encouraged the use of informants who were paid for their accusations and protected with anonymity. Thus, as in Salem, informants would turn in their associates who had angered them, or they would turn in people to "prove" their own loyalty, or they would turn them in for money. Evidence of being a Communist sympathizer was usually supplied by these anonymous informers, who would report what they supposedly heard the accused citizen say. Later, in transcripts of actual cases, one sees the result of their accusations.

FROM *EXECUTIVE ORDER 9835*
(Washington, D.C., Government Printing Office, March 22, 1947)

March 22, 1947
Executive Order 9835

PART I
Investigation of Applications

1. There shall be a loyalty investigation of every person entering civilian employment of any department or agency of the Executive Branch of the Federal Government.
    A. Investigations of persons entering the competitive service shall be conducted by the Civil Service Commission, except in such cases as are covered by a special agreement between the commission and any given department or agency.
    B. Investigations of persons other than those entering the competitive service shall be conducted by the employing department or agency. Departments and agencies without investigative organizations shall utilize the investigative facilities of the Civil Service Commission.

2. The investigations of persons entering the employ of the Executive Branch may be conducted after any such person enters upon actual employment therein, but in any such case the appointment of such persons shall be conditioned upon favorable determination with respect to his loyalty.

• • •

3. An investigation shall be made of all applicants at all available pertinent sources of information and shall include reference to:
    A. Federal Bureau of Investigation files.
    B. Civil Service Commission files.
    C. Military and Naval Intelligence files.
    D. The files of any other appropriate government investigative or intelligence agency.
    E. House Committee on Un-American Activities files.
    F. Local law-enforcement files at the place of residence and employment of the applicant, including municipal, county and state law-enforcement files.
    G. Schools and colleges attended by applicant.
    H. Former employees of applicant.
    I. References given by applicant.
    J. Any other appropriate source.

4. Whenever derogatory information with respect to loyalty of an applicant is revealed, a full field investigation shall be conducted. A full field investigation shall also be conducted of those applicants, or of applicants for particular positions, as may be designated by the head of the em-

ploying department or agency, such designations to be based on the determination by any such head of the best interests of national security.

• • •

PART III
Responsibilities of Civil Service Commission

• • •

C. The Loyalty Review Board shall also:
> (1) Advise all departments and agencies on all problems relating to employee loyalty.
> (2) Disseminate information pertinent to employee loyalty programs.
> (3) Coordinate the employee loyalty policies and procedures of the several departments and agencies.
> (4) Make reports and submit recommendations to the Civil Service Commission for transmission to the President from time to time as may be necessary to the maintenance of the employee loyalty program.

• • •

2. There shall also be established and maintained in the Civil Service Commission a central master index covering all persons of whom loyalty investigations have been made by any department or agency since Sept. 1, 1939. Such a master index shall contain the name of each person investigated, adequate identifying information concerning each such person, and a reference to each department and agency which has conducted a loyalty investigation concerning the person involved.

• • •

> B. The reports and other investigative material and information developed by the investigating department or agency shall be retained by such department or agency in each case.

3. The Loyalty Review Board shall currently be furnished by the Department of Justice with the name of each foreign or domestic organization, association, movement, group or combination of persons which the Attorney General, after appropriate investigation and determination, designates as totalitarian, Fascist, Communist or subversive, or as having adopted a policy of advocating or approving the commission of acts of force or violence to deny others their rights under the Constitution of

the United States, or as seeking to alter the form of government of the United States by unconstitutional means.

A. The Loyalty Review Board shall disseminate such information to all departments and agencies.

• • •

PART IV
Security Measures in Investigations

1. At the request of the head of any department or agency of the Executive Branch an investigative agency shall make available to such head, personally, all investigative material and information collected by the investigative agency concerning any employee or prospective employee of the requesting department or agency, or shall make such material and information available to any officer or officers designated by such head and approved by the investigative agency.

2. Notwithstanding the foregoing requirement, however, the investigative agency may refuse to disclose the names of confidential informants, provided it furnishes sufficient information about such informants on the basis of which the requesting department or agency can make an adequate evaluation of the information furnished by them, and provided it advises the requesting department or agency in writing that it is essential to the protection of informants or to the investigation of other cases that the identity of the informants not be revealed. Investigative agencies shall not use this discretion to decline to reveal sources of information where such action is not essential.

3. Each department and agency of the Executive Branch should develop and maintain, for the collection and analysis of information relating to the loyalty of its employees and prospective employees, a staff specially trained in security techniques, and an effective security control system for protecting such information generally and for protecting confidential sources of such information particularly.

HUAC'S SELF-EXPLANATION

In the following amazing little pamphlet, published in 1954, the House Un-American Activities Committee attempts to explain its purpose and justify its actions. By this time, as in the fall of 1692 in Salem, ordinary citizens had begun to see the devastation and fear bred by the committee and had begun to turn against it. Senator Joseph McCarthy, the notorious head of the committee, had been discredited and censured by the Congress. Yet despite the turning of the tide of support and McCarthy's loss of power, the pamphlet shows that the committee continued to justify its procedures.

Note that, as in the witch trials (where it was claimed that if you criticize us you must be a witch, as in the case of Giles Corey), here, if you criticize us, you must be a Communist or, less dangerous, misinformed. Note also that the committee recognizes that it has been set up with the specific mandate of gathering information with which to propose legislation and argues that it has done this, yet it obviously had also long been merely a way of gathering names and discrediting individuals without much relevance to new legislation. The pamphlet also acknowledges that Congress has given the committee limitless investigative power. Even with all the outrageous misinformation gathered by the committee that has come to light, and even with the abuses encouraged by paying informants and protecting them, the committee insists that all its paid informants have told the truth, and all those who denied being subversives have lied.

THIS IS YOUR HOUSE COMMITTEE ON UN-AMERICAN ACTIVITIES
PREPARED AND RELEASED BY THE COMMITTEE ON UN-
AMERICAN ACTIVITIES, U.S. HOUSE OF REPRESENTATIVES
(Washington, D.C.: U.S. House of Representatives,
September 19, 1954)

Foreword

There has been criticism of the committee and its work. Much of this criticism comes from perfectly loyal American citizens. The committee has

profited from much of the sincere and objective suggestions it has received. Unfortunately, much of the criticism directed at the committee
comes from the Communists and other enemies of the committee, so we
realize that no amount of truth or information is going to alter the views
of such persons.

Some criticism, however, comes from the uninformed or misinformed
individuals. For these persons, the committee hopes that this report may
furnish an answer to questions, or serve to dispel any misinformation or
deliberate falsehoods about the committee.

• • •

Background

• • •

2. What is its purpose?

Its purpose as stated in Public Law 601, 79th Congress, is that, as a
whole or by subcommittee, it is authorized to make from time to time
investigations of: (1) the extent, character, and objects of un-American
propaganda activities in the United States; (2) the diffusion within the
United States of subversive and un-American propaganda that is instigated from foreign countries, or of a domestic origin, and attacks the
principle of the form of government as guaranteed by our Constitution;
and (3) all other questions in relation thereto that would aid Congress
in any necessary remedial legislation.

3. What is un-American or subversive activity?

That activity which attacks the principle of the form of government as
guaranteed by our Constitution is un-American and subversive by seeking
to overthrow it by use of force and violence, in violation of established
law.

• • •

**6. Does the committee conduct investigations and hold hearings by
virtue of a right and duty given it by the Congress?**

Yes. By reason of the express right and duty given it by the terms of
Public Law 601.

**7. Did the Congress specify any fields or areas by which the com-
mittee should not or could not investigate?**

No. The mandate given by the Congress to the committee is probably
broader than that given to any other House committee.

• • •

76. Has the committee actually had the names of more than a handful of persons who were members of subversive groups?

Since 1948, the committee has had positive identifications of 4,151 persons who were members of the Communist Party in the United States. Of this total number, 2,381 have been named during this 83d Congress by witnesses under oath before the committee.

77. Are any of these 4,151 persons still members of the Communist Party?

Many of these individuals have broken with the Communist Party and have furnished the committee with valuable information concerning their knowledge of the Communist conspiracy. The majority, however, refused to testify on the ground that to do so might tend to incriminate them under their fifth amendment privilege.

78. Of this number of persons named, how many were erroneously named?

None that we know of. There have been only 1 or 2 cases where a person has denied Communist Party membership after being named before the committee. In each such instance, the committee refers the matter to the Justice Department for study for possible perjury prosecution. No witness appearing before the committee and furnishing the identification of individuals as members of the Communist Party has been found to have committed perjury.

79. Mention has previously been made of citations for contempt of Congress. How many persons who have been cited for contempt before the committee have been indicted, convicted, and sentenced?

Until the beginning of this, the 83d Congress, there had been 35 persons who, having been cited for contempt of Congress as a result of their appearance before this committee, had been found guilty and sentenced by a Federal court after trial.

Those persons who have been cited for contempt of Congress by this committee and the Congress during this session of Congress cannot be prosecuted for contempt until after adjournment of this 83d Congress on account of required legal procedure.

• • •

Subversive Activities

81. Is the Communist Party a political party?

No. The Communist Party is not in a true sense a political party. There was a period of time during which the Communists did have a place on various ballots and persons sought political office as Communists. Since 1945, however, the "hard core" Communists have dropped almost all pretense of political identity and for the most part operate completely underground.

Finally, the 83d Congress in Public Law 637 stated clearly and emphatically that the Communist Party is not a political party, but is in fact an instrumentality of a conspiracy to overthrow the Government of the United States. It is now outlawed, and is not entitled to any of the rights, privileges, and immunities attendant upon legal bodies created under the jurisdiction of the laws of the United States.

82. Is the Communist Party subversive?

Yes. The Communist Party was cited as a subversive organization which seeks "to alter the form of government of the United States by unconstitutional means" by the Attorney General of the United States in letters to the Loyalty Review Board released December 4, 1947, and September 21, 1948, and so redesignated by the present Attorney General on April 29, 1953.

The Subversive Activities Control Board, established under the provisions of the Internal Security Act of 1950, has recently found that the Communist Party is a "Communist action" group and must register under the provisions of that act. This finding of the Board is presently under appeal and awaits the final decision of the Supreme Court.

83. What does the committee consider a Communist front to be?

The committee has ascertained that a Communist front is an organization, committee, or group of people, or a printed publication created or captured by the Communists to do the party's work in special fields of effort for influence. It does not carry the name "Communist" for this fact is concealed or secret.

84. Why is a Communist front dangerous?

The Communist front is probably the greatest weapon of communism in the country today, because its subterfuge often makes it difficult to recognize its true Communist nature. The Communist front does not hesitate to camouflage its true purposes behind such moral and human appeals as "peace" and "civil rights" while in reality serving the Communist purposes and the aims of the Soviet Union.

85. If it is true that the Communist uses such euphonious titles for its fronts as "peace" and "civil liberties," does this then preclude anyone interested in these humane projects from joining any organization so dedicated?

It most certainly should not. However, some inquiry should be made by those interested in joining as to the background of the organization and those persons promoting or operating it.

• • •

90. Many teachers who have appeared before the committee used the fifth amendment in refusing to tell the committee about past Communist connections. Does the committee know how many of these individuals are still employed?

No. The committee has made no effort to determine what action the institutions employing these persons have taken after their refusal to testify. The committee has never endeavored to exert any influence upon any institution to remove any such witness from employment.

• • •

95. Does the committee believe that a person who pleads the fifth amendment is fit to teach the youth of America?

The committee believes that it is the duty of school officials to determine the fitness of any teacher. The committee does not believe, however, that any person who is a Communist can teach freely and objectively, as must be the case if American education is to be free.

96. Has the committee been charged with attacking "academic freedom" through its investigations?

Yes. In this, as in practically every investigation, there has been criticism from some quarters of the committee's investigations. Naturally, the Communist is going to attack the committee for everything it does. In addition, there is sometimes criticism from perfectly loyal Americans who either do not understand what the committee is doing or who frankly and honestly disagree with the committee's work.

• • •

98. What does the committee consider a "fellow traveler" to be?

A "fellow traveler" is a person who is in complete sympathy with the aims of the Communist Party, and does the work of the Communist Party without actually registering or being carried on the Communist Party membership records.

99. Is the "fellow traveler" dangerous?

Yes. In many respects, he is more dangerous than the actual Communist Party member because of the difficulty in detection and the fact that, when confronted with an inquiry as to party membership, he can deny actual Communist Party membership.

100. Is there any numerical strength in the "fellow travelers" of the Communist Party?

Yes. Mr. J. Edgar Hoover, Director of the Federal Bureau of Investigation, has testified before the committee that:

What is important is the claim of the Communists that for every party member there are 10 others ready, willing, and able to do the party's work. Herein lies the greatest menace of communism. For these are the people who infiltrate and corrupt various spheres of American life. So rather than the size of the Communist Party, the way to weigh its true importance is by testing its influence, its ability to infiltrate.

101. Does the fact that a person has belonged to one or more Communist fronts mean that he is a "fellow traveler"?

No. This is hardly a fair or true test of a person being a "fellow traveler." Many people became associated with Communist fronts through innocence, naivete, and outright stupidity. Fortunately, most of these people immediately disassociated themselves from the fronts when they recognized them as such. The best test for establishing whether a person is a fellow traveler is to determine whether he has ever varied from the Communist Party "line," and especially if he has ever come out publicly against the Communists or the Soviet Union.

102. Is the Communist Party "line" difficult to detect?

No, especially since the many disclosures made in public testimony before this committee. The reference to a Communist Party "line" is actually a misnomer. It could more correctly be referred to as a "corkscrew." In fact, to follow it, a Communist fellow traveler must be prepared to be opposed today to what yesterday he was most fervently advocating. An excellent example of this is in the change of the American Peace Mobilization to the American People's Mobilization within a few hours after Germany invaded the Soviet Union.

PRESIDENT TRUMAN'S VETO

By 1950, Truman realized just what a heavy price he had paid by issuing his executive order, so when Congress passed various other pieces of legislation that curtailed basic democratic rights in the name of fighting communism, he vetoed them. Here one finds his argument that Congress's way of identifying a "Communist front" organization violates fundamental liberties: the bill said that any organization that shared even one goal with the Communists should be labeled a Communist front organization whose members should be suspected of subversion. The same kind of dangerous and faulty logic was used in the witch trials:

Witches like to dance.
Goody Brown likes to dance.
Therefore, Goody Brown is a witch.

or

Communists work for racial justice.
Mrs. Brown works for racial justice.
Therefore, Mrs. Brown is a Communist.

FROM HARRY S TRUMAN, "PRESIDENTIAL VETO OF THE
INTERNAL SECURITY ACT OF 1950"
(Washington, D.C., September 22, 1950)

To the House of Representatives:
I return herewith, without my approval, H. R. 9490, the proposed "Internal Security Act of 1950." . . .

• • •

Insofar as the bill would require registration by the Communist Party itself, it does not endanger our traditional liberties. However, the application of the registration requirements to so-called Communist-front organizations can be the greatest danger to the freedom of speech, press, and assembly, since the Alien and Sedition Laws of 1798. This danger arises out of the criteria or standards to be applied in determining whether an organization is a Communist-front organization.

There would be no serious problem if the bill required proof that an organization was controlled and financed by the Communist Party. . . . However, recognizing the difficulty of proving those matters, the bill would permit such a determination to be based solely upon the extent to which the positions taken or advanced by it from time to time on matters of policy do not deviate from those of the Communist movement.

This provision could easily be used to classify as a Communist-front organization any organization which is advocating a single policy or objective which is also being urged by the Communist Party. . . . Thus, an organization which advocates low-cost housing for sincere humanitarian reasons might be classified as a Communist-front organization because the Communists regularly exploit slum conditions as one of their fifth-column techniques.

• • •

The basic error of these sections is that they move in the direction of suppressing opinion and belief. This would be a very dangerous course to take, not because we have any sympathy for Communist opinions, but because any governmental stifling of the free expression of opinion is a long step toward totalitarianism. . . .

We can and will prevent espionage, sabotage, or other actions endangering our national security. But we would betray our finest traditions if we attempted, as this bill would attempt, to curb the simple expression of opinion. This we should never do, no matter how distasteful the opinion may be to the vast majority of our people. The course proposed by this bill would delight the Communists, for it would make a mockery of the Bill of Rights and of our claims to stand for freedom in the world.

And what kind of effect would these provisions have on the normal expression of political views? Obviously, if this law were on the statute books, the part of prudence would be to avoid saying anything that might be construed by someone as not deviating sufficiently from the current Communist propaganda line. And since no one could be sure in advance what views were safe to express, the inevitable tendency would be to express no views on controversial subjects.

RED CHANNELS

Many publications claiming to inform the government and other employees of dangerous subversives were put together in the 1950s. The most notorious was *Red Channels*, a series of regularly updated books published by three former FBI agents with financial support from politicians who abhorred left-wingers. Much of the information was pure gossip. Almost all of it was irrelevant to a violent overthrow of the United States. To be listed here almost invariably meant to be fired and blacklisted for decades. Mark Goodson, a CBS television producer, reports in an oral history in *Red Scare* by Griffin Fariello (New York: Avon Books, 1995) that the network dropped anyone whose name appeared there, even game-show participants. The following are the entries for three well-known artists. Leonard Bernstein and Arthur Miller survived the listing in *Red Channels*, but actor Will Geer, who had a thriving career at the time, was blacklisted as an actor for eighteen years and was only able to pick up his career at the end of his life as Grandfather Walton on the popular television series "The Waltons." Note that one of his "crimes" is having married the granddaughter of a famous Communist leader.

FROM *RED CHANNELS*
(New York: American Business Consultants, Inc., June 1950)

LEONARD BERNSTEIN
Composer, Conductor

People's Songs, Inc. Sponsor. Letterhead, 3.48

Scientific and Cultural Conference for World Peace. Sponsor. Official Program, 3.49

American-Soviet Music Society

Hans Eisler Concert

Protest Against Deportation of Hans Eisler

Committee for Reelection of Benjamin J. Davis, 1945

Progressive Citizens of America

World Federation of Democratic Youth

Affiliated. Un-Am.Act.Com. Review of Scientific And Cultural Conference for World Peace, 4/19/49, p. 52

Sponsor. Un-Am.Act.Com. Review of Scientific And Cultural Conference for World Peace, 4/19/49, p. 43

Signer. Un-Am.Act.Com. Review of Scientific And Cultural Conference for World Peace, 4/19/49, p. 43

Affiliated. Un-Am.Act.Com. Review of Scientific And Cultural Conference for World Peace, 4/19/49, p. 41

Affiliated. Arts, Sciences and Professions Council, statement in defense of Communist cases. Un-Am.Act.Com. Review of Scientific
And Cultural Conference for World Peace, 4/19/49, p. 37

Affiliated. Un-Am.Act.Com. Review of Scientific And Cultural Conference for World Peace, 4/19/49

WILL GEER
Actor—Screen, Stage, Radio
Communist

Scientific and Cultural Conference for World Peace

May Day Parade, 1947, 1948

Committee for Reelection of Benjamin J. Davis

American Peace Mobilization

Daily Worker Benefit

International Workers Order

Mother Bloor Celebration

People's Songs

Voice of Freedom Committee

Daily Worker

Reported as:

Identified as Communist by Walter S. Steele. Hearings of House Un-
Am.Act.Com, or H.R. 1884 and H.R. 2522

Sponsor. Official program, 3/49

Sponsor. Un-Am.Act.Com. Review of Scientific and Cultural Conference for World Peace, p. 54

Sponsor. Daily Worker, 9/25/45, p. 12

Entertainer. New Masses, 5/27/41, p. 27

Entertainer. Daily Worker, 8/13/37

Sponsor. New Masses, 8/27/40, p. 21

Director of play program. Booklet, front cover

Married to Herta Ware, grand-daughter of Ella Reeve Bloor, veteran Communist Party leader. House Un-Am.Act.Com. Index II, p. S111

Master of Ceremonies. Daily Worker, 9/20/47, p. 11

Participant. House Un-Am.Act.Com. Index II, p. 113

Subject of article. Article states Geer made motion picture in USSR in 1935. Referring to his then current play "On Whitman Avenue," the following is quoted: "Of all the social dramas, agit-prop plays, people's revues and mass chants Geer has ever appeared in during the past two and one half decades, his current vehicle 'is the most educational.' "

ARTHUR MILLER
Playwright—"Death of Salesman," "All My Sons"

American Youth Congress

Book Find Club

Civil Rights Congress

Committee of Welcome for the Very Rev. Hewlett Johnson

International Workers Order

Jewish Life

Reported as:

Signer of call. Official Proceedings, 1/28 30/38

Writer. Book Find News, 5/46, p. 7; 1/46, p. 3

Author of Club Selection. Book Find News, 1/46, p. 3

Signer. Statement in defense of Eisler. Daily Worker, 2/28/47, p. 2

Speaker, "Abolish America's Thought Police." Daily Worker, 10/6/47, p. 8

Member. Daily Worker, 9/22/48, p. 5

Defender of tax exemption for IWO. Fraternal Outlook. 11/48, p. 6

Contributor. Jewish Life, publication of Morning Freiheit Association, 3/49, p. 7

Mainstream and New Masses

National Council of the Arts, Sciences and Professions

New York Council of the Arts, Sciences and Professions

Progressive Citizens of America

Speaker at rally to defend Howard Fast, 10/16/47

New Masses, 10/28/47, p. 2

Signer for Wallace. Daily Worker, 10/19/48, p. 2

Member, Initiating Committee. Writers for Wallace. Daily Worker, 9/27/48, p. 7

Co-chairman. Performance, "The Journey of Simon McKeever," and "I've Got the Tune," Carnegie Hall, 6/21/49. Official program

Sponsor. Committee to Abolish the House Un-American Activities Committee. NY Journal-American, 12/30/48

Speaker. Rally against the "Foley Square Convictions," 10/27/49

Daily Worker, 10/24/49, p. 5

Sponsor. Program, 10/25/47   (49–50, 59–60, 110–112)

QUESTIONING BY SENATOR JOSEPH MCCARTHY

No study of historical documents of the "Red Scare" era would be complete without some sense of what it was like to be questioned by the prominent Senator Joseph McCarthy, whose name is indelibly linked to the temper of the times and the HUAC hearings. What follows is McCarthy's public questioning in official committee of Theodore Kaghan, who was in charge of the State Department's Office of Public Affairs.

The circumstance under which Kaghan was called before the committee emphasizes the parallel between the witch-hunts of the 1950s and the witch-hunts of 1692. We have seen that the motive behind many of the accusations of witchcraft in Salem was revenge. Such was the motive behind McCarthy's calling Kaghan before the committee. Shortly before Kaghan was called, McCarthy had sent two staff members to Germany to see if there were any Communist books in the State Department's Information Program libraries there. Kaghan had labeled the staff members "junketeering gumshoes." McCarthy was out to get his vengeance for the ridicule. As a result of his being called before the committee, Kaghan was fired by the State Department.

UNITED STATES SENATE, 83D CONGRESS, 1ST SESSION,
PERMANENT SUBCOMMITTEE ON INVESTIGATION OF THE
COMMITTEE ON GOVERNMENT OPERATIONS, HEARINGS
(Washington, D.C.: Government Printing Office, April 29, 1953)

The Chairman. You wrote a number of plays. Is that right?

Mr. Kaghan. Yes, I did.

The Chairman. Would you say they followed the Communist line?

Mr. Kaghan. I would not say they followed the Communist line.

The Chairman. Would you say they were acceptable to the Communists?

Mr. Kaghan. I think they were, by and large, not necessarily in detail.

The Chairman. Not necessarily in detail. I have gone over a number of

them, and I have had my staff read the others. I find that they seem
to follow largely the same pattern, that you have someone representing the Communist Party, arguing the Communist line. You have
someone very weakly arguing against it. In the end, you find the man
against the Communist cause has been converted, in practically all
the plays. Is that a correct statement?

Mr. Kaghan. No sir; I do not agree with the statement. You have made
a dramatic judgment about whether the arguments against Communism were weak. I doubt that they were weak. If they were weak,
it wouldn't have been a good play.

The Chairman. Let me quote from one, if I may? You recall the Unfinished
Picture?

Mr. Kaghan. Yes, sir; that is a play I wrote in the University of Michigan
for which I got a $1,000 prize. The University of Michigan is not a
leftwing university.

The Chairman. What was that?

Mr. Kaghan. I say the University of Michigan is not known to be a leftwing
university.

The Chairman. I do not quite get the import of that. Does that mean that
you could not have been leftwing or you could not have attended?

Mr. Kaghan. I mean that the play would probably not have won a prize
if it were a Communist play.

The Chairman. Who awarded this prize?

Mr. Kaghan. The university itself. It was the Avery Hopwood award. I
have forgotten the name of it. Drama, fiction, essay, and poetry. I
won several drama prizes, and that was the last year's prize.

The Chairman. Mr. Kaghan, let me first refer to the Unfinished Picture, and
read a few excerpts from it. Tell me whether you think this would be a
good anti-Communist propaganda or not. These are the words that
you put in your actor's mouth. Page 22 of the Unfinished Picture. Here
is the language, the words, in one of your act[or's] mouth:

How can I enjoy life knowing there is so much misery? What should
I do, get married to some slave? On what? It's just because I want
to live that I am doing this?

The Chairman. Talking about Communist Activity:

I don't want to creep through life like a slave. I don't want to get
married and bring up children to be more slaves. If my children
can't be free, I don't want them to be born.

The Chairman. Would that be good anti-Communist propaganda?

Mr. Kaghan. That sounds like a good American statement.

The Chairman. Let me read from page 24. See if this is a good American statement.

> What is wrong with what we have got? You ought to thank God you have got it.
>
> Thank God? You ought to thank Morgan and Rockefeller for leaving you what they did if you want to thank anyone.
>
> Julia, do you know what you are saying?
>
> JULIA: Of course I know what I am saying. What do you expect me to do? Pray every night for God to let me go to college? I would rather write a letter to the President. At least that might get an answer.

The Chairman. Is that good anti-Communist propaganda?

Mr. Kaghan. Sir, I would rather not discuss excerpts, lines read by you, from the play which I haven't read for years and haven't got a copy of handy. It depends on the rest of the play.

The Chairman. Let me read some more of the play.

> Now, Gordon wouldn't have been shot if he hadn't been a Negro worker. There was no reason for his being shot except the cop didn't think his life was worth anything. It was purely a case of race discrimination of the worst dye, equal to the lynching business going on in the South. The Communists Party is fighting militantly against that, and the mass funeral tomorrow is in protest against discrimination and the rising tide of fascism.   (176–178)

• • •

> The Communist Party wants to unite all workers in a struggle for their rights against a decadent system of capitalism. Gordon was a worker, and because he was a worker he was shot, like many other workers will be shot if they don't organize and put up a united front against their enemies, the capitalist class, which is rapidly becoming a Fascist regime. It's up to us to show our solidarity with all workers, and with minorities, like the Negroes.

The Chairman. Would you say that would be good anti-Communist propaganda?

Mr. Kaghan. Sounds like a long-winded soapbox speech.

The Chairman. No, answer my question. Do you think that is either Communist propaganda or anti-Communist propaganda?

Mr. Kaghan. That would probably be a Communist character speaking.   (199–200)

CASE STUDIES IN PERSONNEL SECURITY

In the late 1940s and throughout the 1950s, the federal government invoked numerous executive orders creating a variety of personnel security programs to deal with what leaders saw as the Red Menace. Executive Order 10450 and Executive Order 9835 were aimed at government workers and civil service personnel with security clearance who were suspected of being Communists or having sympathy with and associates in the Communist Party. There was a Military Personnel Security Program aimed at soldiers, even those of low rank, who because of their opinions and associations were judged to be security risks, that is, at risk for being disloyal under certain circumstances. The Industrial Security Program was aimed primarily at blue-collar government employees, especially those in unions. The Port Security Program was similarly enacted to seek out what were regarded as suspicious politics and associates among seamen and longshoremen, especially union members.

The cases included here are from a book published in 1955 by a group that presented itself as a government agency, the Bureau of National Affairs, but was funded by something called the Fund for the Republic. The book was intended for use by the Committee on the Federal Loyalty-Security Programs, named by the Association of the Bar in New York City, to study security programs and to recommend changes, "if such changes, in its judgment, are needed," this phrase suggesting that it might have had at least some kind of quasi-official government capacity.

In light of what is actually reported of government-approved procedures here and the general climate of intimidation and fear in the country at the time, the student might well see a good deal of irony in the fact that the study had any official status. Today, in a time in which the tactics of the Red Scare have been discredited, it is difficult to read the introduction to such a collection without suspecting that the noncommittal writer was being bitterly sarcastic.

As the compiler of the material tells us in his introduction (without expressing the hint of an opinion), these cases, provided by the attorneys who represented those accused, give us some "understanding of how the security programs operate[d] from day to day." As such, more than almost any available records, these cases bring home to the reader just how radically life for the ordinary person was changed by the witch-hunts of the 1950s. These are not the famous writers and movie stars and high government officials whom we usually hear about who were ruined by the witch-hunts. These were ordinary citizens: a private in the army, a butcher, a plumber, a "sub-professional employee," and a geographer. The cases presented here are just two among hundreds and hundreds of similar cases involving secretaries and electricians as well as scientists and statisticians. When we realize that hundreds more employees just quietly left when they were fired, without making legal appeals, it is not unreasonable to estimate the number of firings on security grounds in the early 1950s to be in the thousands.

The process reported by these attorneys was largely the same in most cases: a government employee would be notified that he or she was fired or suspended from the job; sometimes a reason was given, but at other times the reason was not forthcoming until months later and only when the employee had steadfastly pursued an answer. Usually the employee, now without a salary, would have to hire legal counsel. The general charge of being a security risk would be made known to the employee, but the specific reasons why he or she was considered a security risk would often be six months in coming, delaying painfully the preparation of a defense and a hearing. The more specific charges never included much detail. In the cases presented here, rules of evidence, what we would call common decency, are completely ignored. Never was an accused employee given a chance to know, much less to face, his accusers. "It is reliably reported" was considered sufficient to ruin a person's reputation and livelihood. Sometimes the person was charged outright with being a Communist. More often he would be charged with being sympathetic to communism. Charges were most often based on the employee's supposed associates, his or her family, or what material he was reported to be reading. In short, he was told the judgments reached by the government, but he was never allowed to know how these judgments were reached. With these accusations, the employee, an attorney, and witnesses would appear before a government-appointed review board that would hear the employee's case and then proceed to ask questions. On occasion, a board member would consider it relevant to inquire whether the employee attended church or what newspapers he read or how well he got along with his brother or whom he and his wife invited for dinner. If the board handed down an adverse decision, the employee could appeal the decision.

Sometimes the employee had to wait for two years, without pay, to receive the final decision from the board. If the government restored his job (as was usually the case), the employee received back pay, but emotional equilibrium, harmonious family relationships, reputation, and even financial stability were not as easily restored as a job.

Case No. 10 was a worker in the Department of the Navy who had no access to sensitive materials. He lost his job because someone accused him of being a Communist. It took two years and five months, during which time he was without work, for the loyalty review board to clear him of all charges. His attorney, in reporting his case, indicated that his client had been "deeply disturbed emotionally by this matter."

Another case was that of a geographer who was asked invasive and irrelevant questions by the board and was also asked to turn in to the board the names of others he thought might be Communist or leftist. He also, after several appeals, was cleared of charges and reinstated in his job.

One of the most amazing cases involved a plumber who had worked for his company for three and one-half years before receiving his dismissal notice. Finally, after many months of trying to find out why he had been dismissed, he was told that the reason was that he was "currently maintaining a close continuing association with his wife," who was suspected of having dealings with a Communist organization. Like so many, he also was eventually cleared by the board of all charges of subversion, but only after months of economic hardship and emotional turmoil.

In another instance, a private working as a hospital orderly was charged with subversion because he had a bad attitude and complained about the army and because his family was charged with Communist sympathies. He also was cleared of all charges and reinstated in his job as an orderly.

The similarities between the Salem witch trials and these hearings is inescapable: the false information, the assumption that any mitigating evidence of good citizenship (like church membership) was just being used as a cover-up, the guilt by association, the hidden accusers who might possibly have grudges against the accused, the assumption that to be accused was to be guilty, the assumption that intellectual independence was the same thing as treason, and the failure to accord the accused the rights of proper courtroom procedure. The difference between these trials and the witchcraft trials is that the boards cleared most of these employees of the charges against them, but the procedures the employees were subjected to did not by any means leave them happy and whole.

CASE STUDIES IN PERSONNEL SECURITY, COLLECTED UNDER THE DIRECTION OF ADAM YARMOLINSKY
(Washington, D.C.: Bureau of National Affairs, Inc., August 1955)

Introduction

The 50 cases presented here have been collected in the course of a study of several hundred cases arising under the various Federal personnel security programs. The study is still in progress.

These histories are collected, with the consent of the employees involved, from the files of the lawyers who advised or represented them. The reports are of necessity incomplete, because the Government file, which was not released to the employee, was also not available to our interviewers. While we realize that the usefulness of a study of this kind is circumscribed by the limitations on the available material, we feel that it will provide useful and indeed essential material for an understanding of how the security programs operate from day to day.

CASE NO. 4 (EXECUTIVE ORDER 10450)

Case No. 4 is provided in greater detail than the others so that the reader can get some sense of the general procedure. Note that the employee is scarcely a CIA agent. He is a "sub-professional," but his work supposedly gives him access to classified material. Note also that he has been a government employee for fourteen years and that his loyalty has never before been questioned. Most of the evidence against him cites his friendship with various people who were supposed to be radicals, in some way associated with groups that the attorney general of the United States had labeled as dangerous and subversive. Some of the evidence that he is disloyal comes from the book clubs he belongs to or the magazines he reads. Note how often one finds the phrase "it has been reliably reported" or "several reliable informants have described you." From the employee's response and witnesses called in his behalf, note how much of the information on which the board acted is patently false. At the hearing, note also that a board member "went on to suggest that the appearance of reform 'would be one of the most obvious courses of action for a man to take if he were still actively subversive.' " In short, as with the witchcraft trials, you were assumed to be guilty if charged and were damned if you did and damned if you didn't: to admit to being a subversive was an admission of guilt, but to deny being a subversive was just a way of covering up being subversive. It took seven months after the hearing was over to notify this employee of the board's decision, which was to clear him of the charges.

Excerpt from
Case No. 4 (Executive Order 10450)

This case involves a sub-professional employee who had been employed by the United States Government for fourteen years, the last seven of these in the same Department. The employee's work involved access to classified material.

Late in 1953, the employee received an interrogatory from the Chief of his Bureau. He had not been the subject of any previous proceedings. The interrogatory asked about five associations, one in a former employment, and four with fellow employees.

Charges

The employee submitted a response to the interrogatory, and almost immediately thereafter received a notice of suspension without pay and proposed removal from duty. The basis for this action was stated to be the following charges, which included the substance of the original interrogatory as well as substantial additional material:

"a. That you have been associated with the [housing development] newspaper in various capacities since 1946, and are now serving as Associate Editor of that newspaper. This newspaper was cited as a member of the Washington Bookshop Association which is on the Attorney General's list of subversive organizations. This newspaper has carried several editorials and articles expressing radical viewpoints which were personally defended by you and upheld by you in discussions with fellow residents of the . . . community.

"b. Your personal history statement completed by you in 1944, reflects that you were awarded the [_____ (name misspelled) Fellowship] by [XY (an American architect)]. [XY] is listed by the House Committee on Un-American Activities as being affiliated with various peace organizations and Communist fronts. Reliable sources have disclosed that you know [XY], and that at one time you contemplated working for him.

"c. Reliable sources have disclosed that you were at one time a subscriber to the Daily Worker, as well as other Communist newspapers.

"d. A reliable source has disclosed that at a meeting held at the [_____] School in [the housing development] during National Brotherhood Week in 1943–1944, a motion was made by one Mr. [_____] that 'the Bible should be burned and start building from there', and that you verbally seconded the motion and discussed it.

"e. The personal history statement completed by you in 1940 reflects employment with Mr. [A], during the period February–May 1940. Mr. [A] is on record as editor of the [_____] Publishing Company . . . , a publishing firm that has published books which support the Communist Party line.

"f. It is of record that through your employment with the housing development newspaper you have been closely associated with and personally friendly with the following personnel on the staff of that newspaper who either are known Communists or suspected of having communistic tendencies:

"(1) Mr. [B], who was instrumental in getting you on the staff of the housing development newspaper. Mr. [B] has been reliably reported as a member of the American Peace Mobilization and the Washington Committee for Democratic Action, both organizations are listed by the Attorney General as subversive organizations. It is also reported that Mr. [B] was considered to be a protege of Mr. [C], a known Communist, who allegedly was involved in a Soviet espionage conspiracy in the early 1940's. it [sic] is further reliably reported that Mr. [B] was once listed as editor of the 'UCL Chronicle', a publication described as being controlled by the Communist Party.

"(2) Mrs. [D], alias [_____], a known Communist, who was on the staff of the 'New Pioneer', official publication of the Junior Section, International Workers Order, and illustrator for 'Fraternal Outlook' which is the official publication of the International Workers Order. The International Workers Order was cited as subversive and communist by the Attorney General on 4 December 1947.

"(3) Miss [E], who has frequently upheld communism, and is a regular reader of the communist newspaper, The Daily Worker.

"(4) Miss [F], who is known to have communist leavings [sic].

"(5) Mr. and Mrs. [G], who are reliably reported to have sent 1,000 postcards through the mail 'to save the ROSENBERGS'.

"g. It has been reliably reported that you were closely associated with and friendly with Mr. [H], who is now under suspension from duty with [the employee's Bureau].

"h. It has been reliably reported that you were associated with and friendly with Mr. [I], who resigned from his position in the [employee's Bureau] while charges involving his suitability for employment in the [employee's Bureau] were pending.

"i. It has been reliably reported that you were associated with and friendly with Mr. [J], who resigned from his position in the employee's Bureau while under investigation to determine his suitability for employment in the Bureau. Mr. [J] has been disclosed as an individual having communist tendencies, and it is of record that his wife signed communist nominating petitions during 1939.

"j. It has been reliably reported that you were associated with and friendly with Mr. [K], who resigned from his position in the employee's Bureau while charges involving his suitability for continued employment in the Bureau were pending. Further, that you wrote a eulogy regarding Mr. [K] in the housing development newspaper the day following his resignation from the Bureau, and that you attended a block party in the housing development in farewell of his departure to California.

"k. It has been reliably reported that you were associated with and friendly with Mr. [L], who held a meeting in his home for the benefit of the United American Spanish Aid Committee which is on the Attorney General's list of subversive organizations. Those attending this meeting were required to make donations for this organization.

"l. You have over an extended period of time associated with persons who are known communists. This association applies to Mr. [M] and Mr. [D] and Mr. [E]. It is of record that Mr. [D] was removed from his position at the Government Printing Office on the basis of an unfavorable loyalty investigation.

"m. Several reliable informants have described you as being active in and associated with a radical group in the housing development, and you have been referred to as a 'Red' and 'Pink'. Included in this group are those described as ever willing to defend communism in any discussion of ideology which may occur either verbally or in the housing development newspaper, and who have been extremely critical of the American Legion and of American laws and institutions."

Employee's Response

After obtaining counsel, the employee prepared and filed a 25-page sworn answer. The following summary of the response is keyed to the charges quoted above:

(a) The employee described the circumstances leading up to his joining the staff of the community newspaper, first as a cartoonist, then as a reporter of police news, and after several years, as editor, for about six months until the birth of his first child. He later served as City Council reporter for the communist paper. He denied any expressions of radical viewpoints in the newspaper, and in this connection described his efforts to prevent the publication of a letter to the editor from a Mr. N., a correspondent who was opposed to requiring loyalty oaths of local residents. He said that he had expressed his objection to the letter to residents of the development who discussed it with him.

He said that in the course of his work on the newspaper he had never heard of the Washington Bookshop Association in any connection, nor could he understand how the newspaper could have been a member of the Association; his counsel had told him that membership was essentially a discount arrangement for purchasing books and records.

(b) The employee referred to an interest in architecture, which led him to write to XY about the possibility of an apprenticeship. After an interview with XY, he was invited to become an apprentice, but had to refuse the invitation since, with the birth of his first child, he could not afford the arrangement. He had had no other contact with XY.

(c) The employee stated that he had never read the "Daily Worker" or seen an issue of it and had no idea what it looked like. He pointed out that some two years previously he had been a reader of the newspaper PM, and although he did not regard PM as a Communist newspaper on the basis of his acquaintance with it, he understood from his counsel that it had been criticized as Communistically inclined—perhaps on the basis of its later history. The employee stated that his current periodicals subscriptions were: THE WASHINGTON POST, THE SATURDAY EVENING POST, COLLIERS, THE AMERICAN MAGAZINE, TODAY'S WOMAN, WOMAN'S HOME COMPANION, AND THE SATURDAY REVIEW OF LITERATURE.

(d) The employee denied this charge (relating to his having seconded a motion to burn the Bible) completely; he pointed out that he had not moved to the housing development until August, 1944, and that National Brotherhood Week occurs in February. He described himself as a practicing member of the Jewish faith.

(e) The employee stated that he had been employed as a salesman in Mr. A's bookstore for about ten weeks in 1939 or 1940. He had been hired in the ordinary course of business, and he had been fired because business was poor. The employee stated that he never saw any Communist books in Mr. A's book shop.

(f) The employee denied association with "anyone suspected by him of having Communist tendencies." He stated that he had met Mr. B. once, and that Mr. B. had nothing to do with his joining the staff of the newspaper. As he had explained in his response to charge (a), he had had no contact with Mr. B on the community newspaper; Mr. B had moved away from the housing development some years ago, and he had no knowledge of Mr. B's associations. As to Mrs. D, he had worked with her on the community newspaper and he and his wife had played Canasta with the D's on several occasions. He stated that Mrs. D. tended to become overly excited about minor local issues, but he had no reason to suspect her of Communist tendencies, and, in fact, she had made strong anti-Communist remarks. He added that after he had received charges he had learned from Mrs. D. that she had been a member of the Communist Party for a year, many years previously. The employee pointed out that Mr. D was a business partner of a person who had taken a public role in exposing Communist activities.

As to Mr. E., the employee stated that he had worked with Mrs. E on the local community newspaper, that he disagreed with her on local affairs, that he had "never heard her uphold Communism on any occasion" but that "he had a vague impression . . . that she felt strongly about freedom of expression and was opposed to totalitarianism on those grounds."

• • •

(h) The employee repeated the statement in his answer to the original interrogatory that his only contact with Mr. I had been in a temporary car pool.

• • •

(m) The employee affirmed his belief in the United States Constitution and form of Government, his awareness of the Communist conspiracy and his opposition to "Communism and radicalism."

Hearing

The employee's response was acknowledged with the statement that a hearing would be scheduled. The hearing occupied two and a half days. No witnesses were presented by the Government. The employee's case consisted of testimony by four witnesses, in addition to the employee himself, and thirty supporting affidavits. . . . These affidavits were concerned principally with the charges against the affiants themselves, as well as the nature of their association with the employee, and their judgment of him.

• • •

Mr. B's affidavit, for instance, added the information that his principal activity outside of his employment had for a number of years been in

Boy Scout work and that Mr. B did not think he could recognize the employee if he met him.

• • •

Mr. D's affidavit brought out the information that he had for some time been a confidential informant for the FBI.

• • •

[One witness] was asked . . . whether he noted that the employee "espouses the cause of the underdog in issues." . . .

The minister [a witness] was questioned by board members as to possible sources of adverse information about the employee. Following his testimony that several of the people whom the employee was said to have associated with were active members of his church, he was asked by the board counsel whether he was not familiar with the Communist tactic of becoming a "member in good standing of churches and other worthy organizations" so that "there might be people with 'Communist tendencies' in churches, whether or not such people were "actual party members."

In the course of the cross-examination of the employee himself, toward the end of the hearing, there was an extensive colloquy between the board's counsel and the employee's counsel as to the meaning of "known Communists" and board counsel stated that "known Communists" meant "known to the government." At the conclusion of this colloquy, the Chairman suggested that once it had been disclosed to an employee that a particular individual was a "known Communist" then "the only safe thing for a person to do for his own protection, is to assume that the Government knows what it is talking about." A little later the Chairman observed: "I can only suggest to the employee that he not take it upon himself to decide whether the charges against other people were based on fact or whose files they are based on, but that it might be just as well to assume that what is said is correct." . . . (the information about Mr. G came from the local postmaster, who told the employee that Mr. G was receiving mail with Russian stamps).

• • •

In reviewing the allegation as to the D's, the employee was asked by a board member whether a reformed Communist "would be entitled to complete trust as much as any other person who never had Communist connections?" The board member went on to suggest that the appearance of reform "would be one of the most obvious courses of action for a man to take if he were still actively subversive."

The employee was also asked whether the communist newspaper ever received material from the United Nations; whether he had "any relatives, friends, or acquaintances in foreign countries from whom you receive mail or send mail to?"; whether he ever got a letter from Russia; whether his parents had come from Russia; whether his wife had any relatives living in a foreign country; and whether she had received or sent any mail to anyone in foreign countries.

Result

Following the hearing, employee's counsel received a copy of the transcript, but was unable to obtain a copy of the board's findings. At the close of the hearing, three and a half months had elapsed since the original interrogatory, and almost three months since the formal charges. Some seven months after the hearing, the employee was informed of a favorable decision by the Office of the Secretary, and the employee was reinstated with back pay, after having been suspended for about ten and a half months.

Employee's counsel spent 95 hours of time on the matter. He received a fee of $1,200.

CASE NO. 57

No job seemed to be too menial or manual to escape scrutiny from the government on security grounds. The employee in Case No. 57 had been working as a butcher on a merchant ship for seven years when his papers allowing him to work aboard any ship were withdrawn. Such a restriction was called "screening." Instead of looking for work elsewhere, this employee appealed the decision with the help of an attorney. Note that the Coast Guard refused to provide him with any specific charges whatsoever, but their questions were about his relationship with his brothers and his feelings about the Communist Party. The board got nowhere with questions about communism because the employee seemed to know almost nothing about the party or what he was being asked. Underneath the hearings, the unstated objection seemed to be to the man's and his brothers' memberships in a union. In his case, the board refused to reverse itself on barring him, for security reasons, from serving on board ships.

Excerpt from Case No. 57 (Port Security Program)

The employee was a seaman, working mainly or entirely as a butcher, at a salary of $300–$400 a month. He had been so employed from 1945 to the middle of 1952. He had not been the subject of previous loyalty or security proceedings, and had never been interrogated on loyalty-security matters.

Charges and Hearing

The nature of the charges was not revealed initially. The employee was simply "screened", that is, his papers either were refused validation or were lifted. (Counsel did not recall which.) He filed notice of appeal from his screening, and 6 and 1/2 months later was given 12 days' written notice of a hearing.

At the outset of the hearing Counsel requested the basis for the screening, and the following dialogue ensued:

Chairman: It is asserted by the Coast Guard that he is believed to be sympathetically associated with the Communist Party, or otherwise affiliated with it.

Counsel: And can you tell us when or where?

Chairman: At the present time and for several consecutive years heretofore.

Counsel: Can you tell us anything more than that about the specific charges against [the employee]?

Chairman: I am not permitted under Coast Guard classification prohibitions, to state anything further.

Counsel by reference to a standard objection touched on a demand for amplification or greater specification of charges, which was not granted.

• • •

No evidence was introduced by the Government, the hearing being turned over immediately to the employee's counsel. No oath was given, this being optional. Counsel first questioned the employee, establishing his background—age 42, American-born, 7th-grade education, one of 8 living children, of strong religious belief, a long-time member of his church choir (Greek-Catholic Orthodox). The employee denied membership in, association with, or affiliation with the Communist Party and denied any interest in political theories. Apart from his union, in which he denied any particular activity, he said the only organization he belonged to was the Catholic Sokol.

• • •

The Chairman then assumed the interrogation, with other members interjecting questions. The employee was asked if he had any knowledge of or opinions on the Communist Party and replied negatively.

The chairman opened the interrogation as to the employee's brother.
. . . It was developed that one brother was a Fuller Brush salesman at
home; the employee "thought" that this brother had been screened from
sailing some 10 months previously. A second brother was a vegetable
man in a local hospital who had been screened from sailing some 10
months previously after 13 years of sailing. The third brother, the pa-
trolman, lived locally, and the employee stated that he saw him aboard
ship and had dinner with him at his home occasionally.

Extensive questioning as to the employee's feelings toward the close-
ness with his brothers followed. The Chairman stated, "The relationship
between the brothers is clearly relevant to the Coast Guard classification
here. . . . the Coast Guard believes that a blood relationship between persons, is a basis for, is an association basis for classification or for doubt
as to where loyalty to an individual might lie in an emergency situation
involving one of the members of the family."

• • •

On being asked if he had any reason to believe that any of his brothers
have or would be disloyal to this country, the employee replied negatively; the Chairman then asked if the employee believed that the Communist Party in this country is or would be disloyal to this country. The
employee, as he did throughout the proceeding, stated he knew nothing
about the party. The Chairman then asked, "Well, knowing nothing about
it, have you formed any operating conclusions without any knowledge?"
Counsel thereupon made objection to the question and the proceeding
in general and the Chairman replied, in part: "The basis for the security
program as it is set up, is not to determine whether he is or might be
disloyal, but whether there is any doubt as to his loyalty under any fore-
seeable circumstances."

• • •

Considerable colloquy between counsel and the Board on the propri-
ety of this line of questioning followed; a board member stated that
counsel had no basis for saying that any questions which might be
thought to be irrelevant or unsound necessarily need be the basis of the
Board's judgment, that, in order to arrive at a "workable conclusion", it
was necessary to have all of the elements presented, and that "it's defi-
nitely to the advantage of the appellant to have these questions asked, in
order that we might be better able to understand the nature of the
case."

Counsel stated he was not advising his client not to answer the question. It was rephrased to read, "whether you operated on any hypothesis with respect to Communism or the Communist Party." After Counsel asked if he understood the question, the employee stated he didn't. The Chairman again posed the question in a different form: while the employee had no knowledge and knew nothing about the Communist Party, had he any conclusions as to whether it was good, bad, or indifferent in relation to the interests and security of the country? The employee's response was that he knew nothing about the party.

• • •

Considerable questioning relative to the employee's brothers followed, after which a member asked if the employee could "put your finger on any cause why you would be screened." Appellant stated he had no idea and the member said:

Member: Following that question, I would be perfectly frank. Does it occur to you as at all peculiar, that all of the brothers who have gone to sea, have been screened? Does it occur to you that some one of you, I'm not saying who, some one of the brothers must have done something to arouse the government's suspicion, for some one in the government to put the finger on all of you?

The Employee: Well, I don't know, sire. As far as union is concerned, I don't know, outside of union activities. I haven't done nothing.

Another member added: "And I have been impressed with everything that he has presented and what he has said; but, in keeping with what Mr. [member] has just said, I think it would be well if you perhaps would do a little more thinking along this line to see just what, and where the source of contamination lies; because it doesn't seem reasonable that all of the members of the family would have been screened, unless there would have been some basis for it, and perhaps in the future for your own benefit, you probably would do well to sort of look about a little and see just where this source lies. Even though you are dealing with your own brothers, for your own good, and that would be my recommendation in this particular case."

Result

The employee received no report of the Board's recommendation. He later received a brief notice from the Commandant to the effect that no reason appeared to upset the initial (adverse) determination made by the Commandant. No further appellate steps were taken.

• • •

Immediately upon being screened, this employee was barred from working as a seaman. After being screened, the employee went on unemployment insurance and up to the time of the hearing had about two months work in an Alaskan cannery.

INTERVIEW WITH DAVE AND SOPHIE SMITH

Sophie and Dave Smith, lifelong social activists, have helped shape and have been shaped by a full range of critical issues that prepared for and then characterized the 1950s' "witch-hunts," targeted by Arthur Miller in *The Crucible*. Their lives constitute a social history of modern America since World War I.

The defining event in their lives, as in the lives of so many who lived through it, was the Great Depression created by unbridled capitalism. During this time, in the 1930s, Dave's family was financially devastated, and at a labor demonstration in Michigan, Dave witnessed the killing of fellow workers at a Ford Motor plant by management's hired security guards. Simultaneously he learned that, as the demonstration had been squelched, so had free speech at the University of Michigan, where he was a student (and, incidentally, which Arthur Miller attended at the same time). The university had cancelled an appearance by an invited speaker whose political views were not to the institution's liking. Sophie, whose family had been persecuted for struggling against the corrupt tsarist regime in Russia, found herself, as a university graduate in physics, unable to get a job and observing all around her poverty and injustice, which were just then beginning to be addressed by Roosevelt's New Deal.

We have observed in the previous documents that there were numerous human responses to European oppression and the American depression that were labeled subversive of the U.S. government, chief among them (1) holding membership in the Communist Party; (2) belonging to and organizing labor unions; and (3) being involved in social action, especially civil rights and peace movements. Those who fought against fascism in Spain in the Abraham Lincoln Brigade were also invariably targets of witch-hunts.

Sophie's and Dave's responses in the 1930s and 1940s to the incredible poverty and injustice they saw in the depression would brand them for decades as dangerous subversives. Dave's response was to join the labor movement, where he worked actively as a leader throughout his working years, and to volunteer to fight against fascism in Spain as a member of the Abraham Lincoln Brigade. Sophie's response was to join the Communist Party and be-

Left: Sophie and Dave Smith on their wedding day in 1941—social activists even then. Printed with permission of Sophie and Dave Smith.

Below: Sophie and Dave Smith, at the time of their interview in 1997. Printed with permission of Sophie and Dave Smith.

gin actively and tenaciously to work for economic and racial justice on a grass-roots level.

Their aims were to improve the lives of Americans, especially the poor, the blue-collar laborer, and those suffering under discrimination of all kinds—never to turn the United States over to the Soviet Union. But while those they worked with and those they worked for valued their efforts, by the late 1940s and 1950s, to those who could enjoy power and the unbridled pursuit of wealth, the Smiths were dangerous threats to a way of life bought at the expense of the poor. In the eyes of the political and economic establishment of the 1950s, the Smiths, in short, were something akin to witches.

The fate of many of those accused in 1692 was much more drastic than the suffering of those accused in the 1950s: many of the accused witches paid with their lives on Gallows Hill. But the issues, values, and principles involved in both cases were very much alike, and what was at stake for many in the 1950s was what makes life worthwhile and bearable: one's good name, one's livelihood, and one's self-image and peace of mind.

When the witch-hunts of the 1950s began, the Smiths suffered. Just as Elizabeth and John Proctor are deeply concerned for their neighbors who are being arrested for witchcraft, the Smiths were astounded at the firings and arrests of their associates in the 1950s. As the sheriff finally appears to arrest Elizabeth Proctor, so Dave was soon approached and escorted by an FBI agent to his employer's personnel office to be fired. He was never again to hold a job as a machinist in a sizeable company. Sophie was twice fired as a mathematics teacher.

As John Proctor is asked to name names in order to help himself, so Sophie and Dave were hounded by the FBI with bribes of large sums of money in exchange for information that would hurt others. As Proctor and Corey prepare arguments for the court in defense of their friends, so Dave assisted in the defense of a fellow veteran of the Lincoln Brigade who was threatened with a charge of subversion by HUAC. Like the Proctors, the Smiths had to come to grips with the very real possibility of going to jail and had to wonder what would happen to their children.

The Crucible is about witch-hunts, and it is about how people behave under pressure. Like those heroes of Salem—Rebecca Nurse, John Proctor, Giles Corey, and others—Dave and Sophie

Smith demonstrated extraordinary courage in the face of the immense pressures of the witch-hunts of the 1950s, steadfastly refusing to help themselves at the expense of others.

INTERVIEW WITH DAVE AND SOPHIE SMITH
(Berkeley, Calif., September 1997)

CJ (*Claudia Durst Johnson*): What is your current situation? You've been here for two years in California?

Sophie: Came here September 9th, 1995.

CJ: And you retired at that time?

Dave: Retired in '77.

Sophie: I'll be 85 in a couple of weeks. So I'm retired and Dave also.

Dave: You know, this is a very politically active area. More so than the East. At least on labor history. That's because of the longshore union. The longshore union has always been very powerful and they've never been able to break it. It's small now compared with years ago. There are not so many jobs there now. From the longshore union under the leadership of Harry Bridges back in the thirties came a general strike throughout the country. So the labor history here is very, very rich.

CJ: I don't know whether you know this or not, but when Arthur Miller was asked to participate in the story of "On the Waterfront" about longshoremen, the studio made the proposal to change the "bad guys." Instead of being the mob they would be Communists. (laughter all round)

Dave: You know I was at the University of Michigan with Arthur Miller. Yeah, I was there and he was there during the up-surge of political activity in the area.

CJ: So he was active from his college days?

Dave: Oh yeah.

CJ: What was actually going on in Michigan while the two of you were there? I understand you became interested in social action while you were at Michigan.

Dave: Oh well, that campus was really involved in those days. I followed two guys from my hometown in Massachusetts to Michigan. When I first went there, I didn't need a job. Cost two hundred and twenty-five dollars a year. But after about six months I got a call from home telling me I had to be self-supporting. The depression had done a job on my parents. After that I was completely self-supporting—my board, my room, whatever. It was really rough. And I was a major in science and had to spend a lot of time in the lab. I really couldn't afford the time to work, but I did. So I was working there—I think it was in '32 at a time when they were trying to organize Ford Motor Company. They had a huge plant at River Rouge, a tremendous plant. And there was a large demonstration of people from Detroit— young people walking around with placards, you know, and Ford had security guards there. They came out and killed two or three of the marchers there. Well, the campus went up in arms, and we had big meetings. A lot of the professors spoke. Really, really big demonstrations. Okay, so, as I say, I was a student. I was not political. I came from a small city north of Boston. I just was not political at all, you know. The family wasn't too political either. And I started thinking, "What the hell's going on here?" And then I think the same year John Strachey, a British socialist, member of Parliament, was invited to be a campus speaker. He wrote this book, *The Coming Struggle for Power*. And he was planned as a speaker at the University, but about a week before he came, they cancelled it. Wow! At that time the National Students' League was organized. Well, we had tremendous discussions back and forth. I got drawn in. I joined. And of course on the campus on the corners they were distributing all kinds of revolutionary literature. You had your Communist Party and the Socialist Club, all kinds of things. And I picked up and read some of these things. And, again, I was interested and quite disturbed in my mind, not knowing what the hell was going on. And at the same time working like hell. And then I read about the Scottsboro Boys [black men repeatedly found guilty of rape in Alabama despite overwhelming evidence to the contrary and U.S. Supreme Court reversals]. One professor of cultural anthropology really opened my eyes. Taught me history of religion. And that was an anthropology professor. And that man really took the whole discussion of religion all the way through, and from a materialistic base. He was an iconoclast. He became really well known. And when I finished that course, my mind was in a whirl. I became so confused I didn't know where the hell I was going. So I left school and came home. Very disturbed. I came back to this small, small city of Chelsea, Massachusetts. A school friend of mine, from high school, who had been away all these years, had become a Communist while I was going through all this. And he talked with me and so on, and I also became interested in it. And I was knocking around. It was 1935. And there were no jobs. I finally got a job and started talking union, and well!—I was fired.

CJ: They weren't ready for this in Chelsea?

Dave: Oh, no. You had no labor board or any protection at all. I learned, you know. I got a job with this guy that sold rugs. They were phony rugs, you know. And he sold hot jewelry. He sold it to the police department. I stayed with them for about six months. So I knocked around. I had all kind of jobs. By this time I was reading. And when the Spanish elections took place, a coalition of Independent Parties of the center won and replaced the right-wing reactionary government. General Franco, with the right-wing military establishment and the support of Hitler and Mussolini, led an uprising against the government. This was effectively suppressed by the people in all of the major cities. But with the aid of Hitler's planes Franco's forces invaded Spain from Spanish Morocco. So International Brigades formed in various countries to come to the aid of those fighting Franco. I heard about these and said, "How the hell do I go? I want to go." So my radical friend made the arrangements. And I joined up with Dan Fitzgerald, a University of New Hampshire student.

CJ: I understand you ended up commanding a large group of men.

Dave: Yeah, I eventually became company commander. In the last Republican offensive across the Ebro River, when the Fascists broke through our lines and we were retreating—up behind a little hill. We could see the Fascist tanks up there. But the British anti-tank guns did a pretty good job. There was a lot of firing and so on. But then I heard this Commander Wolf say, "Hey, Smith, take your guys up there and do a job." It was impossible. So I got up there to talk to him and, as soon as I did, machine-gun fire got me in the left shoulder joint. God, I thought I was dead. It went right through— hitting the bone. Funny I didn't feel anything right away, but then, pain enough so I knew I was still alive. . . . I stayed in the hospital until late December of '39. The International Brigades were being sent home by the Spanish government by that time, in the hope that international pressure would force recall of Hitler's and Mussolini's armies. I returned to the U.S. on December 31st, 1939.

CJ: I assume you came back to the States after you were wounded.

Dave: Now I came back to the States. And I came back very angry and resentful of my country and other Western democracies—for their betrayal of Republican Spain—their phony Non-Intervention Pact that embargoed Spain but allowed shipments of U.S. oil and armaments from Hitler and Mussolini to enter Spain to help Franco. I believe World War II began in Spain with the U.S. and other countries' appeasement of Fascist aggression.

CJ: I assume you continued your interest in what was happening in Spain.

Dave: Yeah, we as an organization did everything we could to supply the underground. There was a huge underground there even though the Fascists continued to be in power. We raised all kinds of money for them.

CJ: Dave, how long totally were you in Spain?

Dave: Twenty-two months. But when we got back, we all did everything we could to help from this country. We had picket lines at the consulate here. And one time they wanted to get Fascist Spain into the U.N. And we demonstrated—did everything we could to unseat these Fascists. But, of course, we were not successful. We never stopped and always hoped there would be an overthrow of Franco, but he lasted. But you know he eventually made a big mistake too. He saw to it that Carlos succeeded him because he had royal blood and married a Spanish princess, but Carlos was a liberal! Didn't stand for anything that Franco stood for. He's been a good king. And he has established a constitutional monarchy. In fact, after he came to power and they had an election there, some of the old Franco Fascists tried to have a coup and overthrow the elected government. But it didn't work.

CJ: I wonder if we couldn't bring Sophie up to this period. What were you doing at the time Dave was at Michigan and later serving in the Lincoln Brigade?

Sophie: Well, this was, as Dave said, the depression in this country. I was a graduate of Hunter College. Just to give you the atmosphere: when I graduated I couldn't get a job. Nobody could. There just wasn't any hiring going on. So I went on and took a master's degree in physics from Columbia. Once you were in graduate school you could get loans. Then I tried to get a job. I remember going to the employment office at Teachers College and the guy said, "Well, in the first place they'll never hire a woman as a physicist. Two, you're Jewish." I went to Bell Labs in New Jersey. I told them I was looking for a job and he said, "My dear, you're a woman, and we've not hired a woman in physics at Bell Labs since the World War [I], and we have no intention of hiring one now. And in addition I must tell you that we would not hire anyone of your persuasion." (He knew I was Jewish.) At the Teacher's Agency in New York, all you had to do was present your documents and fill in your application. But they took one look at my name—my maiden name was Kaplan—and I didn't have a chance.

CJ: Dave seems to have been radicalized by his labor experiences at Michigan, the killing of several pickets at the Ford plant, as well as his reading. Did these experiences of yours, happening at the same time, radicalize you?

Sophie: Well, yes. I guess I was involved at about the same time, in the 1930s. I was in the Party—the Communist Party. My parents were better off at that point than Dave's were. They were able at least to support me. But I got loans and worked for the FERA—the Federal Emergency Relief Assistance, which was given to students. I got loans through them and then worked them off. And I joined the Young Communists' League, I guess in about '35 and was active. Incidentally, one of the big goals at that point was to help the guys in Spain.

But I had a quite different background from Dave's. My parents had been socialists in Poland. My father had been exiled to Siberia twice actually, by the czar, for his so-called revolutionary activity. He was picked up twice and he spent quite a long time in Siberia. In this country all of my family were active in the garment workers' union and helped organize there. So in our house politics were always being discussed—at a very high level! I had very excitable families. So I grew up in this atmosphere of "Party" [Communist Party] people. Actually my family were not Communists, but they were close to people (from the same city) who were active Communists in this country. But it was an atmosphere, as I say, which I grew up in where it was accepted that—of *course* you read Marx and of *course* you were for the working class and you were for revolution.

At this point my parents, all my relatives, were storekeepers. They had all left the garment industry. They were comfortable—not rich—but they were all making a living, so to speak.

For a while after college I worked in shops. But it wasn't too successful. I think I was too educated to be really intimate with the workers in the shop. So I worked as a typist for the WPA—the Works Progress Administration put in place by President Franklin Roosevelt. And then I discovered they were organizing teachers. They were organizing WPA arithmetic teachers and WPA reading teachers to help in the schools. So I tried to get switched from typing to teaching. But I discovered that the only way to get a teaching job was to get on Home Relief.

CJ: What was Home Relief?

Sophie: Home Relief? It was really what it sounds like. It was welfare. You had to establish a residence away from home. Well, I was a math major and a physics minor, with a master's degree in physics. And I was hired as a remedial reading teacher! They had no openings at the time in my fields. There was no logic to it, but I became a remedial reading teacher for many years and worked to organize the WPA. We had a teachers' union, a local union. Eventually it was dispersed.

CJ: At what point did you say you joined the party?

Sophie: Oh, I was in what was called the Young Communists' League. I joined that right after my M.A., in 1936. And I was fairly active after that.

CJ: How did you two meet?

Dave: Well, it was about 1940. I didn't want to go back to my hometown in Massachusetts because I couldn't get any work there, so I stayed in New York. My brother was an artist there, an aspiring artist. I was in the office headquarters of the Lincoln Brigade when an opportunity opened to become a business manager of a small newspaper—a labor newspaper—in upstate New York. So I took the job. It was Gloversville, New York, the leather glove working capital of the world, really. So the newspaper was run by the leather workers' union. While I was there they had a really big strike. But the newspaper folded after about six months. And I became active up there with the farmers' union—in upstate New York. They also had a strike. Scabs were driving milk trucks, but soon milk was pouring out of holes in the side and onto the road. And then around about this same time another big demonstration took place in Schenectady. And strikers were throwing roller bearings down the road and these police on mounted horses—they were having a hell of a time with those bearings underfoot. Well, I helped a little bit. And I went around with the farmers' union. At that time the American Labor Party was collecting signatures in preparation for the New York state election campaign. At one time, when something was going on, it was very cold. I was walking down the road and slipped and fell right on my bad arm. Hurt like hell. So, instead of staying there, I went back to New York City. Turned out it was just sprained. Yet some friends said, "Why don't you go up and spend the summer at Camp Unity? A real nice adult camp." So I went up there. I think it was a Labor Day weekend. I go in and Sophie's sitting there. And I looked at her— nice looking, in fact *beautiful* woman. So I spoke to one of the other guys I knew there and he said, "Oh yeah. I know her." And he introduced us. This was in September; in December we got married.

Sophie: When we got married, I had a job as a legal secretary and Dave wasn't working.

Dave: No, no, that's not true. I was working! I was working! (laughter) I was making nineteen dollars a week. I was working in a little machine shop where they made hinges.

CJ: You had moved from being a newspaper man to being a machinist.

Dave: Oh, yeah! I had already worked in a machine shop during a few summers back in the early thirties. But now I came back to the city—New York—from upstate New York. I had joined the Communist Party in Spain. To me, they had the best organization. Funny thing, before the war they got about 14 percent of the vote in Spain. At the end of the war, when the general election took place, they got the same 14 percent. I think of the sacrifice of these people during the war. Because they were the prime movers with the best organization. Anyway, so I joined there. Came back to the city and said, well I possibly *could* go back to school—I was always a pretty good student—but I decided that the working class was for me. And this machine-shop work is something that I had done part-time years before.

CJ: What did the two of you see happening in this country after World War II?

Sophie: Well, first you have to see it in terms of what we did before. In the years right after our marriage when I stayed home, I was active locally in all kinds of movements. Even before I met Dave, I had been active in the Scottsboro Case from New York, raising funds and so on. I had been involved in the unemployment struggles and the unemployment counsels. This was during the depths of the depression when people had to get on welfare or they couldn't survive. We had an organization that helped to get people on welfare. And we also had to get people in decent housing. There was, for example, a street where the working-class blacks lived—and there weren't too many blacks who weren't working class—Flushing discriminated a lot, you understand. And they lived in shacks, literally shacks. And I'm talking now about the 1930s. We had worked on all sorts of issues that involved working people, trade unions, black people. And this was the whole background before the war.

CJ: Did you feel supported by the climate of the country?

Sophie: Well, it wasn't altogether support. You were also fighting a lot. It's true that Roosevelt had done a lot. We had WPA demonstrations. And we got some place, yes. But it was the Communist Party, by the way, and this is before I joined, which was responsible, along with other organizations, for getting unemployment relief as part of life in this country. And that did a great deal to solidify the working class. It was people like me or Dave, college people who were middle class in their basic background, who were the leaders for the most part. Of course, the trade unions were workers, but there were alliances between the Communist Party and a lot of the militant unions. Not all of them. Quite the opposite. Some of them wouldn't have anything to do with Party people. But it was a period in which there was a forward movement kind of atmosphere. And during World War II, I worked for the Brooklyn Navy Yard, and Dave worked for Sperry.

CJ: So you were quite compatible politically from the beginning.

Dave: Oh, yeah. We got married in '41. I was going from job to job. And I was looking for work in a large industry. So I saw the advertisement for Sperry, and I was hired. At that time they manufactured what was called the Sperry gyroscope and other navigational instruments. It was used in stabilizing ships with a gyroscopic motion. A very large plant in Brooklyn. At that time it was about fifteen hundred people. And as soon as I got there an organizing campaign began. Hell, I said, even though I hadn't finished my probationary period, I worked with them. But we lost the election and the company union won. And after about six months, we began to expand. A lot of young people came in. There must have been about seven thousand workers by now. After about a year we won the election and the United Electrical, Radio, and Machine Workers of the United States represented the Sperry workers. Sperry was expanding and built a very large plant at Lake Success in Nassau County. Negotiations for a contract dragged on for many months with no progress. Even though many unions had a no-strike policy during the war, we decided to strike anyway. Here was a company making millions, profiteering, using the facade of patriotism and expecting us to continue working below the pay scale of the industry. And I became chairperson of the Bush Terminal Buildings organizing committee. It didn't take very long—two days—they sat down and really bargained with us and eventually we got a very good contract. Eventually most of the small-plant employees were transferred to the large Lake Success plant. Many, including some of our officials, left for the armed services. I was refused active service because of my wound in Spain, and I became the chairman of the Lake Success plant. I got to be pals with the FBI man. They had an FBI man there. And while all the negotiations were going on there, I had to come into work late and Sophie would take the kids. I took the Long Island Railroad. I met him. I knew him and we got to talking once in a while. A gun-toting FBI man, not a lawyer. And he was there for protection at the plant. And he hated J. Edgar Hoover. He told me that Hoover had a dossier on every politician—complete.

CJ: No problems at this time?

Dave: Oh, yeah. We had some problems. One had to do with the ACTU, Association of Catholic Trade Unions. Their ideological leader was a Jesuit priest in Pittsburgh, Pennsylvania, whose objective was to destroy the left unions and replace them with unions of far-right ideology. By the way, my Spanish War background was well known to Sperry workers, and as a footnote, in the 1960s, this priest made a 180-degree change, as the Jesuits did as a whole, and apologized for his union-busting activity. He became very active in the anti-Vietnam peace movement.

We supported other unions in their struggles to get fair contracts. We were picketing Fairchild Camera of Jamaica, New York, where scabs were trying to enter the plant, protected by some police, a no-no situation. So we took care of some of the scabs. While in action, someone behind us yelled, "Hey, you guys, take it easy." I turned around and there was a policeman who had once worked in my department in Sperry and left to join the New York Police Dept. He looked around and then walked away.

Well, we supported many, many things. I was quite active. Quite busy. I was involved in all kinds of meetings, days and nights, and so on.

CJ: What was your relationship with the Sperry management?

Dave: After the strike it was pretty good. The union was a very democratic organization. It had a system of stewards. Very democratic. The personnel directors of the plants changed. In 1941 and '42 they were army personnel working under management guidance. They didn't know much. That's why we had the strike. The head of Bush Terminal was a marine colonel. During our strike, he came ranting and raving, spouting patriotism this and that. The contract had to go through the War Labor Board. At that time we had a War Labor Board. And they examined it very, very carefully. We ended up after two years with the best contract ever on the east coast. It was a good, $11,000,000 settlement. So our reputation was just pretty good. I had very little to do with the Party in those days, though my history was tied to them.

CJ: I wanted to ask both of you what you found in those days to commend the Party, and what to criticize in the Party.

Sophie: Well, to praise—for one thing—they really fought for the underdog. They really did. There was no question. Your *immediate* activity was a wholesome thing and a healthy thing. The stories about taking over are pretty nonsensical. We didn't take over anything. But we helped direct. Mainly we helped with our backs and our feet. Our kind of life. You have to picture it. In the war years I worked in the Navy Yard as a physicist working on the protection of ships against magnetic mines. For one thing, I had to travel a minimum of an hour and a half to work. No outside child care. I had someone come in to help take care of her. Got up at five in the morning to make the bottle and feed her. I'd work an eight-hour day at the Navy Yard and take another hour and a half to come back. I'd have supper, feed and bathe the baby and then—go to a meeting. Got home at eleven or twelve o'clock. It was a hectic life.

CJ: What were the meetings like?

Sophie: The meetings were where we organized what we were doing, where we channeled our energies. And some of it was stupid. You have to understand that the Party was *not* democratic. But the most productive things we did arose out of the needs of the community. But what was going on—the way the Party functioned—was not democratic. And we knew it then. And we sort of excused it on the grounds that what we were doing was important. The revolution in behalf of the working class was important. And so we excused it. At least that was my point of view.

CJ: What about you, Dave? What is your assessment of the Party?

Dave: Well, the Party operated peculiarly. Community organizations they handled one way. Trade unions they had to be very careful with because when the Party issued directions the union guys could tell them, "No, impossible, to hell with you—we'll go our own way." So the Party could have trouble with the unions. But a lot of people who went into the unions—like the CIO [Congress of Industrial Organizations]—there were a lot of Communists who worked in some of these industries—the mines, in steel, a lot of them. They really worked like hell to organize these workers. They were very good at this.

Then as Sophie pointed out, on the plus side, communism was a way of life that meant *doing* things, keeping in motion. So that excused some of the negative things that we began to question like the structure of the Party organization and the philosophy of the American Communists—their outlook. No question that we had our objections. But we began to question that and decided to leave the Party in about 1954. Should have done it before that.

Sophie: Well, there was also the exposure of what was going on in Russia.

Dave: Well, even before that. Even before Khrushchev came out with his revelations about Stalin—some time in the fifties—I forget the exact year—we began having little discussions about what was wrong with this organization. It can't exist this way. The top leadership was moving in certain ways. We were having all kind of doubts. But we persisted because we were very, very active in what we were doing. However, it was still a number of years before we broke—it was crazy. We made a big mistake in our lives. Well, I shouldn't say that—

a big mistake from the point of view of supporting some of the bigger ideas that they were trying to push over.

CJ: In your own experience, did the American Communist Party have any interest in turning over the United States to Russia? (laughter from both Smiths)

Dave: Really? No! Turn it over to the Russians? Nah. In fact, the American Communist Party early on had as its official stance, not the violent overthrow of the government, but a revolution by peaceful means. And that created quite a split in the Party ranks. No, the Party never had the aim of turning over the United States.

Sophie: Well, I think you could say that there was a kind of fraternal relationship between the Soviet Union and American Communists with fund-raising. Some Americans studied at the Lenin Institute in Moscow. But as far as their teaching the overthrow of the United States or the Party advocating the overthrow of the United States, that was just as far-fetched as anything you could come up with.

CJ: So in preparing to talk about the period of the late 1940s and the 1950s, while Communists wanted to change the economic structure of the country—this was interpreted as subversive of the entire country. In other words, to be subversive of the businessman and of capitalism was to be subversive of the country.

Dave: We're asking what does subversive mean.

CJ: In their eyes.

Dave: In their eyes.

Sophie: We're talking about the Dies Committee and their view of what was going on. In their eyes. Because you were interfering with their idea of what should be the ideal American policy. Basically, communism meant organizing unions, it meant helping blacks, and establishing civil rights. It was anathema to big business and to corporations. I think you're absolutely right.

CJ: We've gotten you through the depression and your organizing years. But things began to change radically after World War II.

Dave: Yeah, a little after World War II. Not me personally, but a lot of the fellows who had been in Spain were harassed immediately. When the harassment really picked up was right after the Korean War. I think that's when we entered the McCarthy period. And that's when I was fired.

CJ: Tell me about that—just as a narrative from beginning to end. Were you getting any signals warning you that something was going to happen before the FBI appeared on your employer's doorstep?

Dave: We felt the political climate change. There's no question about that. The Union of Electrical Workers, the UE, with 600,000 members, was the largest of the progressive unions of the CIO. Of course there were always many election struggles involving the extreme right wing which tried to impose its will, but with very little success. In 1947 the Taft-Hartley Act was passed by Congress to curtail the power of unions. Union officers were required to sign an anti-Communist affidavit. The Cold War Red Menace was in full swing. The CIO under President Murray expelled six international unions including the UE. Hundreds of workers, most of whom helped organize the CIO, were fired from their jobs. New unions were formed to compete with those that had been expelled. The International UE was formed to combat the UE. As the company expanded, many thousands of new workers were hired, and these were taken in by the national hysteria. Eventually the Sperry local lost an election to the IUE. I survived, but as a shop steward, though many attempts were made to unseat me.

Right after that, Truman came through with a loyalty requirement for anybody working in a company that did business with the Defense Department. Anybody who was a leftist working in what was considered a sensitive industry could no longer work there. You were a subversive. And I was working in such an industry. I guess a number of people got fired. Oh, yeah. Throughout the whole country. For example, on the west coast all the seamen in the Union of the Pacific. All of them were blacklisted, off the ships. Back where I was, one day they called a steward, a union steward up to the office. And I was unaware of what was happening. But the right wing of the tool-crib bunch, they were right in the center of the machine shop and they'd keep on looking at me and looking at me. And I didn't know what was going on. It was peculiar. And then I saw one of our stewards come walking up the aisle with an FBI man. And then it seemed to hit me, you know: I'm going to be next. So I spoke to my department men and said, "Hey, you know what's happening here? They're firing people. Just because they don't agree with them." They say, "Yeah, we can't let that happen." So I say, "That's good." Next thing I know, I hear, "Smith, up to the personnel office." I knew what was going to happen. So I said to the FBI, "Let's take a long walk up there. We don't want to go directly up there." So he knew what I was driving at. Everybody knew what was happening. So I walked *all* the way down one side. And circled *all* around. That was a long way. Big long walk. People watched me and they were laying down their tools. Stop work. I was fired and came home. I guess Sophie and I expected something like this. All right, I'll look for another job. But I figured I was going to be black-listed. I knew from the seamen's and other unions what was happening. So I figured the best thing to do was to go to these job shops, these small little shops with five guys, eight guys, that did subcontracting work. These job shops never checked references. And I was a skilled man. I was a toolmaker. You bargain yourself. And I got one job like that. That lasted a couple of months, then petered out. Then I said, "I'm going to go for a big place—see what happens." See an ad in the paper—High Voltage Engineering—not involved in defense work. Toolmakers and machinists Wanted. So I thought hell—I got the job. So I'm working there about a week. Boom. Called up to personnel. I said, "Here it goes." Listen to this, though. Got up to personnel. The guy—personnel director—says, "Got this record from Sperry. What's all this about your background?—a trouble-maker and you're subversive—and should not be hired?" So I said, "Some of it's true." And he said, "You know—that happened to my daughter, too." This is true! (laughter) And I looked at him and I said, "Yeah?" And he says, "You want to stay here?" And I says, "Yeah." And he says, "Okay." Oh, boy, I went home—wonderful! Big time. This place was doing good work—very fine work. But they went bankrupt in a month and a half! (laughter) I'm telling you that was *awful*. So back to—I figure, *now* I'm on the list. So I went back to the job shops. And there was another kind of big ad: Thomas Muffins, English muffins, had a big plant in Long Island—needed machinists—second shift, possible foreman. So I showed up and we had a big discussion. They were interested and were going to make me this and that. And there was a secretary there too. So I went home and waited and a few days later I get a call from the secretary. She said, "You know I worked at Sperry and I'm a great admirer of yours. And the company phoned Sperry for information about you." So I said, "Aw, to hell with it." And after that for a few years I only worked in the small job shops. But what started to happen was that my work required very close movements and my shoulder, where I was wounded, began bothering me and I couldn't control fine movements with that arm. Sophie had gotten into teaching. Of course, she had some unfortunate experiences too. But we managed. She would come home and talk about the kids. And I started thinking, "Jeez, if I went back to school for just six months, one semester, I would have my degree and could get a job teaching biology and chemistry and so on." So we decided. She would continue teaching and I would go back to Columbia. This was a good time because the Russians had just launched Sputnik and there was a tremendous need in this country to get more science teachers to catch up with the Russians. The market was great—lots of ads. When I finished my B.S., I got the first job I applied for—in a small system out on Long Island. My M.A. followed.

CJ: Did you never have problems as a teacher?

Dave: No. It was peculiar. I got hired there and I signed the whole thing about loyalty and figured eventually I would have problems. But I didn't. Certain systems didn't care. And this was one of them.

Sophie: We didn't know that at the time.

Dave: No, I didn't know it. So I went to this job and tried it out. I taught there for three years. You know? And nothing happened. Now with Sophie it was a different story—*two* times bounced. But I wanted to go to a better place. So I finally applied to a school in Westchester County. And they didn't have any loyalty oath to sign! Great! Two months later, called into the personnel office: "Oh, we forgot to have you sign it." So I sign it and think, "Any day." But nothing happened. But I was immediately very active. I was on the organizing committee for the teachers' union, the AFT [American Federation of Teachers]. I became chairperson for the high school for many years, until I retired.

CJ: That's kind of amazing.

Dave: Yeah, it *is* amazing. Just like in actual life. Certain people slip through. And I couldn't figure it out. I was this and that, active in the union and so on and then actually teaching there. And then I could tell some of the people there about my background. Anyways, I was never bothered—before I retired. So I was blacklisted in industry but not in teaching. To this day I don't know how it happened.

Oh, there were any number of people who were blacklisted and bounced around and ended up doing other things. For some people, the blacklisting was a disaster. It was a failure. For *me* it changed my life in a positive way. I was fortunate. Had I continued as a toolmaker, I wouldn't have been able to continue at the trade.

CJ: Just because of your shoulder?

Dave: Yeah. But this blacklisting went on throughout the country and hit hundreds of people—more than that.

CJ: Records at this time show that people were being blacklisted merely for subscribing to the wrong magazines.

Dave: Yeah, if you subscribed to the magazine, *The Nation*. They had a master list down there in Washington of every kind of leftist publication you can name. Or even if some of your family was seen as Communist sympathizers.

Sophie: I was fired from my first two teaching jobs. The main reason I lost my jobs more than Dave did in teaching is that I was a *known* Party person. I led street meetings. I applied to the local police departments for permission to hold street meetings. So there was no secret. They could get me on the loyalty oath business. It was easy.

CJ: Well, you and Dave were very cool headed about all this, but for a lot of people it was a time of terror.

Dave: Yeah, terror. During the Alger Hiss business, the U.S. Treasury Secretary—Joe McCarthy started to go to work on him. He committed suicide. Oh, yeah. A lot of people, many, many people were terrified. I knew many individuals who were deeply concerned, distressed, quite worried. Some lost their jobs and had to just disappear into other parts of the country.

CJ: It ruined a lot of lives.

Sophie: You ended up lying a lot just to get a job. And the loyalty oath. In my book, I was not lying in signing the loyalty oath. I had never thought of doing anything against the United States. So it didn't bother me to sign. But the government and my employers thought differently. Some people were afraid of it. And you never knew. For example, I was offered a job in White Plains. If I had accepted that job, I would have never been fired. But I accepted another job that offered me the opportunity to teach advanced-placement calculus, so I took it. Wrong decision. They did fire me.

CJ: So what were the circumstances of your getting fired?

Sophie: Oh, they call you in and say that the FBI has been to visit and they say that you have a record as a Communist and you signed the loyalty oath. That was a law in New York State. If you had been a member of the Communist Party, you had falsely signed the loyalty oath.

CJ: How often did you get bounced?

Sophie: I got bounced twice. And then I ended up in a private school, because a private school didn't have to abide by the New York State requirement.

CJ: So neither of you were ever charged and had to hire lawyers and counter allegations?

Dave: Well, the Veterans of the Spanish Civil War as a whole had a big deal with the House Un-American Activities Committee. They wanted to put us on the list of subversive organizations. What happened was that the whole executive committee resigned and left only two guys in charge. And we got some very good lawyers. Still, we ended up being named a subversive organization. We appealed and were in court for a number of years and some kind of ruling came down, leaving it up to the attorney general to do something about. The attorney general looked at it and let it lay. He recognized that his case was lost.

Sophie: The case went on for three years.

Dave: We went down to Washington and had demonstrations there. And the guys didn't take any crap from them. Some guys were called before the HUAC and took the Fifth Amendment. And we also had some guys testifying down there. They did a good job. They said, "I'm a vet." And we did this and we did that.

Sophie: The average person was not called before the House Un-American Activities Committee. Mostly the ones they called were those who were known nationally. The average person was just fired.

CJ: Did either of you have any experience with naming names?

Dave: Well, yeah.

CJ: What did that involve?

Dave: You walk out of your house and you're walking down the street and suddenly there are two guys right beside you. "Hi, Dave." Nice, good-looking men—young guys. "You could help the country a lot. In fact, we'd be willing to offer you as much as, well, twenty-five thousand dollars! Who do you think's going to be on the next central committee?" (laughter) And then the other guy would become tough—a pair, you know. And I'm walking down to the subway or something. And I say, "Okay, what are you guys doing around here? I want to make a living. You're wasting your time." Two or three weeks later, I'm walking up the street: "Hello, Dave."

CJ: There they are again, huh?

Dave: Two different ones. "We've got a car up here. You want to come and sit down and have a little chat with us?" I said, "What have you got—a microphone in the car?" I talked to them a little bit, just chatting. Some of the guys had a policy of just cutting them off short. But I wanted to find out what the hell they were up to. Three times they came up to me.

CJ: So naming names to help yourself was a live issue.

Dave: Oh, yeah, this movie director, Kazan. How pathetic.

CJ: What about you, Sophie? Were you ever asked to name names?

Sophie: Not exactly in the same way. They tried to visit me at home to find out things. But I refused to talk to them. Mainly, it wasn't a case of meeting them on the street; it was that my children were home. So I never admitted them and never made an appointment to speak with them.

CJ: So they did approach you?

Sophie: Yes, I was approached by the FBI.

Dave: One time I got a call: a Treasury Department official wanted to see me. I didn't know whether to see him or what—so I saw him. Well, they had something to do with immigration, and some of the guys had come here from other countries, and gotten citizenship and the government was trying to deport them. I said, "What do you want me for?" They said, "We want you to testify—help us." I said, "I don't even know the guy." "Well, you could," they said, "you could." I said, "You got the wrong guy. Are you going to offer me $25,000, too?" (laughter)

Sophie: And then there was the FBI list of dangerous subversives, published as *Red Channels*. Actually, *I* was listed in *Red Channels*. An important person! (laughter) Under my party name of Sophie Stern.

You know the Party in my experience—anybody could join the Party. You weren't required to do a presentation and nobody checked up on you. You just joined. In terms of the average member. There were thousands who went through the Party who were members for a few months, a few years, and left. Now to be a state or national leader in the Par, presumably you had to be tested to some degree at least. But it wasn't hard for the FBI to infiltrate the Party or even to pass some kind of test to become leaders in the Party. So it is not surprising that there were lots of informers because the Communist Party was not a secret organization.

CJ: So, Sophie, you never felt any panic either?

Sophie: Oh, not really. I guess I was pretty lucky. I had parents who had enough of a background in revolutionary thinking to accept our kind of life. And I never was hungry. I may have had a lot of hand-me-down clothes, but outside of that I had everything I needed. I had the education. And I had a whole group of friends. And I had Dave. I was luckier than Dave because Dave had a hard time with his parents at first. But they accepted it afterwards. In general, essentially I was cushioned. I could see it as much more of a problem for the young women whom I lived with. And I tried to be of help. I could draw them in when their husbands were away and they had problems. But no, we didn't panic. Not in that sense.

Dave: We were lucky.

Sophie: We only worried about our children. And the effect on them. I mentioned our friends. Our friends took care of the kids lots of times when we were busy with political activity. We worked in the neighborhood, so we had a whole corps of people who were around us—women like ourselves, children—you didn't feel isolated. And if you don't feel isolated, you don't panic as easily.

Dave: Although some people didn't speak to us during these times. Some of the guys I worked with. I would bump into them on the street. Some of them would greet me and say we miss you. Others would take off and didn't want to even talk to me.

Sophie: Well, it was kind of the other way around when we left the Party, Party members wouldn't speak to us. (laughter)

CJ: Did either of you ever feel that there was a danger of going to prison?

Dave and Sophie: Yeah. Yes.

Dave: One time we discussed about our kids—who would take care of our kids if both of us ended up in prison. And one time we talked to some friends about it. And I had two brothers and a sister who were sympathetic. But we didn't panic or anything. We just talked about it for a couple of days and then we laughed about it all.

CJ: In your experience, were there valid parallels—like Arthur Miller draws in *The Crucible*—between the Salem witch-hunts and the witch-hunts of the 1950s?

Sophie: There certainly were parallels: the ignorance of people, the readiness to accept falsehood, the ease with which the stories spread and were accepted. And the panic. People did panic.

Dave: There's no question that we made some mistakes in our lives, but the real regret I have is that we didn't spend enough time with our kids. Jeez, we spent our time at meetings and so on, and I look at our daughters and the way that they handle their kids and we talk about it sometimes at night—there's a real family there, you know? But when I talk to our daughters, they admire the way we lived our lives. Because we used to take them to May Day parades, picnics, etc., and they remember that! These big, big parades, Sophie pushing this little carriage along. These are their memories. But when I think back, from my own point of view, I wish I had known a lot more about handling kids. When I see how these younger people handle their kids, I realize what we missed the most back then.

But we made a contribution. There's no question about that. Take the CIO and how the Party helped in that situation. Back then John L. Lewis broke away from the AFL [American Federation of Labor].

Some of our leaders of the Party—especially William Z. Foster—was a key labor organizer in the 20s. This was after Debs.

Sophie: You don't regret the immediate things you did. And I think that it's interesting that wherever we worked, we had the same sort of response. Dave has *always* been respected by the people he worked with. He was an important figure to them. And I know he was quite liked. And I had the same kind of experience. People respected me and felt that I was a good person even though I was a Communist. Of course, a few may not have known, but most of them knew that I was active. Still, they had the utmost respect for us. Partly because what we did was good and partly the work we did. Dave was a good machinist. I was a good teacher. Whatever we did, we threw ourselves into it. I don't like to say I have regrets. There's no use saying, "I was a damned fool." And there are people who say that and turned bitterly against the Party. I mean bitterly to the point that they have nothing but animosity toward the Party and the whole situation. That's not true of us. At least it's not true of me, and I'm pretty sure it's not true of Dave. We have a lot of respect for who we were and a lot of pride in what we did.

PROJECTS FOR ORAL OR WRITTEN EXPLORATION

1. By reviewing the documents presented here, make a study of the things that could bring one under suspicion in the 1950s witch-hunts.

2. Write a paper on the topic of guilt by association using *The Crucible* and materials in this chapter.

3. How does guilt by association (in an unofficial way, not necessarily a legal way) operate in your own world?

4. Have a class discussion on the topic of guilt by association in your own sphere. To what extent is "association" a valid matter of concern for parents and others? Should one's associates be valid legal evidence? Why or why not?

5. An earlier exercise asked you to research "rules of evidence" and apply them to the Salem witchcraft trials. Do the same thing for the hearings in the "Red Scare" years; then compare the tactics used in both 1692 and the 1950s.

6. Write a research paper on the case of Alger Hiss, former State Department employee accused of spying, looking carefully at all the arguments you can find as to his guilt or innocence.

7. Write a research paper on the Hollywood writers and performers who were blacklisted by the movie industry.

8. Secure one of the films written by one of the Hollywood blacklisted writers and analyze it. Does it appear to represent reality well, or does it distort reality? Who might be angered by the movie? Suggestions for films: *Ruthless* (Alvah Bessie, 1948), *Backdoor to Heaven* (William K. Howard, 1939), *The Sound of Fury* (Joe Pagano, 1951), and *Watch on the Rhine* (Lillian Hellman, 1943). Do some research on the film you choose and its writer.

9. Read Arthur Miller's *Death of a Salesman*. Speculate about why many people found this play politically objectionable in the 1950s atmosphere.

10. Choose one of the following subjects for a research paper: the Korean conflict, the Spanish Civil War, China's Cultural Revolution, Roosevelt's New Deal, or labor unions in the 1940s.

11. Secure videotapes of some of the McCarthy hearings and write an analysis of what you see.

12. Read Arthur Miller's *After the Fall*. Write an analysis of the political issues in the play. Compare pertinent aspects of the play with *The Crucible*.

13. Write a paper on the "reversals" in public opinion that occurred after the Salem witchcraft trials and the McCarthy years in the 1950s.

14. Find a list of standard logical fallacies. How many of these fallacies were in operation in the hearings documented in this chapter? Explain.

15. Review the general introduction to this chapter to note major historical events that are pertinent to the topic of the chapter. Then create an oral history with someone who experienced some event linked to the background of the Red Scare of the 1950s. Your most likely sources will be retired persons, and the most easily accessible event will likely be one related to the labor movement, but do not rule out other possibilities.

SUGGESTED READINGS

Allen, Woody. *The Front*. Columbia Pictures, 1976.

Brown, Ralph S., Jr. *Loyalty and Security: Employment Tests in the United States*. New Haven: Yale University Press, 1958.

Fariello, Griffin. *Red Scare*. New York: Avon Books, 1995.

Fried, Richard M. *Nightmare in Red*. New York: Oxford University Press, 1990.

Kutler, Stanley I. *The American Inquisition: Justice and Injustice in the Cold War*. New York: Hill and Wang, 1982.

McWilliams, Carey. *Witch Hunt: The Revival of Heresy*. Boston: Little, Brown, 1950.

Navasky, Victor S. *Naming Names*. New York: Viking, 1980.

Radosh, Ronald. *American Labor and United States Foreign Policy: The Cold War in the Unions from Gompers to Lovestone*. New York: Random House, 1969.

Trumbo, Dalton. *The Time of the Toad*. New York: Harper and Row, 1972.

5

1990s Witch-Hunts

Many issues raised by *The Crucible* are very much alive in the 1990s:

1. The problem of the destitute and homeless, especially those with mental illness. In 1692, these were the first targets of the children—old women whose eccentricities were frightening and who were too confused to realize the seriousness of the charges against them, too confused to answer the judges' questions, and so weak minded that they were easily led to confess and name others as witches. In the 1990s, these same types wander the streets of our towns, frightening passersby with their aberrant mannerisms, filthy attire, and muttered obscenities and annoying everyone with their sometimes aggressive begging. The question about how to treat the insane persist: Should those whose behavior is eccentric, even frightening, though clearly not dangerous to themselves and others, be locked up? Should the insane who commit crimes be punished in the same manner as the sane?

2. The seduction of a young person by a much older (and frequently more powerful) person, as in the case of John Proctor and Abby Williams, is as old as time, but has only more recently been exposed as serious misconduct, not to be ignored or laughed at. The peculiarities of the academic situation, in particular, give rise to young, awe-stricken, impressionable students allowing them-

selves to be drawn into affairs with older professors who use their authoritative positions to take sexual advantage of those over whom they have influence. This has been the subject of many an academic novel (see especially *Professor Romeo* by Anne Bernays). Seduction has also been a frequent matter for the courts of the land in spheres other than the academic. In the daily news in the spring of 1997, to cite one example, a young politician from a powerful New England family was being investigated by a state prosecuting attorney on the grounds that he had allegedly had an affair with his children's fourteen-year-old baby-sitter.

3. The validity of the legal system, which came into question in both 1692 and 1952, arises again in the 1990s. To what extent are money and position able to buy leniency from a legal system that much more readily convicts the poor? The public began questioning the way the legal system was influenced by money and race in a 1990s trial for murder of a wealthy and famous athlete. As in 1692, so in the 1990s, it is charged, injustices in the courts only seem to come into question when someone with influence and money gets caught in the machinery. As so often in Salem when socially respectable people were able to escape when charged, so in the 1990s, one reads statistics about which criminals end up serving jail time and being executed: they are, not surprisingly, the very poor without the means to hire expensive legal assistance.

4. Political and monetary ambitions continue to influence "investigations" of public figures as in 1692, when one local political faction led by Thomas Putnam and Samuel Parris set out to put its rivals in their place, and as Republicans in the 1940s and 1950s set out to put the New Deal Democrats in their place. In the 1990s, investigations into wrongdoing by a Republican Speaker of the House and into dealings by a Democratic president seem more than a little motivated by politics.

5. Fear and hysteria based on natural events perceived as irrational or supernatural phenomena are seen even in the last decade of the twentieth century. In 1692, the hysteria came from attributing the sickness of children and the death of animals to witchcraft. In 1996 and 1997, various misfortunes and even visions of the end of the world were confirmed in the minds of many people by the appearance of the Hale-Bopp comet. A sizeable portion of one cult even committed suicide as a result.

HYSTERIA AND WITCH-HUNTS

By far the most persistent and frightening issue suggested by *The Crucible* in the 1990s is the mass hysteria or community terror that gives rise to modern-day witch hunts. Sometimes the differences between hunter and hunted are dramatically clear, as when people of one color hunt down and persecute those of another color. More often, distinctions between hunter and hunted are less dramatic, as when those of one religion or culture or tribe or clan are driven by hysteria to hunt down those unlike themselves, whether it be Catholics and Protestants hunting down one another in Northern Ireland or the Hutus and Tutsis hunting down one another in Africa. A graphic example is Nazi witch-hunts of Jews during World War II.

Witch-hunts also still occur on smaller, more local scales, as they did in Salem. A striking example of what has been called a witch-hunt in the late twentieth century involves charges of mass child abuse on the part of churches and schools, especially day-care centers.

It is indisputable that child abuse is a wide-ranging problem of the most serious magnitude, but demonstrable cases of abuse are clearly distinguishable from instances of mass hysteria arising from dubious cases and spurious charges. Such cases developed with alarming frequency in the 1980s and early 1990s as the day-care system was beginning to burgeon, as sexual abuse in general was coming out of the closet, and before social services had the common sense and expertise to deal with the testimony of children. Several horrendous cases developed from the mental instability of the accusers (like Salem's Ann Putnam) and/or from a desire for vengeance (like Thomas Putnam and Samuel Parris) by those who used children to mount grossly unjust witch-hunts in which innocent people were charged with mass sexual abuse of children.

In every one of these cases, there was an initial determination of guilt on the part of the courts, but later expert testimony has brought all of these convictions into serious question, raising doubts that have reversed many guilty decisions. In other cases, guilty decisions are now seriously challenged. While the public tends to assume with the courts that a jury verdict of guilty implies wrongdoing on the part of the accused, revelations since the early

1990s lead one to question the verdicts in these peculiar cases, much as the citizens of New England began slowly to question the court verdicts in the witchcraft cases.

Guilty verdicts in these cases have been called into question for several reasons. In 1995, expert studies began to come to light regarding the suggestibility of children as witnesses, especially in the hands of poorly trained police interrogators. Children, it is argued, are easily led into fantasies by adults, just as they had been in Salem. One of the first studies to issue a warning about the testimony of tiny children in such cases was Angela Dunn's "Questioning the Reliability of Children's Testimony" (*Law and Psychology Review* 19 [Spring 1995]: 203–215). Many other studies in the same vein have followed. The validity of a child's testimony, Dunn writes, is seriously damaged by suggestive questioning, by repeated interviews, and by lapses of several months, even years, between the so-called abuse and the child's testimony.

The McMartin Case

One of the first cases to receive national attention was the McMartin Preschool case in Manhattan Beach, California. The trial, which lasted for over two years, was the longest and costliest criminal prosecution in the history of the United States at the time. McMartin Preschool had been in operation for twenty years when in 1983 a mother reported to police that her two-and-one-half-year-old boy had indicated that he had been sexually abused by the one male worker in the preschool, the son of the owner. Although the man, Ray McMartin, was arrested, he was released for lack of evidence. Yet at the persistence of the accusing mother, the police sent out two hundred letters to parents of students and former students who, after very suggestive interviews, also charged the McMartins with sexual abuse, including having taken part in satanic rites, mutilating animals, and forcing children to touch corpses, all of which purportedly took place in secret passageways. No evidence was ever presented, and no secret rooms were ever discovered. Although none of those charged were ever convicted, Ray McMartin spent five years in jail awaiting trial, and Peggy McMartin, the owner, spent two years in jail awaiting trial.

The Amirault Case

Another case came to light in 1986 in the Fells Acres Day School that Violet Amirault had been running in Malden, Massachusetts, for close to twenty years. She employed her son Gerald as a bus driver, her daughter Cheryl, and five other teachers. In 1984, after Gerald had helped a little boy who had wet his pants, the boy apparently told his family that Gerald had touched his penis and that all manner of sexual abuse had taken place in a secret room. In following up, the police instructed all other parents to quiz their children about irregularities that might have taken place in a secret room. More and more children came forward with stories about sexual abuse involving robots, rape by clowns, ritual slaughter of animals, penetration by knives, and pornographic filming. The physical evidence presented at trial would not be considered sufficient today for a conviction since the "proofs" of abuse on the children's bodies were invariably attributable to poor hygiene, and no secret rooms or films of any kind were located. Nevertheless, Violet Amirault and her daughter were found guilty and sentenced to from eight to twenty years in prison, and Gerald Amirault was sentenced to a maximum of forty years in prison. The three served eight years in prison before the court ordered the two women to be released on bail in 1997 for a new trial. Gerald Amirault remains in prison.

Wee Care Nursery School

In 1988, a young female employee of the Wee Care Nursery in Maplewood, New Jersey, was charged with sexual abuse of a four-year-old boy who casually mentioned that his teacher took his temperature rectally. As the charges of abuse spread, the children were examined by being asked leading questions, along with promises of gifts and candy if they told stories of abuse. Some of the children claimed that she had turned them momentarily into mice. The employee was found guilty and sentenced to forty-seven years in prison. After five years she was released on bail, her conviction was overturned, and charges against her were dropped. However, litigation goes on as parents of some of the children launched suits against the employee and she herself filed a $10-million suit against the state and county for malicious prosecution.

The Little Rascals Day Care Center

The most meticulously documented case of a modern-day witch-hunt is the Little Rascals Day Care case, which began in Edenton, North Carolina, in September 1988. The Little Rascals Day Care facility, by reputation the most respectable day-care center in Edenton, was owned and run by Betsy Kelly and her husband Bob Kelly, who employed several workers. The trouble began in September when Jane Mabry, the mother of a child in the center and a woman who had regarded the center's owner, Betsy Kelly, as one of her best friends, became hysterical over her son's complaint that Betsy's husband, Bob, had slapped him. Looking back, Jane said of her son's complaint, "My world just crumbled. . . . I just knew that life as I knew it would never be the same" ("Summary," *Innocence Lost*, on *Frontline*, www.pbs.org., 3).

Bob explained that the slap was an accident, and both Kellys apologized to Jane Mabry. However, believing that they were not sufficiently contrite, she became even more incensed, especially when the Kellys failed to react to her decision to withdraw her son from their day-care center. She continued to pursue the matter, calling other parents to probe what she was convinced was physical abuse. One of these parents was Audrey Stever, who decided to speak with a policewoman, Brenda Toppin, who had just completed a seminar on child sexual abuse. Between Audrey Stever's constant conversations with Jane Mabry and her contact with Brenda Toppin, who obviously had sexual abuse on her mind after the seminar, physical abuse became an issue of sexual abuse, and Audrey Stever filed the first complaint.

In January 1989, when Bob Kelly was informed that a complaint had been lodged against him, he met each parent at the door of the day-care center to inform them of what had happened. Most of the parents at this time thought that the suggestion of child abuse was outrageous, and they defended the Kellys. The children themselves denied any sexual abuse at first.

The case began to escalate, however, after three or four therapists with inadequate and poor training, as well as what many believed were ulterior motives, became involved. They examined the children by suggesting to them ways in which they might have been abused, using "anatomically correct" dolls. The first small group of children began reporting that others had been molested, and then the parents of the newly involved children took them to the same therapists and became convinced that the Kellys had molested *their* children. Another parent was convinced, after her own intense investigation, that the children were not abused. She described her own child's treatment by the therapists. They asked if he knew what sex meant, for example, and he said that it meant you stayed within the lines when you colored. They also asked him if he had ever played "doctor," getting very excited when he said, "yes," only to learn that he meant that Bob Kelly had put a bandage on a scrape he had gotten on the playground. This parent also reported that children were told that they would not get dessert unless they told about sexual abuse, and described how the therapists would ask leading questions, such as "Did he ever touch you on your bottom?" This same mother claimed that her son could not remember who had worked with him when he was so little at the day-care center, but that when the therapists wrote up their reports, they indicated that he had identified all the workers. Furthermore, she said, her son had testified that the sheriff had molested him, and said that "Mr. Bob" was a good man.

By April 1989, when Bob Kelly was actually arrested, the number of children who had been taken to therapists and claimed that they had been molested reached ninety. Both sides of the case testified that the entire town was completely obsessed by the charges, with parents on the telephone or meeting with one another for much of the day, with parents and therapists continually quizzing children and examining their every action and word, with constant communication between lawyers and police, and with additional "molested" children and additional charges surfacing. It was the only topic of conversation, waged at a fever-high pitch of shrieking hysteria.

In September 1989, Betsy Kelly was also arrested and sent to prison to await trial. Following her arrest, three other women who taught at the center were arrested. There were also two inexplicable arrests made on the strength of children's accusations of people who had no direct connection with the center. Betsy's bail was

so high ($1.5 million) that she remained in jail for two years await-
ing trial until her bond was reduced. Scott Privott, the Kellys'
friend, was in jail for three and a half years waiting to go on trial.

Bob Kelly's trial went on for eight months, with twelve children
testifying. Despite the evidence that no children had complained
until Jane Mabry began her investigation and the therapists became
involved and despite the fact that there was no physical evidence
of abuse and no eyewitnesses of abuse, Kelly was found guilty on
ninety-nine counts and sentenced to twelve consecutive life terms
in prison.

Part of the testimony included statements from Brenda Toppin,
the policewoman who had taken a seminar on sexual abuse and
had first interviewed the children, that she had not kept notes of
the interviews and that she had lost or misplaced every single tape
of every interview with every child. Children testified that they had
been taken up in spaceships, that they had seen babies killed rit-
ualistically, hamsters skinned, and sharks circling them in salt-
water ponds, that they had been choked in a boat, that one of the
women had put a tractor toy "in his butt," that Bob had cut their
necks and licked the blood, that Bob had broken into their houses
and threatened to break their toys, and that children had been
thrown into the ocean. All this supposedly occurred in a facility
where parents and tradesmen were constantly going in and out at
all hours of the day. One of the children testifying had been one
and a half years old when the abuses, described by his brother,
had taken place.

One female worker was sentenced to life in prison. As a result
of seeing the outcome of two previous cases, Betsy Kelly pleaded
"no contest," while still maintaining her innocence. She was sentenced to one more year in prison and then was released on probation.

At the end of 1995, Bob Kelly's conviction and that of a female
teacher were overturned by the appellate court of North Carolina.
Both were released. Charges were dropped against three other
workers, and Scott Privott, like Betsy Kelly, took a no-contest plea
and was released after three years in jail.

In April 1996, the state brought a new charge of abuse against
Bob Kelly—one that had allegedly taken place nearly ten years
earlier, in 1987, and was unrelated to the Little Rascals case. On
May 23, 1997, all charges were dropped against the accused re-

garding the Little Rascals case. However, the new charge against Bob Kelly remained, and the state made clear its intention to proceed against him on the new charge.

PARALLELS

The comparisons between the witchcraft trials in Salem and these cases of alleged mass child abuse are impressive.

- Both involved children as accusers.
- Convictions were determined almost solely on the basis of the children's testimony.
- Everything escalated rapidly—the number of children involved, the number of the accused, and the different kinds of charges.
- The minds of the children were in both cases manipulated by adults.
- Charges were instigated by adults who held grudges against the accused.
- There was an absence of corroborating evidence.
- "Fanciful" testimony was regarded seriously. In Salem, it was spectral evidence. In the twentieth-century cases, it included children's stories of spaceships, sharks, and ritual murder.
- Community hysteria arose from the feeling that evil—witches and sex abusers—had access to their children.
- "Poppets" or dolls were involved. In the Salem trials, little dolls were immediately seized upon as poppets used by witches to pierce with pins with the object of inflicting torture. In sexual abuse cases, "anatomically correct" dolls were used by psychologists to coach details from the children.
- There were charges that satanic rituals were conducted.
- The prosecution showed a single-minded determination, by threat or bribe, to get the accused to confess.
- The prosecution showed a single-minded determination, by threat or bribe, to get children to disclose more and more details of misconduct without regard to truth.

DOCUMENTS

The following documents are from transcripts of the Edenton trials. First is the testimony of Officer Toppin, the woman who first examined the children. There are also excerpts from interviews with two of the mothers of children who attended the day-care facility, several bits of testimony from children, and excerpts from the closing arguments of the defense. The final document is an editorial from the *Wall Street Journal* written by Dorothy Rabinowitz, who had for years been investigating charges of mass sexual abuse of children in nursery schools.

OFFICER TOPPIN'S TESTIMONY

As was made clear repeatedly upon testimony by experts, the very first reports of the children were the ones that would be most critical in determining whether sexual abuse had indeed occurred. Yet in the first interviews, the children said almost nothing of any interest with regard to sexual abuse, and the police officer who conducted these hearings destroyed all of her notes and all of her tapes of what happened before the case went to court. She was approached by several of the mothers initially because she had taken a short course in investigating cases of child abuse. Officer Toppin was crucial to the whole process because she was the one who escalated the case from a minor complaint by one parent into a case of massive sexual abuse of dozens of children by scores of day-care workers.

The prosecution argued that the child's willingness to point to the anatomical parts of the doll rather than to verbalize sexual abuse merely showed that he had been too traumatized to speak about something that he could express with the use of the doll. The defense argued that Officer Toppin had led the child—had planted the suggestion of child abuse with repeated, suggestive questions. Certainly, psychologist Angela Dunn would say that Toppin's suggestive questioning, her long and repeated sessions with the children, and the years that intervened between the testimony and the supposed abuse would severely taint what the child had to say.

FROM OFFICER TOPPIN'S TESTIMONY
(Edenton, N.C.: Court Trial Transcript, 1989)

[Toppin is asked about the accusation of a three-year-old boy whom she had examined]

Defense Attorney: When you said to him, "How do you play doctor? I don't know how to play," what was his response?

Officer Brenda Toppin: He just—he would just sort of—he sat there, sort of just kind of went down in a little ball, like, and just—not actually a ball, but just sort of withdrew and wouldn't say anything.

Defense Attorney: He did not say anything.

Officer Toppin: Would not say anything.

Defense Attorney: When he didn't say anything, did you pursue that any further?

Officer Toppin: Just asked him if—if he—if we were to let him use our special dolls or special tools—I don't know which terminology I used—that could he show us how he played doctor.

Defense Attorney: So after the one question and the one failure to respond, you went to the dolls?

Officer Toppin: No, it was not after one question and one failure to respond. There was quite a length of time there that we just sat there. He would not respond at all.

Defense Attorney: Okay. So after he failed to respond, you both sat there. There were no further questions?

Officer Toppin: It was very obvious that he was—he was not going to be able to tell us, but maybe he would be able to show us.

Defense Attorney: So you assumed, at that point, that there was something he could tell you further and he just wasn't able to do it. It wasn't a question of a lack of knowledge on his part?

Officer Toppin: It was—in the look on Kyle's face, and because I knew him, there was—he couldn't tell us how to play doctor, however the way was. So we asked him if he could show us on the dolls and—

Defense Attorney: And he pulled on the doll's penis?

Officer Toppin: That's correct.

Defense Attorney: What else did he do with the doll?

Officer Toppin: He had pulled the pants down of the doll.

Defense Attorney: Now, it's my understanding from your testimony that before you began using the dolls, you could not get him to say anything.

Officer Toppin: That's correct.

Defense Attorney: You could not get him to describe anything.

Officer Toppin: That's correct.

• • •

Defense Attorney: Do you keep your original notes?

Officer Toppin: Not as a usual rule, no, sir.

Defense Attorney: Have you destroyed the notes you used to prepare the reports in this case?

Officer Toppin: I have kept everything since I had gotten the order to keep everything, but before that I did not.

Defense Attorney: So all of the notes that you made during the period of time you were actually interviewing the children for the first time are now gone?

Officer Toppin: Yes, sir.

Defense Attorney: When did you destroy them?

Officer Toppin: As these were typed.

Defense Attorney: And do you know approximately when that was?

Officer Toppin: Shortly after the interviews.

Defense Attorney: Is that your standard practice, to destroy your notes—

Officer Toppin: Yes, sir.

Defense Attorney: As you go along?

Officer Toppin: After I type them, yes.

Defense Attorney: And do you do that in every case?

Officer Toppin: Yes, sir.

Defense Attorney: And is that something you were taught in your law enforcement training, to destroy your notes as you had typewritten reports prepared?

Officer Toppin: I don't believe that was covered.

Defense Attorney: Pardon?

Officer Toppin: I don't believe that was covered.

• • •

Officer Toppin: So I just destroyed—it's just a lot of extra paper, so I just destroy those.

Defense Attorney: I just have not been involved in any type of a criminal case where what is basically crucial evidence was simply discarded. Anyone that knows anything about this field will tell you that the first contact with the children, the initial interviews with the children, are the most critical. How they were conducted, what the individual conducting the interview said, what they asked, how the children responded are the most critical things in these cases and they were just gone forever. There was no effort to either create them or preserve them at all.

• • •

Officer Toppin: Sometimes the children when I was talking with them, they would just come right out and just say it. I didn't even have to ask a question.

Defense Attorney: Is that what happened on this occasion?

Officer Toppin: I cannot tell you exactly if that's what happened. I know that has happened.

Defense Attorney: But you do not know, on this occasion, whether that's what happened or whether you asked some question or made some remark to Laurie?

Officer Toppin: I feel like that's what happened on this occasion.

Defense Attorney: Do you know that?

Officer Toppin: I can just tell you my recollection.

)

DEBBIE FORREST'S INTERVIEW

Debbie Forrest was one of the few parents who doubted the children's charges of sexual abuse at the day-care center. She revealed the extent to which Officer Toppin mishandled the children, making suggestive remarks to them and misrepresenting what had actually happened during her examination in order to support charges of sexual abuse.

FROM INTERVIEW WITH DEBBIE FORREST
(Edenton, N.C.: Aired by PBS, 1997)

Debbie Forrest: [speaking of her son, Frankie] They asked him if he understood the dolls and the various parts of the anatomy and that these were just like little boys and girls, and he said that was disgusting. They asked him if he knew what the word "sex" meant and he said he wasn't stupid, that it meant you colored and you stayed in the lines. They asked if they watched movies or did anybody take pictures and he said yeah, they got to bring movies from home, and they had movie day, and he had his picture taken for school. But they constantly asked him the same thing over and over again and they would rephrase it. And he's very outspoken and very blunt sometimes and he just continually told them he—you know, he already answered that question. They asked him a lot of things about, you know, taking your clothes on, taking your clothes off. They—they asked him about had anybody ever played doctor and did they play doctor. And he got excited and said yes, you know, Mr. Bob is the doctor, and they got real interested in that and asked him again and again about it. And he finally told them that when they got hurt on the playground, he went and got the first aid kit and brought them out Flintstone Band-Aids and G.I. Joe Band-Aids. They talked to him—it had to be an hour and a half or so before we interrupted and they wanted to continue to talk to him. I guess the same questions were asked five or six times.   (18)

INTERVIEW WITH BETTY PHILLIPS

Betty Phillips, one of the parents whose children had attended the day-care center and who had worked there herself taking care of the babies, at first listened carefully to what the other mothers were saying and doing about the charges of sexual abuse. She even took her child to be examined by Brenda Toppin, the police-woman who had had a course in investigating child abuse. But she very soon became skeptical of what was happening and took her child to a Duke University psychologist for examination. In the opinion of the Duke specialist, her child had not been abused. In the following interview, Betty Phillips makes plain that the children were being led by Officer Toppin, their parents, and court-appointed therapists and that their reports misrepresented the truth.

FROM INTERVIEW WITH BETTY ANN PHILLIPS
(Edenton, N.C.: Aired by PBS, 1997)

Mrs. Phillips: [about her son's interview with the police] He said absolutely nothing to Brenda [Officer Toppin]. He wanted to play when
she was there talking to him. He was just running around. It was,
you know, something that he just didn't want to sit there and talk
to her about. So finally I asked her, I said, "In your opinion, has my
child been sexually abused?" And she said, "I can't tell you this on
the record," she said, "but off the record, yes, he has," and she told
me to expect the worst because there was a lot more to come. I
asked her would charges be brought and she said she was going to
bring this tape to H. P. [the district attorney] and let H. P. listen to
it and then H. P. would decide. Well, there was nothing on the tape,
because Daniel hadn't said anything.

• • •

[Mrs. Phillips, speaking of how other mothers elicited accusations from
their children]

Mrs. Phillips: The parents refused to give the child her dessert unless she
told her. When the child had told her for three weeks that this per-

son did nothing to her, then the parent refused to give the child her dessert, "unless you tell me that this person did something to you." . . . Do anything for your dessert!

• • •

Mrs. Phillips: [about her son's reaction when showed a picture of the accused a year later just before the trial] They had these little pictures of them in the paper. . . . So I said, "Daniel," I said, "You know, you know who those people are," "No, I don't, I don't know who they are." . . . Well, he didn't know who they were. He was getting them all mixed up. I mean, this had been a year, you know. He didn't remember what they looked like really. But when she [the therapist] wrote up her therapy report for him, he had gotten every one of them right the first time and she hadn't had to tell him who they were. . . . I said, "My child is confused. I have confused him." And Judy kept on saying, "No, he's not confused." And H. P. and Brenda would say, "No, he's not confused. He knows what he's talking about. You're the one that's confused." So I said, "Well, then we need to investigate the sheriff," I said, "because he has pinpointed the sheriff as being upstairs when this was happening, too." (18–23)

CROSS-EXAMINATION OF SUSIE, ONE OF THE CHILDREN

The testimony of Susie, one of the children making charges of sexual abuse, reveals just how suspect any of the children's stories were. Remember that most of the children were between two and one-half and three and one-half years old when they first left the school with charges of sexual abuse. Susie had told the court-appointed but minimally trained therapists (who admitted having asked leading questions repeatedly in a thoroughly unprofessional way) that she had seen the owners of the day-care center kill babies in outer space. Susie changes her testimony several times during Spivey's cross-examination, confused about just what she was supposed to say and just what the truth was. Her testimony at first is that she saw day-care helpers beat babies until they bled from their eyes. Then she claims that the owners shot the babies in open daylight out on the playground, eventually admitting that she had told the therapist that all the baby killing occurred in outer space.

FROM CROSS-EXAMINATION OF SUSIE BY MR. SPIVEY FOR THE
DEFENSE
(Edenton, N.C.: Court Trial Transcript, 1990)

Q: Okay. Now did you remember Ms. Betty Ann, Ms. Betty Ann Phillips?

A: Yes.

Q: Okay. And she worked in the baby room, too, right?

A: Yes.

Q: What did she do to the babies?

A: I can't remember.

Q: Did you, ah—did you tell Ms. Judy that Ms. Betty hurt four of the babies, that she beat them until blood came out of their eyes?

A: Yes.

• • •

Q: Now, did you tell Ms. Judy that she beat their knees and toes and legs, too?

A: Yes.

Q: And that they were bleeding from their knees and toes and legs?

A: Yes.

• • •

Q: Okay. Susie, do you remember seeing anybody kill any of the babies at the day care?

A: No.

Q: Well, now, you told Ms. Judy that they killed babies at the day care, didn't you?

A: Yes.

Q: Okay. And where did that happen that you saw babies killed?

A: I can't remember.

Q: Okay. Who killed the babies?

A: Sometimes Ms. Betsy or Mr. Bob.

Q: And how did they kill them?

A: With a gun.

Q: Okay. Did they shoot them?

A: Yes.

Q: Did you really see the babies shot?

A: Sometimes.

Q: Sometimes you did?

A: Yes.

Q: When you really saw it, where did that happen?

A: Outside.

• • •

Q: Okay. And were you outside when the babies were shot?

A: Yes, we were playing on the playground.

• • •

Q: Did they really kill real babies?

A: Sometimes.

Q: Sometimes. Well, now when you talked to Ms. Judy you didn't tell her that happened at the day care, did you?

A: No.

Q: You told Ms. Judy it happened in outerspace, didn't you? Susie, isn't that what you told Ms. Judy that Mr. Bob and Ms. Betsy killed the babies in outerspace?

A: Yes.

Q: And you told her that you went to outerspace with Mr. Bob and Mrs. Betsy in a hot air balloon, right?

A: Yes.

Q: Did you really do that?

A: It was a spaceship.

Q: Okay. It wasn't a balloon; you went in a spaceship?

A: Yes.

CROSS-EXAMINATION OF JAIMIE, ONE OF THE CHILDREN

Jaimie, one of the primary children who lodged stories of sexual abuse, was about three at the time that he made or was led to make the charges. He was four at the time he testified. Jaimie made the extraordinary claim that Mr. Bob put a six-inch knife in his rectum, but that it just hurt a "little bit," not enough to make him cry. He also testified that Mr. Bob forced him to eat feces at night after all the children had gone home and that he told his parents about both occurrences at the time that they happened.

While most members of the jury interpreted Jaimie's story as true, one has to ask: could a child be forced to eat feces, immediately tell his parents what had happened (as he said he did), and yet exhibit no tell-tale odor or other suspicious physical evidence that would lead them to an immediate investigation? The likelihood of a child's being raped with a six-inch knife without drawing his parents' attention to serious physical damage is remote, to say the least, especially in light of the child's claim that he immediately told his parents about both events.

FROM CROSS-EXAMINATION OF JAIMIE BY MR. SPIVEY FOR THE
DEFENSE
(Edenton, N.C.: Court Trial Transcript, 1990)

Q: Okay. Tell me about [Mr. Bob] sticking a knife in your butt?

A: Well, he just stuck the knife in my butt and that's all.

Q: Okay. What kind of a knife was it?

A: A play knife.

Q: Okay. Do you know how big it was? Can you show me with your hands?

A: (Indicating), about that big.

Mr. Hart: Let the record reflect, Your Honor, that he's indicating a distance of about six inches.

• • •

Q: When Mr. Bob stuck the knife in your butt did it hurt?

A: Yes.

Q: Okay. Did you cry?

A: No.

Q: Okay. Why didn't you cry?

A: Because it didn't hurt that bad, it hurt a little bit.

• • •

Q: Jaimie, do you remember telling your mom that Mr. Bob made you eat poopie at the day care?

A: No.

Q: Okay. Did that ever happen?

A: Yes.

Q: Tell me about that.

A: Well, someone used the bathroom and didn't flush the toilet. Then he saw it and then he took some out and put it on the floor and he made me eat some.

• • •

Q: What did the other children do when that happened?

A: They weren't in there.

Q: Where were they?

A: They were at their houses.

Q: Okay. Was this in the daytime or at nighttime?

A: Nighttime.

Q: This was at nighttime?

A: Yes.

Q: Okay. How did you get to the day care at nighttime?

A: Um, all the other children left and it was close to nighttime.

TESTIMONY OF ANDY, ONE OF THE CHILDREN

Some of the more outlandish testimony was provided by Andy, one of the children, who made or was led to make charges of sexual abuse. In this instance, however, he spoke of Mr. Bob taking them out at night on a boat that was surrounded by sharks that his friend kept in a salt-water pond behind his house, occasionally carting the sharks out to Albemarle Sound for outings before taking them back to their pond.

FROM CROSS-EXAMINATION OF ANDY BY MR. SPIVEY FOR THE
DEFENSE
(Edenton, N.C.: Court Trial Transcript, 1990)

Q: Did he say anything about the sharks?

A: No, because one of his friends kept—had—had those sharks for a pet and had them and that friend was with him and he let them go.

• • •

Q: Where did he keep the sharks?

A: He kept them in a salt water pond. He had a pond behind his house and he put lots and lots of salt in it so the sharks could live.

Q: Okay. And when he took the sharks out there so they could circle around the boat, how did he get them out there so they could circle around the boat?

A: He picked them up and put them in his big aquarium and took them out to the sound and let them go out and surround the boat.

DEFENSE ATTORNEY SPIVEY'S CLOSING ARGUMENTS

Attorney Spivey points out the obvious inability of the children, most of whom were between two and one-half and three and one-half, to distinguish truth from fantasy and the ineptitude of the court-appointed therapists who asked the children suggestive questions and encouraged their parents to ask suggestive questions. He also draws the jury's attention to the numerous preposterous claims made by the children. He asks, in effect, "How can you disbelieve these preposterous claims, yet believe other accusations relating to sexual abuse?" Are not all of the children's claims suspicious, arrived at long after the fact and in the parental hysteria of the moment?

FROM DEFENSE ATTORNEY SPIVEY'S CLOSING ARGUMENTS
(Edenton, N.C.: Court Trial Transcript, 1990)

Do you believe the stories about, ah, from Beth Bateman about a black man being upstairs skinning hamsters at the day care? Do you take that at face value? . . . Do you believe the stories about sharks and machines that scooped them up out of the water and salt water ponds behind people's houses where they kept sharks? And children being hung by the neck in a tree and yet living to testify about it? Obviously, those are things that are simply not true. But they are all coming out of this same process.

DEFENSE ATTORNEY MILLER'S CLOSING STATEMENT

Attorney Miller tried to show the jury in his closing statement that what was presented as evidence at trial was often the testimony of adults, the parents, who were scarcely disinterested parties, and the prosecution's inept therapist, who had asked the children leading questions repeatedly until they had received the answer that would make a good case for sexual abuse. He also argued that much of the testimony by children was in the way of either "yes" or "no" answers.

FROM DEFENSE ATTORNEY MILLER'S CLOSING STATEMENT
(Edenton, N.C.: Court Trial Transcript, 1990)

How many "Yes" or "No" questions have we had in this case? How many statements that are being made by parents to you that sound like full-blown statements out of a child's mouth are actually their reconstructions of conversations? . . . Well, for the most part the child didn't say it. And for the most part the child didn't say the things when they were on the witness stand. Remember that. Remember those issues. Those are critical issues because they do make a difference, because they're important in this case. Because you remember, it's not what the children said so much as it is how do they come to say it.

PROSECUTORIAL SELF-INTEREST

Just as in the witchcraft trials in Salem, so in many cases of supposed massive sexual abuse of children in nursery schools, it was
the state prosecutors supported by a formidable bureaucracy who
insisted that the children's fantastic stories be believed without
question or corroborating evidence. Reporter Dorothy Rabinowitz
has done more than any other person to expose the ambitions of
prosecutors in the more notorious and unjust child-abuse cases
involving nursery-school personnel. In the article reprinted here,
she pays homage to a district attorney, Alan Rubenstein of Pennsylvania's Bucks County, who saw as his first obligation to see justice done rather than to enhance his own career by seeking to
prosecute in a case that would have guaranteed him national attention. Unlike other prosecutors, in the Breezy Point case, he de-
manded corroborating physical evidence, and held consultants in
the case to a level of competent performance. As a result, the case
was dropped for lack of evidence and the accusers were forced to
pay the teacher a settlement after she won her suit for defamation
of character. The editorial also illustrates the gullibility and hysteria
of the parents and their unscrupulous manipulation of their children. Like Martha Corey and Rebecca Nurse, Dorothy Rabinowitz
was one of the few people who took a stand to point out the
danger of using—without question or investigation—the fantastic
testimony of children.

DOROTHY RABINOWITZ, "JUSTICE AND THE PROSECUTOR"
(*Wall Street Journal*, Friday, March 21, 1997)

In April 1989, investigators began looking into charges that appalling
acts of sex abuse had been committed against children at the Breezy Point
Day School in Bucks County, Pa.—only the latest in the steady eruption
of sensational molestation charges brought against day care centers in
the 1980s. By the time the Breezy Point story had begun, Violet Amirault
and her two children, Gerald and Cheryl—proprietors of the Fells Acres
School in Malden, Mass.—had long been convicted and imprisoned, on
the basis of accusations obtained by the prosecutors' appointed experts

in child abuse. By this time too Grant Snowden of Miami was making his way through the Florida prison system after State Attorney Janet Reno's office prosecuted him on similarly extracted allegations. Charged with assaulting children for whom his wife baby-sat, the Dade County police officer had been sentenced to five life terms.

The new target of allegations was a 35-year-old teacher who had two children and, also, a husband employed by a publishing house—which fact the accusing parents would view as substantiation of their charges that the family was engaged in nefarious undertakings. The teacher's problems began some eight months after she began working at the school, with a report of a complaint that she had violated a four-year-old girl by penetrating her vaginally with a cream: specifically, the allegation had it, a "cinnamon cream."

In the days that followed, events proceeded in a way that had become routine after such accusations. Child welfare agents questioned other children—who denied that they had been touched or abused in anyway. A few months more, nonetheless—months of questioning by their parents, a caseworker, and a psychologist working for Bucks County Children and Youth Services—brought forth two more four-year-old girls now saying they had also been abused vaginally with cream.

As usual, too, there were far more interesting charges to come, and an enlarging number of molesters. As parents of the three alleged victims held more meetings—with one another, the caseworker and the psychologist—there soon developed an entirely new list of accusations. The four-year-olds, it was reported, now said they had been beaten by the teacher and her aide, locked in cages, and made to ingest feces and urine and to watch rabbits being slaughtered while the teacher held the animals' beating hearts. They had, furthermore, been abducted to various hotels to take part in group sexual activities, and had seen the teacher cut and stab other students. They had been raped by the teacher's husband and her two children, been photographed nude by the teacher's husband and been forced to set fires and to bury animals.

By now, the investigation was in the hands of Bucks County District Attorney Alan Rubenstein, who saw the possibilities of a spectacular case involving sex and child victims. Mr. Rubenstein had taken over at the request of the Northampton police while the allegations were still in the assault-by-cream stage. While still looking into these charges, for which he [District Attorney Alan Rubenstein] could find no evidence, there came the new ones—rapidly multiplying communiques from parents reporting rape, mutilation, stabbing and the rest supposedly committed by the Breezy Point schoolteacher, her 68-year-old female aide and other conspirators.

"I *Like* Breezy Point"

All of which was quite enough for the district attorney, who had already viewed with interest a video tape made by the mother who first reported her child had been assaulted. In it, the mother presses her laughing four-year-old to tell what happened, for which the child receives lavish praise and assurances that these terrible things would never happen again and that she would be taken to a much nicer school. But, the girl objects, "I *like* Breezy Point." The child had been raped, beaten, abused and ter-rorized, Mr. Rubenstein noted—and she *liked* going to this school?

Confronting a mounting tide of accusations, and parents' demands that the teachers be arrested, the district attorney ordered an inquiry into the merits of every allegation—no small task. In the course of this extraor-dinary investigation, Mr. Rubenstein had his detectives sweep all the areas in which the children had supposedly been abused. They gathered hair samples, groveled in the school sandbox for remains of mutilated ani-mals, and checked the accused's car and house, and hotels and rooming houses near and far where children said they had been attacked. They investigated the secret rooms identified as sites of abuse and demonic rituals, which children had described in vivid detail, including in one case a large working fireplace.

Faced with glaring discrepancies between the children's descriptions and the actual layout, parents argued that the school owners had re-moved the fireplace and remodeled the room to avoid detection. There was no such evidence of remodeling, the district attorney in turn re-ported. He had every child at the school questioned separately; no child corroborated any of the charges, or could tell about anything bad that happened at the school. When one of the accusing children told of cer-tain identifying marks on the teacher's body, Mr. Rubenstein asked the woman—now in an advanced torment—for photos and an examination. No such marks were evident—which fact, the complaining parent charged, only meant that the teacher had taken care to have them sur-gically removed. There was no evidence of any such surgical removal, district attorney Rubenstein observed. Not least, he had the complainant children examined for physical evidence of abuse—of which doctors found none. The findings, the district attorney reported, were clearly inconsistent with charges of forcible rapes against children. False claims that a pediatrician had found evidence of abuse, Mr. Rubenstein point-edly noted, had been accepted at face value by Children and Youth Serv-ices and their consulting psychologist.

In the midst of it all, there arrived an expert—as so often in these cases—recommended as having special capacities in dealing with child sex abuse cases. Dade County prosecutors had the Bragas, Joseph and

Laurie, represented as psychologists. In Massachusetts, then-District Attorney Scott Harshbarger had nurse Susan Kelley, whose expertise was amply illustrated in interrogations in which she pleaded with children to tell about the bad things that had happened at Fells Acres, the way all their little friends had. In Bucks County, parents enlisted the aid of one James Stillwell, who had developed something of a following as a consultant.

This expert now counseling the parents examined their children's drawings and shared his conclusions with the consulting psychologist for Children and Youth Services—that there was a pedophile preying on children at Breezy Point. Introduced as an investigator experienced in child abuse cases who had worked with the FBI, Mr. Stillwell soon came to the attention of the Bucks County district attorney, who ran a check on his credentials. The results were instructive: The expert advising the parents on pedophilia at Breezy Point was an unemployed plumber, unknown to the FBI, whose past experience consisted mainly of jobs in heating and refrigeration. In due course the president of the National Agency Against the Organized Exploitation of Children, Inc. would offer his services to the district attorney.

"I'll call you," Mr. Rubenstein informed him, "when my refrigerator light burns out."

When Mr. Stillwell claimed that a promotional video tape put out by the Breezy Point school revealed acts of perversion, the district attorney issued a statement denouncing him as a quack. He further advised the parents' consultant, who operated from Maryland, that he would arrest him for fraud if he set foot in Bucks County.

In the meantime Mr. Rubenstein's investigation continued. So, too, did calls from the parents, looking for an arrest. One wanted to know if the district attorney had drained the pond to look for bodies of children. There were no missing children. Mr. Rubenstein told the father: 20 children walked into the school, 20 children walked out. Eight years later, his detectives still go around mordantly asking one another if they've drained the pool yet.

The nearly year-long investigation into events at Breezy Point finally came to a close with the district attorney's announcement that the charges were baseless. So ended what had seemed at first a spectacular case to a prosecutor as ambitious as any; as ambitious, say, as District Attorney Scott Harshbarger of Massachusetts, who had brought the case against the Amirault family, or Dade County State Attorney Janet Reno, whose office prosecuted Frank Snowden. In District Attorney Rubenstein, the workings of ambition were of a crucially different order—the sort that required a prosecutor to ask, first of all, whether there was any truth to the charges against the accused. The accused in this case—who could never again bring herself to work as a teacher—began efforts to return to a normal life. The accusers ended up paying teacher and school an undisclosed sum in settlement of a defamation suit.

How easily all this might have gone otherwise, had these allegations been made, say, to the office of Scott Harshbarger, is clear enough in the fate that befell the Amirault family of Massachusetts. Violet, Gerald and Cheryl Amirault, too, were alleged to have tortured children in secret rooms and committed fantastic crimes involving a bad clown, mutilated small animals, stabbed children, nude pictures and the rest—all as in the Breezy Point case. An investigator could search the length of the case Mr. Harshbarger and prosecutors brought against the Amiraults without finding any reference to matters like lack of evidence, and findings "Inconsistent with forcible rape" such as filled the pages of Mr. Rubenstein's Breezy Point report. The same can be said of Janet Reno's prosecutors, otherwise busy unearthing new charges of abuse till they succeeded in their effort to convict Frank Snowden.

In place of evidence, prosecutors had gone to trial in these cases armed with explanations about dark skills and matchlessly clever wiles: talents that had allegedly enabled Gerald Amirault, for instance, to rape a child with a butcher knife, as one complaint had it, without leaving marks. After the Breezy Point case, the Bucks County district attorney made strong objection to the reappointment of the County Youth Services psychologist, on grounds that he had endorsed baseless charges of abuse. Such experts were not in short supply—as was evident in the Amiraults' trials, where numerous authorities appeared to offer their testimony to the absurd, among them the pediatrician who supported the butcher knife story.

No experts, to be sure, did more to prepare the way for conviction of the innocent than those interviewers who conducted interrogations of four- and five-year olds. In the Snowden case [in Florida], no child had a single word to say about sexual abuse, till the prosecutor's expert Laurie Barga [*sic*] put the words in the child's mouth. In the Amirault case [in Massachusetts], the interrogator similarly pleaded and cajoled children who initially had nothing to say, until they finally yielded. Someday, in some more rational time, members of the public can gather to hear public readings of these bizarre interviews—in which adults offer police badges, gifts and trips to McDonald's if children will "help" by telling.

Servant of the Law

It was on the basis of testimony obtained just in this way, of course, that Gerald Amirault and Frank Snowden were convicted and fated to be locked in prison, by now for 11 years. There their prosecutors are determined to keep them. In 1935, Supreme Court Justice George Sutherland held that a prosecutor is not an ordinary party to a controversy, whose interest is to win a case, but a servant of the law, whose interest is "that justice shall be done." This precept perhaps comes as news to prosecutors now working so assiduously to preserve their convictions in these child abuse cases.

Within the next few months, the Supreme Judicial Court of Massachusetts will rule on Gerald Amirault's appeal. The court will decide, at the same time, whether to uphold Violet and Cheryl Amirault's reversal of conviction—or whether, as the state is bending every effort to assure, the women are returned to prison. While the state automatically moves to strike his appeal brief, Grant Snowden in turn awaits the judgment of the U.S. Circuit Court in Atlanta.   (A18)

PROJECTS FOR ORAL OR WRITTEN EXPLORATION

1. Write a paper on the manipulation of children by adults using, in part, materials on the Salem witchcraft cases and the Edenton case.

2. Write a paper on one's being found guilty merely by accusation, using materials on Salem, on the Red Scare years, and on the Edenton case.

3. Write a paper on the role of confession, especially forced confession, in all three cases—Salem, the 1950s, and Edenton.

4. In the 1950s, "subversives" were the "witches." In Edenton, supposed sex abusers were the "witches." Prepare carefully for a discussion on what other "witch-hunts" have occurred throughout history, but especially in the 1990s.

5. If you were a jury member or the judge in the Edenton case, what would you demand as evidence to corroborate the children's stories?

6. Write a paper on the theme of community hysteria using the three cases documented in this book. Make sure you define the word *hysteria* carefully, using examples. You may want to avail yourself of some books on the subject of hysteria.

SUGGESTED READINGS

Bottoms, Bette L., and Gail S. Goodman, eds. *International Perspectives on Child Abuse and Children's Testimony*. Thousand Oaks, Calif.: Sage Publications, 1996.

McNaughton, Janet. *Portable Guide to Investigating Child Abuse: An Overview*. Washington, D.C.: U.S. Department of Justice, 1997.

Myers, John E. B. "New Era of Skepticism Regarding Children's Credibility." *Psychology, Public Policy and Law*, June 1995.

Showalter, Elaine. *Hystories*. New York: Columbia University Press, 1997.

Index

About the Authors

CLAUDIA DURST JOHNSON is Professor Emeritus of English at the University of Alabama, where she chaired the English Department for 12 years. She is series editor of the Greenwood Press "Literature in Context" series, which includes her works, *Understanding The Red Badge of Courage* (1998), *Understanding Of Mice and Men, The Red Pony, and The Pearl* (1997), *Understanding Adventures of Huckleberry Finn* (1996), *Understanding The Scarlet Letter* (1995), and *Undersatnding To Kill a Mockingbird* (1994).

VERNON E. JOHNSON is Academic Dean, California Christian University–Berkeley. In an extended career in theatre, he has worked in every phase of production in professional, education, and community theatres.